ALPHABETS
AND THE
MYSTERY
TRADITIONS

"Nothing excites me more than the origins and magic of the early alphabets. The alchemy and mystery of language, of vibration, or image from above, below, and around the world contains the story of consciousness. Here is a compendium of magic and mystery. Judith Dillon has made a masterful assemblage of languages, including the *heka* (or magic) of each language and the power of word vibration. Heavens! What a book!"

REV. NORMANDI ELLIS, AUTHOR OF
HIEROGLYPHIC WORDS OF POWER

"A stunning cross-cultural portrait of the sacred order of letters. So many signs and symbols surround Judith Dillon's astounding account of an inner pathway dictated by letters of the alphabet. A beautifully illustrated new addition to the literature!"

DAVID APPELBAUM, PROFESSOR IN THE
DEPARTMENT OF PHILOSOPHY AT SUNY NEW PALTZ
AND FORMER EDITOR OF *PARABOLA* MAGAZINE

"*Alphabets and the Mystery Traditions* is a fresh and exciting anthropological investigation of the origins of the alphabet. Judith Dillon has unveiled a compelling story of renewal and resurrection in the ancient Mysteries. I particularly enjoyed her descriptions of the role of the Goddess in the spell of the alphabet."

BETHSHEBA ASHE, CRYPTOGRAPHER AND
AUTHOR OF *BEHOLD! THE ART AND PRACTICE OF GEMATRIA*

ALPHABETS
AND THE
MYSTERY
TRADITIONS

The Origins of Letters in the Earth,
the Underworld, and the Heavens

A Sacred Planet Book

JUDITH DILLON

Inner Traditions
Rochester, Vermont

Inner Traditions
One Park Street
Rochester, Vermont 05767
www.InnerTraditions.com

Sacred Planet Books are curated by Richard Grossinger, Inner Traditions editorial board member and cofounder and former publisher of North Atlantic Books. The Sacred Planet collection, published under the umbrella of the Inner Traditions family of imprints, includes works on the themes of consciousness, cosmology, alternative medicine, dreams, climate, permaculture, alchemy, shamanic studies, oracles, astrology, crystals, hyperobjects, locutions, and subtle bodies.

Cataloging-in-Publication Data for this title is available from the Library of Congress

ISBN 978-1-64411-665-4 (print)
ISBN 978-1-64411-666-1 (ebook)

Printed and bound in the United States by Lake Book Manufacturing, LLC

10 9 8 7 6 5 4 3 2 1

Text design and layout by Debbie Glogover
This book was typeset in Garamond Premier Pro with Horus and Gill Sans MT Pro used as display typefaces

To send correspondence to the author of this book, mail a first-class letter to the author c/o Inner Traditions • Bear & Company, One Park Street, Rochester, VT 05767, and we will forward the communication.

Scan the QR code and save 25% at InnerTraditions.com. Browse over 2,000 titles on spirituality, the occult, ancient mysteries, new science, holistic health, and natural medicine.

Contents

Acknowledgments

I would first like to thank my friend Sue Langman, and my family—Chuck, Lusya, Michael, and Emily—who patiently supported and listened to my multiple (many, many multiple) attempts to research and write this book over the years. I owe a debt of thanks to David Appelbaum, who was an early supporter of a raw form of my emerging book, and Rabbi Barbara Cohen, who gave me a forum to discuss some alphabet ideas. Also, to the great Marija Gimbutas, who gave me permission to use some of her drawings. Other friends cheering me on include Carol Wright (who took my photograph) and Jayne Prabhudas.

I would also like to thank Ross Hamilton and Richard Grossinger, who suggested my research for publishing and advised me on how to submit the book. Then, my thanks to all the helpful people at Inner Traditions who have walked me through the steps to create a new book. I want to give special thanks to my very brilliant editor, Kayla Toher, whose suggestions have added a coherence to my story. I also salute Nancy Ringer, the very thorough copy editor who corrected my numerous mistakes and made a poetical approach more user-friendly to those of a literal bent. My proofreader, Will Solomon, did an incredible job. I also thank my very creative typesetter, Debbie Glogover, who created a wonderful book design. Thanks to many others, too numerous to recount, as well.

Introduction to the Alphabet
as a Spell of Resurrection

Our alphabet, the ABCs we learn almost as soon as we begin to chant "Pat-a-Cake," may have begun life as a calendar for celebrating rituals: a star-guided mnemonic for the timing of seasonal chants. There remains a memory trickling down from this long-ago world that by following the correct order provided by our alphabet, the proper sequence of a great "Spell" would renew both Earth and the fragile butterfly souls of her children. Charms spelling out this promise hold Earth's gift of life, her alchemical secrets of spinning new gold from worn straw, if we can but remember their names.

Early alphabets used pictures of objects to represent sounds: an ox head (aleph) as the letter A, for instance. I began wondering why creators of ancient alphabets chose each symbol to represent the orderly letters of our ABCs. Investigating physical and mythological qualities associated with each object, I uncovered a story. Before embarking on our journey through this story, I must describe several traditions I compared to unearth a widespread Mystery hidden in our alphabet.

A picture is not confined to a single language. Each viewer names a picture according to their own language. Our numerals, for instance, are such pictures. Seeing the shape 3, we might say "three," but a French speaker would say "trois." The shape gives no hint of the sound, but if we write "t-h-r-e-e," we pronounce "three." True writing is a way of visualizing speech: sound represented by symbols. The magic of oral enchantments eventually evolved into the spells of writing. Objects becoming our letters described a "Spell" long before they began to record linear history.

Although my journey is about the discovery of a path, there are few literal paths to follow, only numerous clues derived from seemingly unrelated stories. They include Mother Goose rhymes and carefully guarded recipes for gold, magic, bread, and vinegar—which begin, like all of Earth's magic, with a mother.

Originally enchantment, letters were eventually engraved or inscribed. As Maurice Bouisson tells us in his 1961 exploration of the history of magic, "Writing . . . like incantation had magic power. The transference of this power from the chanted word into the written word represents the second stage."[1] Enchantments maturing with the magic of time eventually evolved into proper spells. Correct spelling, of course, demands letters placed in the proper order. The spells hidden in our first alphabet are revealed by the order of the objects, the attributes of the objects chosen to represent their letters.

The story of the alphabet begins with ancient skywatchers marking the passing stars over Earth. Recognizing the age-old maxim "As above, so below," these observations led to measurements and calendars. As these calendars became more complicated, our ancestors needed a way to record them. I believe they did so by encoding them into our alphabet, and at its root, the order of our letters hides this Spell. Each object chosen to represent a letter was determined by its position in the series: first letter, second letter, third letter, et cetera. In this way, the alphabet became a form of number magic, a Spell whose symbols, given in the proper order, come together to create the revolving Creation, just as proper spelling, putting letters together in a proper order, creates a word.

Adepts of Mystery traditions have long recognized the relationships between their various practices and the symbols of the alphabet, a Mystery itself as the original Spell of Creation. In 1839, Victor Hugo, an initiate of the Mysteries of Masonry, noted, "Human society, the world, and the whole of mankind is to be found in the alphabet. Freemasonry, astronomy, philosophy, all the sciences find their true, albeit imperceptible, beginnings there: and so it must be. The alphabet is a wellspring."[2]

This is not a history of writing in the usual sense; it is not a linear story of the transformation of speech into symbols to record that speech. Instead, we will examine the wisdom and reasoning behind the choice of objects to represent early letters. Evolving story rather than random selection mandated choice of symbol in each position. Why, for instance, did the early Hebrews choose an ox (aleph) as the first letter of their alphabet, while the ancient Celts chose a birch tree? Why does Mercury, the youngest (and oldest) of the Greek gods, occur at the start of a pack of Tarot cards, while an androgynous vulture leads an Egyptian alphabet? And why does a fey bull (Fe) promise money as the first Germanic rune?

The choice of ancient alphabet symbols lies in a pattern inherited by numerous traditions. They include the alchemy of turning a dark Earth to gold and a black night into a shining new day. Comparison of the mythic attributes of numbers and symbols across varied traditions reveals a common order: a connection across ancient cultures revealed in the ordering of symbols to create an alphabet for the communication of not just words but meaning, ritual, and Mysteries.

As the alphabet spread widely throughout the ancient world, Mystery traditions followed along. For the wise, travel through the unfolding Spell of letters promised the initiate the wealth of the material world as well as an enlightened return from the dark. But, over time, people came to use the new technology of the alphabet simply to record business transactions and communicate across distance and time. The deeper reason for the order of the symbols making up the alphabets was largely forgotten, passed on to only a few.

> *Heaven rained down ripe grain the day that [letters] were first invented.*
>
> H. N. HUMPHREYS, *ORIGIN AND PROGRESS*
> *OF THE ART OF WRITING*

In this book, we will examine several ancient alphabets and traditions associated with divination and magic, including ancient Hebrew, Germanic runes, and Celtic Ogham, comparing them to unravel the stories and secrets hiding among our letters. We begin with the Phoenician alphabet, the oldest alphabet known to human civilization. First appearing c. 1800 BCE in the lands of Egypt and Canaan, it became known as Phoenician around 1050 BCE. Shortly after, the script was adopted by the Hebrews and in this early form was known as Old Hebrew (Ketav Ivri). This ancient alphabet seems to group its letters into three families: the letters of the Earth, those of the Underworld, and those of the Heavens. We will use this structure as our own template for investigating the symbolism and secrets of each letter of our alphabet.

The first family describes the natural year: an undivided Earth splitting apart, being purified, plowed, planted, and delivered through the dalet (door) of our fourth letter D, a sharing of the harvest, and finally a dying back before rising through the gate (heth) of the eighth letter.

The next eight letters guide the mythic hero's journey through the Underworld. Beginning with the ninth letter, the labyrinth of teth (translated as wheel or coil), we then continue through judgments and paying our debts by the eleventh hour. In time the serpent-fish (nun) of the fourteenth letter travels safely over the waters of death: letter thirteen (mem/water). After growing stronger, we emerge into the light of day through the opening eye of the sun (ain/sixteenth letter).

The last letters hint at astronomical cycles, beginning with control of the North Star: pe (commandment) as the seventeenth Phoenician letter.

Letters of the Earth

1. Aleph (ox): A Guide at the Gateway
2. Beth (house): Adolescence and the Purification of the Virgin Spring
3. Gimel (camel or rope): Impregnation and the Bonds of Time
4. Dalet (door): Deliverance from Knots and Bonds

5. Hey (window): Teachings, Pupils, and a Gift of Tongues
6. Vav (hook or nail): Marriage of Heaven and Earth and the Throne of God
7. Zain (weapon): Floods, Apocalypses, and Pregnant Pauses
8. Heth (gate or fence): Happy Gate of Heaven

Letters of the Underworld

9. Teth (wheel or coil): Entering the Labyrinth
10. Yod (hand): Judgments of Fate
11. Kaph (palm of the hand): Visionaries and Payment of Debts
12. Lamed (ox goad or rod of the teacher): Upside-Down Teacher and L's Name of God
13. Mem (water): Breaking Waters and the Deluge
14. Nun (serpent-fish): Return of a Messiah and Allotment of Fortune
15. Samekh (prop or fish): Devas, Devils, and Protection
16. Ain (eye): Opening Eye of the Sun

Letters of the Heavens

17. Pe (mouth or commandment): Pi's Control of the Circle
18. Tsade (hunt or fishhook): Tsadiks, Moons, and Midwives
19. Qopf (monkey): The Number of the Sun
20. Ros (head): New Year after Sun/Moon/Mercury Nineteen-Year Cycles
21. Shin (tooth): A Triangular Number of a Sinuous Moon God
22. Tav (mark): Escape from Death and the Promise of a Good Return

As we explore the symbols of various scripts and patterns, I cannot emphasize enough that we must compare attributes associated with the *mythology* of each symbol. Do not be fooled by the shape occupying each numbered position. There is almost no correlation between shapes or sounds of the letters (using the word loosely) of these various traditions. However, each position in an ordered series contains certain powers associated with that placement. All symbols in the same position share a family resemblance of qualities. Looking at what each ordered object represents provides a clue to the alphabet's evolving story. The traditions I explore emerge from a common source, though not necessarily a common use of the powers inherent in each position.

We will pull apart secrets from the most luminous soul journey of a Jewish mystic or Taoist adept to the more prosaic calendars of a farming year and the ill-tempered uses of letter magic by Norse hags and Viking warriors. Our work ascribes no value on use. We simply compare widespread traditions to demonstrate that there *is* a pattern: that each letter contains a group of attributes or "powers" associated with its position in the sequence, and that the pattern carries a message of renewal and resurrection. Although various cultures chose symbols from their own word-hoards, it is the number placement of each letter, its position in the sequence, that mandates the choice of symbol.

This is surface exploration only. I am not competent to discuss the deeper uses of alchemy and Kabbalistic Mysteries nor to determine an ultimate origin for the secrets hidden in our alphabet. I only claim they share a common ancestor—and I hope that you will come to understand these secrets.

PART ONE

Origins of Our First Alphabet and Later Traditions

INTRODUCTION TO PART 1

At some point in time, a poetic genius ordered random symbols into a pattern and created an alphabet—not just for spelling out speech, but for recording the Spell of Creation. In early alphabets, two factors appear most important. First, each symbol must represent a sound in the language: A is for apple. But our first letter was not A but aleph, represented by an (androgynous) ox—and as we shall explore, cows and sky bulls are associated with the gift of writing in many traditions. The second factor important to our story is order: it is always ABC not ZBD. Each symbol represents attributes determined by its order of appearance, by its number in the series of symbols that make up the alphabet. (We will explore these attributes, letter by letter, in the second part of the book.)

Many early adaptors of the alphabet chose from their own hoard of symbols to represent the sounds of their languages, but they followed an unvarying common pattern. The symbols of these alphabets were not chosen by chance; their order was never arbitrary. Early writing was too special, too sacred, for symbols to be carelessly determined.

> *God drew the Hebrew letters, hewed them, combined them, weighed them, interchanged them, and through them produced the whole Creation.*
> SEFER YETZIRAH (c. 500 CE) AS QUOTED IN SCHOLEM,
> ORIGINS OF THE KABBALAH

Among its mysteries, our alphabet contains secrets of calendars and alchemical transformations lost when magic became hidden and then forgotten. Properly spelled, with the letters in their proper order, the alphabet holds the story of creation and re-creation, of birth, death, and resurrection, in which seed and soul continually emerge into a new light of day.

Some scholars dismiss the idea that the ancient creators of alphabets chose and ordered their symbols with an intentional mystical, magical, or alchemical purpose. Though mine is not the usual approach, my insights about alphabets as spells are based on extensive research and documentation.

The Phoenician/Old Hebrew alphabet is our oldest, and for this reason we will use it as our template. We will also look at numerous other patterns of writing to learn the full story of the relationship between alphabets and Mystery traditions. Not all of these patterns are true alphabets or even writing systems, but each has named symbols, and each symbol is placed in a set order. This makes comparison possible.

Although citing scholarly opinions, I am not trying to translate ancient script nor spelling out occult uses for its magic. Instead, I am writing from deep in my belly and over my finger bones as I trace Earth's order from her awakening in early spring through the birth and death of her golden children. In her winter-cold womb, the seed sleeps until her lover kisses her awake and she circles again with the Lord of the Dance. Once more souls slip like words through the opening door (our letter delta) of her warming womb.

1

Alphabets as Rosaries
of Letters

Historically, writing developed and spread with the need for record keeping by city storehouses. Symbols incised on tokens were used as counters to identify the owners of items long before the appearance of true writing. But our interest is not in the history of writing but in the mythology underlying the objects chosen to represent early alphabet letters.

In addition to its early use in record-keeping, our orderly alphabet served mystical purposes. Describing a yearly Great Round of agriculture, from seed to golden harvest and back again, it outlined a path for a spiritual journey through life and the afterlife, guiding the soul toward the light of resurrection.

The sequence of letters in ancient alphabets follows a pattern evolved long ago in the almost forgotten era of the Earth mothers. Square, squat, deep-breasted, and full-bodied, these charming goddesses brought abundance and peace to their people. The people in turn played their part in the seasonal festivals, ensuring the land's continued fertility. The magical spells manifested in that celebration—the appeals to the Earth mother to nurture the cycle of birth, growth, death, and resurrection—formed the pattern that, in turn, took concrete form in the symbols of the alphabet.

Some Earth goddesses were depicted with necklaces. *Zodiac* is the

Fig. 1. The Lady of Saint-Sernin, a statue-menhir of an Earth mother with necklace and breasts, c. 3000 BCE, housed at the Musée Fenaille in Rodez, France

Photo by Erwin Corre, CCO 1.0

name of one such necklace; *Cosmos* is another. *Cosmos* means both "ornament" as cosmetic as well as "universe." Our universe is built from elements, a word the Oxford Universal Dictionary describes as meaning both "building blocks" of the universe and "alphabet letters." Some necklaces were composed of alphabet letters or symbols of astrology's zodiac calendar. The necklaces show that these goddesses possessed the proper spell, the correct order of revolving letters and stars, to return a dead Earth and her seed to new life. They provided the elements needed to spell each new world into existence after the dying of the old.*

Although alphabet stories hint at rebirth, eternal life was never promised, only motherly (material) help along the journey. After each harvest, it is Earth's seed that returns after passing through the dark. In the ancient Mystery traditions, the end is always embedded in the beginning. Of all the early alphabets I investigated, the last letter hints at this return. The ancient Phoenician/Old Hebrew alphabet ended with the letter tav (meaning "mark"), originally written as *T*,

---

*Examples include Diana of Ephesus, who wears a zodiac as a necklace. The Norse goddess Freya has a necklace of shining stars; the Hindu goddess Kali wears the Varnamala of alphabet letters around her neck.

Fig. 2. A to T
watermark

From Harold Bayley,
Lost Language of Symbolism, 1912

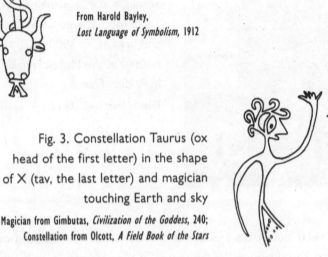

Fig. 3. Constellation Taurus (ox
head of the first letter) in the shape
of X (tav, the last letter) and magician
touching Earth and sky

Magician from Gimbutas, *Civilization of the Goddess*, 240;
Constellation from Olcott, *A Field Book of the Stars*

X, or +. This symbol—the multiplying cross of resurrection, the plus sign of additional returns—promised that death was never final. In its season, this mark of salvation circles back as the bull (Taurus) as letter A.

In his investigation of secrets hidden in early images, British scholar Harold Bayley noted that the combination of A and T is the first and last letter of the Hebrew alphabet, and went on to say, "The expression 'last' is generally misunderstood . . . the truer implication being the end of the last days and the dawn of a new era or beginning."[1]

Discussed later, Hebrew remembers a tradition that God created the alphabet letters (A–T) before creating Heaven and Earth (Genesis I). Remembering we begin our alphabet with an ox head, it must be noted the Bull of Spring, Taurus, is also depicted with the X shape of tav. That is, the first and last letters join in a continual rosary of seasons.

We continue our investigation with one source for the numbers that underlie the alphabet magic: the Heavens.

2
Astronomy and Calendars

And now they do not see light, it is brilliant (Bahir)
in the skies.

THE BAHIR (TWELFTH CENTURY),
TRANS. ARYEH KAPLAN*

After eons spent watching the changing sky, people began to recognize and ultimately record repeating patterns. Planets migrate past fixed stars at regular intervals. Fixed stars revolve over Earth, marking the changing seasons. Stars circle a seemingly fixed pole star, but, slowly, they too change position. These patterns underlay the discovery of mathematics and measurements and influenced the choice of symbols in our alphabet. Our earliest alphabet recorded these calendars, these ordered cycles of revolving seasons, in the sequence of their letters.

Fig. 4. Figure of the Magician, touching Earth and sky, as Above and Below, Hungary, c. 5500 BCE. Five thousand years later, the shape linking Earth and sky became the Hebrew aleph (א).

From Marija Gimbutas, *Language of the Goddess,* 16

---

*This is the first verse quoted in *The Bahir,* a twelfth-century Kabbalah text that discusses, among other things, the secrets of the Hebrew alphabet. The word *bahir* means light or illumination.

Time measured by the revolving lights in the sky mirrors the seasons changing the face of Mother Earth. The seasons on Earth mirror the changing bodies of all her children: plant, animal, or human. We, in turn, share with the rising and falling stars not only the same atoms of creation but also the cycles of birth, growth, fertility, old age, and death. With each death comes a disappearance into the dark and then a rebirth: energy and light returning to the circle from out of nature's black womb.

A cycle can begin with the shadows of a gentle Eve or with the brightness of Earth's returning sun. Reflecting this, most of the first symbols of the mercurial hermetic patterns we explore are black, white, or black and white.

Numerous circles guide the paths of stars and planets crossing our skies. One circle is the undulating path of our Milky Way. Another is the ecliptic, a narrow band of stars providing the path followed by the zodiac stars as well as the sun, the moon, and the five wandering planets (Mercury, Venus, Mars, Jupiter, and Saturn) that can be seen by the naked eye.

The zodiac circle of 360 degrees has in our time been divided into twelve astrological houses spanning 30 degrees each. Each house is named for a constellation of fixed stars that, rising with the sun, rules for one month. After their morning (heliacal) rising, they disappear into the glow of the sun. Circling Earth over twelve months, the stars of each house should return to their proper season each year. Helpful in my study, each house in the series has certain attributes, which, like the attributes assigned to the symbols of alphabets, become useful as a means of comparison to other ordered patterns.

PRECESSION OF STARS

But Earth has a faint wobble in her body. Like a spinning gyroscope, she slowly changes the orientation of her north pole and hence the pole star visible to her northern gaze. Observed from Earth, all our stars revolve around the command of our pole star: now the North Star, the Nail of the North, an apparent whirlpool, eye, or mouth. About

6,000 years ago, the pole star was among the stars forming the constellation of a Dragon, a humpbacked camel-serpent covering much of the northern sky.

Shifting slowly, Earth's northward gaze drifted toward the Wagon stars, also known as the Dipper or Great Bear. In time, she will turn back, reclaiming her former pole star. The cycle takes about 13,000 years in each direction, an entire passage taking 25,800 years. The year 2012 was halfway through the cycle. We are now heading slowly back toward the lost stars of the Golden Age once described by Plato.

This migration of our north pole has the added effect of "precessing" the equinoxes, a slow backward movement through the zodiac. This movement occurs at an average rate of one degree every seventy-two years. This is one source of the number seventy-two, which appears numerous times in our study of alphabet myths. Because of the precession, every 2,200 years the zodiac sign rising with the New Year's sun changes, its Age passing. As each Age ends, the nature of the world also changes. Around 4000 BCE, the farmer's Bull of Taurus rose with the spring equinox. By 2000 BCE, the warrior Aries ruled the spring sky. Finally, we entered the Age of Pisces, which now, 2,000 years into the present era, is moving toward the unsettling Age of Aquarius.

Twelve Signs
of the Western Zodiac

Reflecting a solar calendar of twelve months, each sign rules for one month. The Western zodiac begins with the constellation's rising at sunrise in the spring equinox. Due to the precession of the equinoxes, the slow backward movement of the stars as seen from Earth, the zodiac signs no longer correspond with the stars ruling the spring equinox. Because of this, the Western zodiac is said to be "frozen" at Aries. In reality, the equinox stars are now in Pisces and moving slowly toward the Age of Aquarius. Like other ordered symbols, each sign has characteristics associated with its position.

Number	Sign	Ruler	Month of Rule
1	Aries	Mars	March 21–April 21
2	Taurus	Venus	April/May
3	Gemini	Mercury	May/June
4	Cancer	Moon	June/July
5	Leo	Sun	July/August
6	Virgo	Mercury	August/September
7	Libra	Venus	September/October
8	Scorpio	Mars or Pluto	October/November
9	Sagittarius	Jupiter	November/December
10	Capricorn	Saturn	December/January
11	Aquarius	Saturn	January/February
12	Pisces	Jupiter or Neptune	February/March

A tower built to mark the rising of a star in the sky or to predict a seasonal rising of the sun or a planet against a fixed star (on the solstices and equinoxes, for instance) ultimately goes out of kilter. The tower's calendar can no longer be trusted; the center no longer holds; the ages shake apart. While the faithful sun will continue to rise in its proper season, the ruling stars change, losing their command of the sky. (The icon of the Fallen Tower will reappear later in our story.)

Descriptions of zodiac time concentrate on the new year of the spring equinox (March 21). I believe our pattern developed much earlier than the above dates suggest. Oral traditions have long memories extending back thousands of years before written history. Around 10,500 BCE, the date Plato (c. 400 BCE) declared the lost Golden Age, the twin stars of Gemini and the nearby constellation of the giant Orion rose on the winter solstice. This was the period (c. 9000–8000 BCE) when settled villages appeared in the Near East and around the Black Sea area of Anatolia. This was the period when an even older hunter-gatherer people created a ceremonial center of stone pillars richly carved with animals (known as Gobekli Tepe, c. 10,000 BCE).

THE CHINESE ZODIAC

The Chinese zodiac is a lunar calendar. The signs, each named for an animal, begin with the rising of the full moon between 11 p.m. and 1 a.m. Traditionally beginning around February 4, each sign rules for a year, rather than a month as in the Western zodiac tradition. In the list below, I include the names of the Western constellations for comparison only. The Western and Chinese traditions each ascribe very different attributes to these constellations.

1. Rat (Aquarius)
2. Cow (Capricorn)
3. Tiger (Sagittarius)
4. Hare (Scorpio)
5. Dragon (Libra)
6. Serpent (Virgo)
7. Horse (Leo)
8. Sheep or Ram (Cancer)
9. Monkey (Gemini)
10. Fowl or Rooster (Taurus)
11. Dog (Aries)
12. Pig or Boar (Pisces)

ORION AND THE WOMB OF THE WORLD

Orion will play a large part in our mythic history. His journey through the sky is just outside the zodiac circle. Orion and his faithful star Sirius were important markers of many calendars and their measurements. In a calendar used by astronomers in ancient Egypt, thirty-six bright stars traveling the same path as Orion were identified. Known as decan stars, they appear in the morning sky for ten days. After disappearing into the light of the sun, they finally reappear to set in the west. After seventy days they are born into the night sky.

Closely connected with alphabet symbols and the measurements of Heaven, Orion traveled under many names, including Algebra; Saturn (ruler of the rings of time); the Bull of Heaven; Frigga (spinning stars with her spindle); Lao Tsu (returning order to a corrupt world); Tammuz (dying after fertilizing his Lady of the Dates); and Osiris (both bull and rising barley of Egypt).[1]

Orion was also known as El, supreme god of the early Semites. The son of this Ancient of Days was Baal (lord). Early protean gods became more concrete, more static, as our world aged. The Bull of Heaven as Baal and the supreme El may originally have represented the same being. Ancient gods once changed aspects with the seasons. Harvested in their time, they returned young, re-emerging with the Virgin Springtime of each new world.

In our alphabet, for example, the name El appears as L, our twelfth letter, a number associated with (twelve-inch) rulers, wise kings, and measurements. As the twelfth letter, L dies upside down on Twelfth Night. We will first meet him in the form of an alphabet letter as the potent third letter, the Greek gamma (Γ), and then again as the aging ruler of the seventh letter. In Phoenician, the ancestor alphabet preceding Hebrew and Greek, the third letter is ᒣ (Old Hebrew's gimel); the twelfth is an upside-down teacher (ᒪ, Old Hebrew's lamed). The belt stars of Orion's constellation, the "El-wand," contain L's shape.

One hundred and eighty degrees away from Orion is the constellation of Scorpio. Between them runs a river, a road of stars, a Milky Way marking the path of a wandering cow goddess consorting with Orion, the Bull of Heaven.* During Plato's Golden Age (c. 10,500 BCE), this starry road touched Earth on the winter and summer solstices, two of

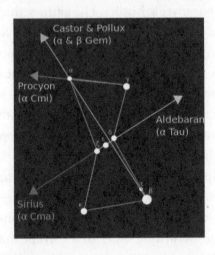

Fig. 5. The constellation of Orion

Mysid, CC BY-SA 3.0

---

*Orion has also been associated with the giant Nephilim who once married the daughters of man.

the quarter days* marking the corners of the year. Touching Earth, it was the Road of Souls, allowing giants, ancestors, and angels to wander and make merry among the children of man.

Eventually (c. 6000 BCE), the precession brought the rising of these stars to the spring equinox. The starry Road of Souls still touched Earth on a quarter day, but world ages and star-measuring towers continued to topple. With the backward shifting of the zodiac, the star path running between Scorpio and Orion eventually lost contact with Earth on the important corners of the year.[2]

THE WOMB OF THE BLACK GODDESS

The stars of the Scorpion are associated with myths about the death of Orion, with the giant dying in the west when the Scorpion rises. Tradition places the fierce form of the Goddess, the Hag or Black Goddess aspect of the goddess, in the constellation of Scorpio. The Black Goddess has important implications for stories of birth and rebirth. The actual womb of Earth, our galactic center where our cosmos physically originated, lies among the stars of Scorpio-Sagittarius. Here the stars of our galaxy began to sing as the sounds of energy first became light and then coalesced into the material world of matter (from *mater,* "mother"). This navel, this Root Star, this womb, opens directly across the sky from the Bull of Heaven. He disappears from Heaven when she rises. Numerous ancient peoples describe the Black Goddess taking her dying consort's seed into her womb to store until another Creation.

In the long-gone Golden Age around 10,500 BCE this Black Queen of Heaven rose on the summer solstice (June 25), just as her dying sun began his journey toward the dark. Summer marks the prime of Earth's sun. After midsummer, his days grow shorter, and he must die to be reborn. Orion once returned with the sun, six months later, on the darkest night in the dead of winter. Due to the implacable precession, Scorpio's Hag now rises around Halloween, and her lover Orion on May Day.

---

*Winter and summer solstices, and spring and fall equinoxes, are the quarter days marking the corners of the year.

Fig. 6. The Scorpion Goddess opening her womb, Ur, c. 2400 BCE

From Buffie Johnson, *Lady of the Beasts*, 333

Fig. 7. Sheela Na Gig, Herefordshire, England, ninth century

Photo by John Harding, CC BY-SA 3.0

Fig. 8. Stone drawing, Algeria, Paleolithic period

From Erich Neumann, *The Great Mother*, 114

The Bull of Orion disappears from the sky when Scorpio's receptive womb appears. After traveling the night of the Underworld, he reappears in the morning sky. Each time he returns, he brings fertility to his land. The Hag also renews, growing young with each spin of time's wheel. Thousands of years after the Scorpion Goddess (fig. 6) was painted, her image still appears over the doors of medieval churches. Like her ancestor, she stretches her labia wide to offer protection, a place to rest until resurrection.

The stars of the protean Bull of Heaven, here known as Orion, have also represented a hunter. It is not beyond imagination that the image in figure 8, showing a hunter, his penis connected to the womb of his Lady of Animals, depicts Orion, the path of the Milky Way, and the Goddess of the Womb (the galactic center in Scorpio), 180 degrees and six months away from the stars of Orion. From black Earth's fertile womb, multitudes of plants and animals emerge when she is pleasured by her giant.

BULL OF HEAVEN

Bulls and wandering cows, domesticated around 6000 BCE, are associated with the gifts of both writing and calendars in several cultures. Needing to track cattle may have led to symbols as brands predating the tokens of early storehouses; tracking the Bull of Heaven led to the measurements of calendars. The bovine's head shape of the inverted letter A is equally the shape of a woman's womb, intensifying the association of the material world that will emerge from A.

In many ancient cultures, the Bull of Heaven, sometimes known as the Sky Bull, was paired with the goddess of Earth as the progenitors of life. There is an image of a giant bull covering a pregnant goddess from Paleolithic Spain, around 12,000 BCE.[3] This bull covering a fecund Earth is a giant aurochs, predecessor of domestic cattle. Starwatchers of Mesopotamia, from around 3000 BCE, a long way in time and space from Spain, tell a similar story. They held that the Sky Bull, the Bull of Heaven, fertilized Earth with his semen falling as rain. Early gods not yet solidified, he was also female, and her breasts poured forth their nourishment. Tracking this bull and the changing constellations across the sky was the basis for a calendar that would mark the times of year.[4]

3

Anatolian, Mesopotamian, Egyptian, and Early Semitic Scripts including Phoenician

The ancient civilizations of the Black Sea area have long been associated with mother goddesses, giant bulls, black vultures taking the dead into their bodies, and early script-like symbols. Farming, metallurgy, and the art of the Vine originated near the Black Sea of Asia Minor. The temples of Gobekli Tepe, built by Neolithic hunter-gatherers in what is now Anatolia, Turkey, contain massive stone pillars covered with animals and people. They were carved around 10,000 BCE, the same period as Plato's lost Golden Age. One of the carvings depicts a vulture by a headless man, a motif appearing again as our story unfolds. At some point in prehistory, the builders buried their temples and left them. Researchers believe that the need to feed and house these wandering hunters as they returned over many years to build the shrines perhaps led to the formation of local farming—among the earliest examples of farming in the world.

Çatalhüyük is another ancient Black Sea site. The cosmopolitan civilization here made use of extensive trade routes, city planning, weaving, metallurgy, farming, and animal husbandry. No signs of violence have been found, but the inhabitants disappeared from their land

Fig. 9. Çatalhüyük,
Anatolia, c. 6000 BCE

From Marija Gimbutas, *Language of the Goddess*, 188

around 6000 BCE, for unknown reasons, to unknown destinations.*

Their shrines contained bull heads combined with the beaks of vultures as well as multiple paintings of vultures consuming the dead of the inhabitants. Vultures cleaned the bones of the dead relatives, which were then buried within the homes as company for the living. Figure 9 shows a vulture by a headless body. I have uncovered no information on where the heads were placed. Perhaps they were placed in niches of stone like those of later Celtic heads. If exposed, they would have furnished calcium to pregnant squirrels and mice. Centuries later, both Celts and northern gods claimed they learned the divining art of letters in these lands of the goddess Asia. Feathered bird-maidens also carried off the dead of these later peoples.

The people of Çatalhüyük also "painted representations of the goddess of fertility, showing her as a young girl, as a mother giving birth, and then as an older woman," historian Sanford Holst writes.[1] In our unraveling of alphabet Mysteries, this repeating cycle of the seasons of life represented by young, maturing, and aging deities, is widely shared.

Unfortunately, although script-like symbols from Gobekli Tepe and Çatalhüyük exist, there is no ordered pattern available for them. Therefore, I am unable to include them in my study and cannot use them

---

*Ian Wilson, author of *Before the Flood* (2001), suggests that climate change affected farming in the area, necessitating a move. The people of Çatalhüyük might have gone to the then-freshwater Black Sea. When the Mediterranean Sea broke through the land bridge (c. 5600 BCE), it caused a great flood, destroying their new cities and sending the survivors wandering again.

to compare to other ordered alphabets. As noted earlier, in researching the evolving "Spell" of the alphabet, order is of utmost importance.

The early scripts of China, Mesopotamia, and Egypt appeared around 3200 BCE, about 3,000 years after the symbols of the Black Sea communities. These were true writing systems, composed of images of hundreds, if not thousands, of characters. But, like the Black Sea scripts, the cuneiform script of Mesopotamia, the Chinese script, and most hieroglyphs of Egypt were not ordered, so we cannot make use of them for comparison. The myths and divinations of these skywatchers, however, are relevant in uncovering the stories unfolding among later alphabet traditions.

EARLY PHOENICIANS AND THE DEBT TO EGYPT

The Phoenicians, eventual source of all Western alphabets, including that of the ancient Hebrews, settled the area south of Anatolia, along the west coast of Canaan, in what is now known as the Levant: Lebanon, Syria, Israel, Palestine, and Jordan. By convention, although their seafaring culture quickly became distinct from that of other Canaanites, they were called Canaanites before 1200 BCE and eventually re-named Phoenicians by the Greeks. Their cities, inhabited since Neolithic times, included Byblos, Tyre, Sidon, and Ugarit. These became seaports confined to narrow strips of land by the Mediterranean Sea. Preferring the wealth of trade to the spoils of war, these maritime traders eventually sailed as far as Scandinavia and Britain, around Africa, and possibly to the Americas.

The Phoenicians, as they became known, were master craftsmen: builders, metal workers, winemakers of a much prized Byblos wine, weavers, and dyers with the secret of a deep purple in demand by royalty. Along with the cedar lumber of Lebanon, they traded their own handiwork for the wealth of the known world. Beginning an early trade with Egypt, large groups of these western Semites eventually settled in Egypt. Some arrived as slaves; others came as craftsmen, settlers, traders, and warriors. Some known as the Hyksos (c. 1630–1523 BCE), the "rulers of foreign lands," even reigned briefly as pharaohs before their forced exodus (1523 BCE).

As early as 3000 BCE, Egypt's Sinai region contained turquoise and copper mines worked, over time, by different bands of Semitic Canaanites.

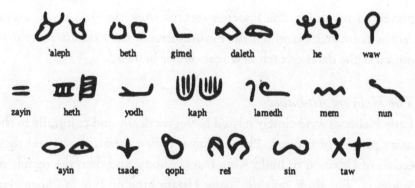

Fig. 10. Proto-Sinaitic script

As shown on the Codex 99 website

Around 1800 BCE an early alphabet developed in this area. The script, originally called Proto-Sinaitic, simplified a selection of Egyptian hieroglyphs and adapted them to represent sounds in a western Semitic language. Now, no longer needing years of training to learn the vast array of hieroglyphs, even common men could learn to write using a few simple symbols to represent single sounds. Despite the usefulness of this simple script it was not openly employed for nearly another thousand years. Then around 1050 BCE, its descendant known as the Phoenician alphabet came into open use. Its name is derived from the Canaanite traders transmitting it around the ancient world. Phoenician, evolved from the earlier Proto-Sinaitic example, had twenty-two letters, set in a specific sequence, and each letter represented a certain sound. Generally acknowledged as the world's first true alphabet, this alphabet, which could be used to write numerous unrelated languages, quickly spread across much of the ancient world.

I believe that while the alphabet was simmering for several hundred years, evolving from its Proto-Sinaitic origins of 1800 BCE into what became known as the Phoenician alphabet, its symbols were finalized. This alphabet served not only as a way of writing the sounds of a language but also as a mnemonic for the secrets of measurements and a return, a resurrection, after death—that is, the foundational elements of the Mystery traditions.

Greeks, after acquiring the alphabet with its Mysteries, renamed the Canaanites: the Phoenicians. Like Canaan's ancestor Cain whose mark prevented his death, the Phoenix returns from the fires of his ashes. As the palm tree on which the bird resurrects, the *Phoenix dactylifera* produces the dates of each new year on her branches.

The Hebrew Alphabet

Early Hebrews were closely related both genetically and culturally to the other peoples of Canaan. Phoenicians supplied the architects and their cedars of Lebanon to build King David's home and then the temple of Solomon. The Bible tells us, "Now Hiram king of Tyre [a Phoenician city] sent envoys to David, along with cedar logs and carpenters and stonemasons, and they built a palace for David" (Samuel 2: 5–11). Phoenician queens once married the kings of Israel, their temples to Baal and his consort existing until late in Israel's history.

In addition to supplying expertise, raw materials, and queens, the Phoenicians also supplied the early Hebrews with an alphabet. Indeed, the early Hebrew alphabet was essentially identical to the Phoenician one. Phoenician deities included a Bull and his consort Baalat, known as Hathor or Isis in Egypt. Although the related Hebrews eventually demonized these Baal-El worshipers and their golden calves, originally their cultures were close. The Hebrews of Israel were not fully monotheistic until late in the period of the Second Temple of Jerusalem (539 BCE–70 CE).

Hebrew stories about their alphabet are remembered in mythic stories. Abraham, patriarch of Jews and Muslims and traveler in Egypt, was said to know the Mysteries of the alphabet, including its power to create new life. Abraham studied with Enoch, ancestor of Noah, who saved the arcana in his ark.* There is another story that Moses (c. 1200 BCE), after leaving Egypt and ultimately wandering for forty years in the wilderness of Sinai, received the script inscribed on the Torah, the Five Tablets of the Law.

The Hebrew alphabet, alone of all later alphabets, retained the Phoenician objects used to name letters (e.g., an ox for aleph, the first letter, a house/beth for the second). The Hebrew tradition also

---

*See Noah's story in the fourteenth letter in part 2.

retained a memory of the magical luminous qualities of the early symbols; the Hebrew alphabet never lost the Mystery inherent in each of its letters.

The Greek Alphabet

Important to the story of our own alphabet, which begins with the ox head as letter A, the ancient turquoise mine at Serabit el-Khadim in the Sinai is one site where the early Proto-Sinaitic script appeared. It had a temple of the cow goddess Hathor. Appearing under many names, the only Sinaitic word that has been translated is her Semitic name, Balaat (lady) written on a carved sphinx. On the opposite side, hieroglyphs write "beloved of Hathor."[2]

Reminding the reader of the frequent association of cows and sky bulls with the origins of writing, the wandering cow goddess Hathor, also known as Isis, is associated with the stars of Sirius, Orion, and the Milky Way. She is also known as Io of Greek mythology, the White Cow. Her descendant Cadmus is said to have carried the Phoenician alphabet and its Mysteries to Greece after stealing the knowledge from his ancestor (see chapter 5).

Some Mystery traditions of Greece included the number secrets of Pythagoras, the trance-inducing rites of Dionysus, and the metalworking of the Cabeiri. Also including the spirits of winemakers, these secretive Mysteries involve a passage through the dark before the spirits are released into the light—the same resurrection hinted by the attributes associated with the Phoenician letters as they evolve from first to last letter of the alphabet.

The enthusiasm with which Greeks welcomed this foreign tradition may have roots in the Greek concept of death: listless shades wandering aimlessly about a sad gray Underworld. As the Homeric "Hymn to Demeter" tells us, a few Greeks were lucky enough to learn those Mysteries which no man may speak about: "Happy is he among men upon earth who has seen these mysteries; But whoever is uninitiated in the rites, whoever takes no part in them, will never get a share [aisa] of those sorts of things [that the initiated get] once they die, down below in the dank realms of mist."[3]

THE TWENTY-FOUR LETTERS OF
THE EGYPTIAN ALPHABET

1		Vulture (mother goddess; represents "A" sound)
2	or	Reed (appears as one or two reeds)
3		Forearm
4		Quail
5		Leg
6		Seat
7		Snake with horns
8		Owl
9		Water
10		Mouth
11		Reed shelter (11 as 1 + 1 is mirror of 2, whose symbol is the reed)
12		Plaited wick (upside down)
13		Placenta
14		Belly of animal with teats (i.e., a nursing mother)
15		Bolt (associated with Set, Devil-like god of Egypt)
16		Folded cloth
17		Lake or sea
18		Hill
19		Basket with handle
20		Stand for jugs
21		Bread (rising bread, not a flat wafer)
22		Hobble for cattle
23		Hand
24		Snake (represents a djT sound)

4

The Egyptian Twenty-Four-Hieroglyph Alphabet

Writing first appeared in Egypt around 3200 BCE. It comprised hundreds and eventually thousands of hieroglyphs representing a "nearly complete panoply of alphabetic and multi-consonantal signs" along with numerous other shapes and images determining the meaning.[1]

When writing appeared in Egypt, the script appears to have manifested as a mature system. It is possible that the idea of writing was derived from the Mesopotamian cuneiform and translated into a uniquely Egyptian format of sacred script. It is equally possible that the fragile papyrus used by Egyptian scribes, with which we might have been able to establish a record of development, has been lost to time.

At some point in history, someone ordered twenty-four hieroglyphs into a phonetic alphabet, with each hieroglyph representing a single sound. Because this alphabet has a traditional order, with each symbol naming an object, we can thus compare it to other ordered alphabets.

Although the hieroglyphs used for this alphabet are among the earliest known, I have been unable to find a date for the first appearance of the order as it appears in scholarly books. Perhaps Isidore, archbishop of Seville (c. 600 CE), is correct: "As for the Egyptian alphabet, Queen Isis . . . coming from Greece to Egypt brought them [alphabet letters] with her and gave them to the Egyptians."[2] It is possible this ordering occurred during the period Greeks ruled as the pharaohs of Egypt: the Ptolemies (320–31 BCE). Cleopatra was the last of the Greek pharaohs.

As the order of the twenty-four hieroglyphs represents the same unfolding story of death and resurrection appearing in the Phoenician alphabet, I believe the scholar(s) who ordered the Egyptian alphabet was aware of the hermetic Mysteries. Perhaps the Phoenician alphabet and its Mysteries that Cadmus carried to Greece returned to Egypt to order this Egyptian alphabet. As discussed below, the ordering of the twenty-four letters is unlikely to have been random. Caveat: I have seen the twenty-four symbols pulled out of its original order to mimic the ABCs of our own alphabet. This destroys the pattern, obscuring the story.[3]

Despite the development of twenty-four phonetic letters rather than hundreds of symbols to write speech, this was not commonly used; Egypt continued to use the more elaborate hieroglyphic script. Eventually, slightly simpler hieroglyphic scripts, known as Demotic and Hieratic, were developed, but they were still complex and difficult to learn. The ancient Egyptians ignored the democratic simplicity of being able to write with a few phonetic hieroglyphic letters, reserving that alphabet mainly to write foreign names. The earliest appearance of the name Israel was written in this hieroglyphic alphabet around 1200 BCE on the Merneptah Stele. The educated scribes of Egypt were a wealthy class, their skills bringing them power, prestige, and money. They would have been reluctant to employ a simple script easily learned by the common man.

BLACK MOTHER GODDESSES
AND RISING SERPENTS

A vulture leads this script of twenty-four hieroglyphs. A serpent sleeps at its base. Snakes, renewed by annually shedding their skins and becoming briefly blind in the process, symbolize regenerating life. As described earlier, the circular patterns we explore promise a return into

Fig. 11. A and T, the start and end of the
Egyptian hieroglyphic alphabet

life. The use of a vulture as the first hieroglyph, and a serpent as the last, makes it impossible to suppose the order and choice of symbols was random. The serpent goddess Wadjet, one of the earliest Egyptian deities, was depicted as a cobra. Joined with her sister the Vulture goddess, the Two Sisters protected the lands of a united Egypt as well as uniting the "Egyptian alphabet." The alphabet's first hieroglyph, the White Vulture (*Neophron percnopterus*), represented the sound of A.[4] The serpent hieroglyph, usually representing the sound *dj,* can also represent the sound of T. As Jim Loy notes, "The resting serpent (djT) is the word for cobra. It is pronounced DjT and can be spelled out with a T sign, and may be another determinative sign showing a cobra."[5] That is, this script begins with A and ends with T, just like the Hebrew and Phoenician aleph-to-tav sequence.

In ancient Egypt, the vulture was a symbol of motherhood. As French Egyptologist Christian Jacq notes, "The father is terrestrial (the snake), the mother is celestial . . . a vulture. . . . [To] the Egyptians it embodied the most excellent mother . . . although she is celestial, the mother vulture does not hesitate to dismember carrion and transform death into a vital food so as to transmit life."[6]

Egypt preferred to preserve its dead, but the Canaanites, like the peoples of Asia Minor, were no strangers to vulture funeral rituals. Excavations of Rogem Hiri (c. 4500–3500 BCE) in the Golan Heights revealed stone rings that may have been observatories. They may also have been places to feed vultures as well as offering homes for rock-dwelling serpents. Archaeologist Rami Arav argues that the site "was a . . . sanctuary, built specifically for the purpose of . . . exposing the bodies of the dead to vultures. . . . [This ritual] was widely practiced in cultures and civilizations that for one reason or another were interested in saving the bones of the deceased and not their flesh."[7]

Eventually, the black Griffon Vulture (*Gyps fulvus*) joined the White Vulture as Egypt's protective mother. This huge vulture is depicted on the walls of Çatalhüyük. It became associated with the goddess Mwt (mother), whose worship arrived in Egypt with the Semitic Hyksos. She merged with the older Egyptian White Vulture goddess to become the sister of the cobra.

Just as the sound of A gives birth to the following letters, the vulture gives birth to each new generation. The ancient Egyptians believed that the vulture was impregnated by the wind. As a black (or white) mother goddess, she takes the bodies of the dead into her womb and births the next generation. (The thirteenth hieroglyph is the symbol for placenta, indicating womb symbolism. Not coincidentally, the thirteenth letter of the Hebrew alphabet is the watery womb of mem, or water.)

The large serpent of the final hieroglyph is one of the aspects worn by ancient Earth gods. Apophis, also known as Apep, a serpent god, came to Egypt with the Hyksos and ultimately became an evil serpent-dragon in Egyptian mythology. The serpent also came to represent the storm god Set (who himself was identified with Baal, the Phoenician bull god who might also appear as a snake or bull-headed serpent). Although Set, an early Egyptian storm god adopted by the Canaanites as a form of their own god, was, like other serpents, ultimately demonized, Egyptian gods continued to carry the was scepter of Set to symbolize their authority. This was a staff with the head of the Set animal on top of the forked stick. The trade city of Thebes, Egypt, near where the early Proto-Sinaitic script appeared, was known as Waset, the city of Set. Cadmus, the Phoenician who carried the alphabet descended from the Proto-Sinaitic script to Greece, "was the son of Agenor, king of the Phoenician city of Tyre. Yet

Fig. 12. Serpents rise above the heads of feather-skirted women, Ukraine, c. 3800–3000 BCE

From Gimbutas, *Language of the Goddess*, 242

according to Diodoros, Kadmos [i.e., Cadmus] was also a citizen of Egyptian Thebes, which implies that he lived in Egypt."[8]

Figure 12 shows serpents rising above the heads of feather-skirted women. The archaeologist and anthropologist Marija Gimbutas notes, "Many authors have interpreted such dancing figures as 'mourning figures,' which . . . does not reflect the real meaning. . . . They witness energetic regeneration rites, not mourning or wailing of women."[9] In other words, the vulture and snake, representing cycles of life and death, imply rituals of a Great Round of regeneration.

Thousands of years later, and in another culture, the Black Mother and her serpent are still associated with letter magic. In India, it is said that the resting serpent as Kundalini is awakened to ascend the twenty-four vertebrae of the human spine to emerge, enlightened, through the crown of the head. She encounters the entire range of Sanskrit letters along her journey (see chapter 10).

Germanic tribes were another group finding magic among their twenty-four letters. In the Norse *Saga of Bosa* (c. 1300 CE), one of the hero's tasks was to locate a vulture's egg covered with golden letters.

Fig. 13. Orphic egg, 1774. The Mysteries of Orpheus included a return from death, the egg and serpent image promising this rebirth.

Drawing by British mythographer Jacob Bryant (1715–1804), *A New System*, plate iv, 243

From this egg emerges a serpent. (Note: Ancient symbols derive from close observation of nature. Serpents are not above feeding upon vulture eggs.)

EGYPTIAN CALENDAR

Egypt measured her twenty-four-hour day by choosing thirty-six decan stars. Each of these thirty-six Righteous Ones were visible for ten days before disappearing into the light of the sun ($36 \times 10 = 360$). They begin their cycle with Sirius, the star associated with Isis/Hathor, mother goddess of Egypt. That is, like the letter A as the Hebrew aleph (cow/bull), a mothering cow leads the circle of Egypt's year.

Included among my patterns are five gods chosen to rule the five Egyptian holidays. The Great Round of the sky measured 360 degrees; these five were needed to make a calendar of 365 days, closer to the actual sun's cycle of 365.25 days. The attributes of the five gods fit closely with those of our first five alphabet letters. Myth following the reality of a calendar regulated by the changing sky and seasons on Earth, Egypt's sky (Nut) and Earth (Geb) gave birth to these gods. In order, they are Osiris, Horus, Set, Isis, and Nephthys. The Egyptian sky,

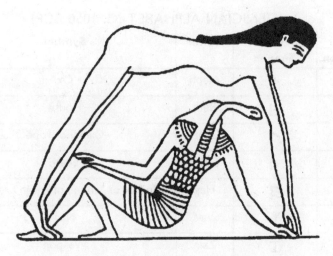

Fig. 14. Geb as the serpent and Nut as the sky

From E. A. Wallis Budge, *The Gods of the Egyptians*

usually depicted as a woman arching over her Earth, was also depicted as a cow. Her consort Geb sometimes appears as a serpent, an ancient form of the Earth gods. To allow the creation of the world, they were separated by the young air.

PHOENICIAN ALPHABET (C. 1050 BCE)

Letter Position	Phoenician Shape*	Name†	Symbol
1	⪤	Aleph	Ox
2	⪦	Beth	House
3	⺄	Gimel	Camel or rope
4	◁	Dalet	Door
5	⪛	Hey	Window or "sound of rough breathing"
6	Y	Vav	Nail
7	I	Zain	Weapon
8	⊟	Heth	Gate or fence
9	⊗	Teth	Wheel or coil
10	⅂	Yod	Hand
11	⪥	Kaph	Palm of the hand
12	∠	Lamed	Ox goad/rod of the teacher
13	⟆	Mem	Water
14	⅄	Nun	Serpent or fish
15	⩱	Samekh	Prop or fish
16	O	Ain	Eye
17	⌐	Pe	Mouth or commandment
18	⼁	Tsade	Hunt or fishhook
19	Φ	Qopf	Monkey
20	◁	Ros	Head
21	w	Shin	Tooth or bow
22	X	Tav	Mark

*The Phoenician shapes are essentially identical to the shapes of Old Hebrew (Ketav Ivri).
†Because there are multiple spellings for Phoenician letters, throughout this book I (technically incorrectly) use Hebrew and Greek names for letters, as they are the most accessible to the reader.

5
Spread of the Phoenician Script

Phoenicians from the coast of Canaan traveled and traded everywhere their increasingly sophisticated boats could sail. Though they are said to have carried an alphabet to all the ports built around the Mediterranean, the Phoenicians themselves left few writings beyond accounts of trade items and storehouse records. This secretive, cosmopolitan people began a lucrative trade with Egypt as early as 3200 BCE.[1]

Their alphabet, which came to be known as Phoenician around 1050 BCE (though it appeared earlier and developed over time), descended from the letters associated with the cow goddess Balaat as Isis/Hathor in the Sinai, which first appeared around 1800 BCE. The ultimate source of all Western alphabets, including Hebrew, Greek, and Arabic, the Phoenician alphabet also influenced later syllabaries ("alphabets" in which characters represent syllables), including India's sacred scripts of Brahmi (c. 300 BCE) and ultimately Sanskrit.*

Phoenician's brilliance is that each letter represents a simple sound. Other writing systems of the time used hundreds if not thousands of symbols to write language, limiting the use of writing to elite scholars.

---

*Thought to have been a spoken language by 1500 BCE, Sanskrit did not appear in writing until much later. Sanskrit was preserved for thousands of years in such oral traditions as the Ramayana, the tales of Sita and Ram described in other chapters. It is often written today in the north Indian script, Devanagari, developed around the seventh century CE.

Democratic Phoenician allowed anyone to write in any language with only a few simply drawn letters. With just twenty-two symbols, it could be quickly learned. Traveling along the trade routes, it was rapidly adapted for use by numerous unrelated languages.

According to the Greeks, Cadmus (Kdm), the "man from the east" mentioned earlier, carried Phoenicia's alphabet to Greece and established his city of Thebes in Boeotia after following a cow. He was not the inventor, having, according to some stories, stolen the letters from a White Cow. While myth is a vastly underutilized source of linear history, it is not clear on the ultimate source of the Phoenician Spell. One of Cadmus's ancestors is said to be the Nile River (Egypt); another is Isis/Io, hinting at the Phoenician connection with Egypt. Some of the earliest alphabet letters, dedicated to the Phoenician cow goddess Balaat, appeared in the temple of Hathor, the goddess as a cow, in the Sinai.

On the way to Greece, Cadmus married Harmonia on the island of Samothrace. Like many Earth goddesses, she owned a necklace of stars. "It was a snake shot through with stars, a snake with two heads, one at each end," says Roberto Calasso in his book about the event.[2] Harmony implies music, but the vibrations of musical notes, like the mathematics of masons orienting temples toward fixed stars, contain measured mysteries outside this investigation. In a fusion of alphabets, cows, bulls, and serpents, Cadmus and Harmonia, like the last of the twenty-four Egyptian hieroglyphs, become serpents at the end of their days.

Cadmus's sister was Europa, a Phoenician princess whose ancestry, like that of her brother, included the Nile. A great bull kidnapped her and carried her to the island of Crete. There she married the king, Asterion (starry one), and became the mother of the Minoan dynasty. Cadmus's name can translate as "east" or "orient"; Europa is sometimes said to represent the cow goddess Hathor, and her name may derive from the Akkadian erebu, meaning "to set" (in the west, opposite her east-rising sun).[3]

An early Cretan script, called Linear A, is not yet deciphered, its language unknown. I don't have an order for the pictographs so can't

Fig. 15. Vulture goddess with serpent,
Crete, c. 1500 BCE.
(Recall that these are the first and last hieroglyphs
of Egypt's alphabet.)

From Marija Gimbutas, *Language of the Goddess,* 37

include the symbols. Given that few archaeological dates are truly firm, Linear A (c. 1900 BCE) may or may not have preceded Proto-Sinaitic (c. 1800 BCE). A descendant system of pictographs, Linear B, wrote a Greek language used by the later Mycenaeans. Their culture was c. 1750 to 1050 BCE. According to historian Sanford Holst, the Phoenicians became known as the seagoing Minoans for the several hundred years they lived in, and influenced, the culture of Crete.[4] There is genetic proof that a founding male of Crete came from the Levant or Anatolia.[5] Weakened by earthquakes, they left when the Mycenaean Greeks conquered Crete (c. 1500 BCE), sending the wandering Phoenicians back to their cities in Canaan.

After the collapse of the Mycenaean empire (c. 1050 BCE), the Phoenician script arrived in Greece, replacing Linear B. Phoenician possibly arrived around 800 BCE, although the date is widely debated. While the Greeks changed the letters from symbols to meaningless sounds, our alpha-beta, they kept the Phoenician order of letters. They also adopted Phoenicia's number magic hidden among the letters, which was inherited by multiple descendants, including the mathematician Pythagoras and later users of a tradition known as the Kabbalah (discussed later).

If we are to understand ancient traditions, we must learn something from their astronomical knowledge. Linear history often conforms to mythic templates, like our own Camelot. The constellation Taurus and the giant Orion are both Bulls of Heaven. With the precession of the equinoxes, Taurus replaced Orion as the ruler of spring before eventually moving into a May Day rising.

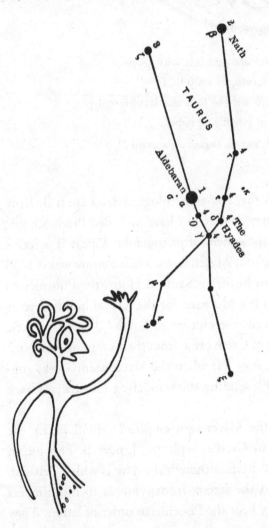

Fig. 16. Taurus, linking Heaven and Earth, and the Magician, Crete, c. 1500 BCE

Magician from Gimbutas, *Civilization of the Goddess*, 240; Constellation from Olcott, *A Field Book of the Stars*

According to myth, May Day was when cattle arrived in Ireland, homeland of another script, known as Ogham, hiding secrets (see chapter 8). According to the archaeological record, domesticated cattle arrived in Ireland around 3500 BCE.

Taurus, usually depicted by the bull head as letter A, is also sometimes depicted as tav's mark of renewal (written X, T, or +). Promising a return into the circle, tav is the last letter of the Phoenician/Old Hebrew alphabet. That is, the last shall be first. (See Tarot Magician and square Hebrew's first letter, aleph: א.)

PHOENICIAN/OLD HEBREW AND MODERN SQUARE HEBREW

Letter Position	Phoenician/ Old Hebrew/ Ketav Ivri Script c. 1050 BCE	Familiar Hebrew Name	Square Hebrew/ Ketav Ashuri Script c. 250 BCE
1	⪤	Aleph (ox)	א
2	⪦	Beth (house)	ב
3	⟋	Gimel (camel or rope)	ג
4	◁	Dalet (door)	ד
5	⪔	Hey (window or "sound of rough breathing")	ה
6	Y	Vav (nail)	ו
7	I	Zain (weapon)	ז
8	目	Heth (gate or fence)	ח
9	⊗	Teth (wheel or coil)	ט
10	⅂	Yod (hand)	י
11	⪤	Kaph (palm of the hand)	כ or ך
12	∠	Lamed (ox goad/rod of the teacher)	ל
13	ⱳ	Mem (water)	מ or ם
14	⅂	Nun (serpent-fish)	נ or ן
15	≢	Samekh (prop or fish)	ס
16	O	Ain (eye)	ע
17	⟅	Pe (mouth or commandment)	פ or ף
18	ⱱ	Tsade (hunt or fishhook)	צ or ץ
19	Φ	Qopf (monkey)	ק
20	⪦	Ros (head)	ר
21	W	Shin (tooth or bow)	ש
22	X	Tav (mark)	ת

6

Traditions from Hebrew and the Kabbalah

There exists an occult and sacred alphabet which the Hebrews attributed to Enoch, the Egyptians to Thoth or Mercurius Trismegistus, the Greeks to Cadmus and Palamedes. This alphabet, which was known to the Pythagoreans, is composed of absolute ideas attached to signs and numbers.

ELIPHAS LEVI, *LA CLEF DES GRANDS MYSTERES*

According to one tradition, Abraham, patriarch of both the Jews and Muslims, studied the Mysteries with Enoch, who created the alphabet that Noah saved from the Flood (Enoch is an ancestor to Noah but possessed an eternal life). Another tradition has Abraham studying with Shem, son of Noah.

Followers of the Mystery traditions never forgot the association of the alphabet and number magic, but the knowledge was hidden from common men. During Europe's Inquisition, hiding the Mysteries became a matter of preserving one's very life. Modern scholars attempting to interpret ancient practices are often handicapped by their ignorance of the natural world, astrology, palmistry, and number magic.

KABBALAH AND SQUARE HEBREW LETTERS

Hebrew words and the letters from which they are formed
are much more than mere symbols. Each letter is like an
element of the periodic table, with individual properties of
density and conductivity.

RAV P. S. BERG, *THE ESSENTIAL ZOHAR*

The original Hebrew alphabet, called Old Hebrew or Ketav Ivri, was essentially undifferentiated from the Phoenician. Its shapes gave overt homage to the Golden Calf of Baal worshiped by the Phoenicians: ⟨. This was the script originally used to write the Torah received by Moses on a mountain in Sinai. But around 250 BCE, Jews began abandoning the shapes of the original Phoenician alphabet to adapt the Aramaic shapes of Assyria, learned during their exile in Babylon. This "modern" Hebrew script is known as the Ketav Ashuri. I believe there were both political and religious reasons for this change of script.*

When the Torah finally adapted the Aramaic script, it was not as a translation into Ketav Ashuri, but rather as a replacement, letter by letter, following the original order. As scholar Joseph Naveh notes, "We are faced with an extraordinary phenomenon: the Jews, a conservative nation which adhered strictly to its traditional values, abandoned their own script in favour of a foreign one."[1] Before this change, languages always appeared in their own script: Hebrew in the Old Hebrew script, Aramaic in the Aramaic script. Now we have a Hebrew script—the sacred Torah—written in a foreign script. Even after the replacement of the letters, the four-letter name of YHVH

---

*According to Joseph Naveh, "The earliest Hebrew manuscripts written in the Aramaic type of writing . . . were probably written in the second half of the third century BCE" (*Origins of the Alphabets*, section 6, "The Jewish Script," 35). On the Stack Exchange discussion board "Which alphabet were the original Torah scrolls in?" one participant notes, "According to Pritchard's *Ancient Near East* and A. Mazar's *Archaeology of the Land of the Bible*, they have no surviving Land of Israel inscriptions from before the Babylonian conquest—royal inscriptions, letters, jar handles, grave markers, you name it, that are not in the Ivri script."

continued to be written in the old script until after the fall of the Second Temple in 70 CE.

The new letters continued to be imbued with the qualities inherent in each original symbol. Aleph (א) was now formed from two hands (the symbol for a hand being the tenth letter, yod: י) attached by a line, the vav of conjunction. One hand reaches for Heaven, the other toward Earth.

Preceding the Creation of Genesis, God spoke the letters A–T into existence. Vav, the nail linking Heaven and Earth, first appears in the Torah as the twenty-second letter in the story of Genesis when God created Heaven and (vav) Earth (Genesis 1:1). The order of the letters used to write the Torah is never to be altered. Changing even one letter would destroy the proper spell rigorously followed by the *sefer*, the order/scribe transcribing each new copy of the Torah. The order of both the alphabet and Torah are never arbitrary. A correct spell mandates letters placed in the proper order.

The new alphabet (Ketav Ashuri), now known as square Hebrew, retains the extensive tradition of meditation and magic of the older twenty-two letters that eventually became part of Kabbalah. Abraham is said to have received this wisdom. Born in Ur of the star-watching Chaldeans, he traveled north toward Anatolia and eventually to Egypt, following the commands of his One God. The first known book of the Kabbalah, *Sefer Yetzirah,* is attributed to Abraham, and Rabbi Ayreh Kaplan claims that since "Abraham was the greatest mystic and astrologer of his age, it is natural to assume that he was familiar with all the mysteries of ancient Egypt and Mesopotamia."[2] (I find that extensive travel and genealogies of the ancestors denote awareness of cultural debts rather than literal history.)

Transmitted orally for generations, the *Sefer Yetzirah* appeared in written form early in the Common Era. Scholars usually date it between the second and seventh century CE. Further elaborations and commentaries on the Kabbalah appeared in Spain after the seventh to eighth centuries. Spain during this time blossomed under the Arabs, who were translating Greek texts. Keeping with the idea that it is the numerical placement of letters in an order, the proper "spelling," that empowers each symbol, sefer includes the meaning of counted "order," as does the term for a scribe (sefer) properly and faithfully transcribing the letters in a Torah scroll.

Included among the Kabbalah's teachings are astrology, physiognomy, palmistry,[3] and the transmigration of souls. Historian Gershom Scholem posits, "The Cabbalists created images and symbols; perhaps they revived an age-old tradition."[4] Kabbalah includes a Tree of Life composed of ten lights and the twenty-two letters of the alphabet. The tree is said to manifest in the body of the Primal Man, Adam Kadman. Kadman is the Phoenician name for Cadmus. The Semitic root *kdm* means "east," but east implies both "Orient" as well as "orient" as in a guide, in addition to the luster of a pearl of wisdom.

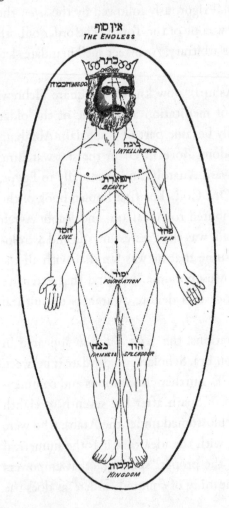

אין סוף
THE ENDLESS

Fig. 17. Adam Kadman as a Tree of Lights

From Isaac Myer, *Qabbalah*, 1888, as reproduced in Christian Ginsburg, *The Kabbalah: Its Doctrines, Development and Literature*, 1920

There is a prayer, the Akdamus or Akdamut (c. 1095 CE), celebrating the gift of the Torah. Written during a period when the Jews of Europe were being massacred, it may also have been a wish for a return to a better life. Each verse ends with T-A. That is, as soon as the letters finish (T as last letter), they return to A. I think it is outside of chance that the similarity of the prayer's name to kdm is accidental.

Again, I wish to emphasize that I am not implying that the extensive traditions of Jewish mystics, alchemists, ancient musicians, Druids, Phoenician mathematicians, Viking warriors, Taoist scholars, Hindu sages, or others all seek the same goals through the magic contained in our letters. I am merely unraveling threads from an ancient pattern to demonstrate that such a pattern exists and that it included an enlightened return into the circle.

7

Various Western Traditions

While I am not attempting to write a linear history of Mystery traditions, that history "leads us to the underside of Christianity . . . [and is] viewed as heresy. . . . This diverse group includes the Gnostics, the Cathars, the Knights Templar, the Cult of the Holy Grail, and the Church of Mary Magdalene."[1]

TAROT

Tarot is an alchemical revelation, revealing the descent and ascent of Hermes/Mercurius/Thoth.

JOSEPH CAMPBELL AND RICHARD ROBERTS,
TAROT REVELATIONS

Twenty-two Tarot card images are among my resources to develop the stories of the letters described in part 2. Perhaps created as playing cards, they are now used for divination. Tarot, whose name has been linked to both the Torah and the Latin *rota* (wheel), includes twenty-one numbered Major Arcana cards plus a Zero, the Fool. Like Orion, whose Hebrew name is Kis'l (Fool), traveling outside the zodiac circle, the Fool of the Tarot wanders outside the circle of the other cards; but his appearance still brings his Mother's material wealth. Although a nothing, a naught, a zero, each time he returns he brings a tenfold increase (1-10-100-1000). As a hidden cipher (zero) remembered for his measurements, one of Orion's many names is Algebra.*

The Tarot illustrations included in this book are from the Rider-Waite deck, a set designed at the end of the nineteenth century. The designer, A. E. Waite, and the illustrator, Pamela Colman Smith, had connections with Mystery cults whose symbolism is reflected by the cards. The oldest surviving Tarot cards were commissioned by the Visconti family of Milan in the fifteenth century. Although they were not numbered, the characters of the allegorical cards, the trumps, appeared in most later decks, including the Rider-Waite deck.

The Tarot is attributed to multiple origins, including the secrets of Jewish magicians, gypsies from India, Arabs, and Egyptians. My own investigation indicates a pattern so widespread and so ancient that all of the above are possible. Preceding Tarot cards, packs of playing cards began appearing in Europe in the late 1300s, shortly after the destruction of the Knights Templar (1312 CE).

THE KNIGHTS TEMPLAR

During the Crusades, the Knights Templar headquartered at the Temple Mount of Jerusalem, which is possibly located above the Temple of Solomon. There, they may have discovered ancient secrets promising both gold and enlightenment. Accused of heresy by later popes, many Templars were tortured and executed, their riches seized by the Church, their secrets (and most of their wealth) disappeared underground. They have been linked with numerous Mystery traditions, including Masonry, masons from Egypt having built Solomon's Temple. I repeat: I am not aiming for literal history, only following myths to uncover trails left by a Mystery.

Templars, like Masons and witches, were heirs to the measurements of ancient magic. As researchers Michael Baigent, Richard Leigh, and Henry Lincoln write in their book *Holy Blood, Holy Grail,* "There are unquestionably mysteries associated with the Templars . . . and secrets

*Algebra and geometry include the measurements of the Earth mother Ge (Gaia).

of some kind as well. . . . Symbolic carvings in Templar preceptories . . . suggest that some officials in the order's hierarchy were conversant with such disciplines as astrology, alchemy, sacred geometry, and numerology, as well, of course, as astronomy."[2]

ADDITIONAL WESTERN TRADITIONS

The letters described in part 2 also draw from such diverse traditions as alchemy, palmistry, and Mother Goose rhymes.

Alchemy

My primary alchemy text is *The Six Keys of Eudoxus of Cnidus,* written around 400 BCE. Eudoxus was a Greek philosopher and mathematician who studied astronomy in Egypt. One of his teachers was Pythagoras, teacher in another Mystery school who, like Cadmus, was born to a Phoenician. Like the Creation myth of Genesis, the cryptic keys follow the symbolism present among our ABCs.

Mother Goose

The ancient bird goddess now known as Mother Goose supplies a divination poem counting blackbirds. Since the pattern closely recalls the numerical secrets hiding among our alphabet letters, I include her verses as we explore the first ten letters.

> *One for Sorrow,*
> *Two for Mirth [Joy],*
> *Three for a Wedding,*
> *Four for a Birth [Boy].*
> *Five for Silver,*
> *Six for Gold,*
> *Seven's a Secret n'ere to be told.*
> *Eight's for Heaven,*
> *Nine for Hell,*
> *and Ten for the Devil's ain self.*

An alternate form not found in children's books concludes with:

Seven for a Witch,
Eight for a Whore,
Nine for a Burying,
Ten will be a Dance.

PALMISTRY

Palmistry, another divination technique, reads one's fortune revealed by the hand. The lines and shapes of hand and fingers all are considered. Each of our five fingers is said to represent a deity and is endowed with certain qualities. Their numbering mimics the stories of the first five letters of our alphabet. Saturn as third (middle) finger, for instance, was an ancient deity once responsible for fertility: the "sower of the seed." In Genesis, seed-bearing plants appear on the third day. Traditionally, for an aspiring couple hoping for offspring, the third day (Tuesday) was the best day to marry.

The Five Fingers

1. Little finger—Mercury
2. Second finger—Apollo, the healer
3. Third finger—Saturn
4. Fourth finger—Jupiter
5. Thumb—various deities, including a strong aspect of Mercury or Hercules

SEVERAL OGHAM SERIES

Position, Shape	Tree Ogham	Bird Ogham	Assistant Ogham	Fort Ogham	Lin (Water) Ogham
1, ⊢	Beth/Birch	Besan/Pheasant	Babel	Bruden	Banba/Barrow
2, N/A	Unspoken	Unspoken	Unspoken	Unspoken	Unspoken
3, ⊨	Luis/Rowan or Fire	Lachu/Duck	Loth (Lot)	Liftey	Lumneach Shannon
4, ⊫	Fearn/Alder	Faelinn/Gull	Foraind	Femen	Foyle
5, ⊯	Saille/Willow	Seg/Hawk	Saliaaath	Scolae	Shannon
6, ⊰	Nion/Ash or Hook Nin/Forked branch	Naescu/Snipe	Nabgadon	Nephin	Nith
7, ⊣	Huath/Hawthorn	Hadai/Night Raven	Hiruad	h-Ocha	Othain
8, ⊣	Duir/Oak	Droen/Wren	Dabhid (David)	Dinn Rig	Dergderg
9, ⊣	Tinne/Holly or Ingot	Truith/Starling	Talamon	Tara	Teith
10, ⊣	Col/Hazel	Unspoken	Cae	Cera	Catt
11, ⊣	Quert/Apple	Querc/Hen	Kaliap	Corann	Cusrat
12, ✚	Muin/Vine or Neck	Mintan/Titmouse	Muriath	Meath	Muintin
13, ✚	Gort/Ivy or Gart/Garden	Geis/Swan	Gotli or Gad	Gabur	Gavel
14, ✚	Ng/Reed or Pethboc/Guelder Rose	Ngeigh/Goose	Gomers	nGarman	Graney
15, N/A	Skipped	Skipped	Skipped	Skipped	Skipped
16, ✚	Straif/Blackthorn	Stmolach/Thrush	Stru	Streulae	Sruthair
17, ✚	Ruis/Elder	Rocnat/Rook	Reuben	Roigne	Rye
18, ✛	Ailm/Elm, Palm, or Fir	Aidhircleog/Lapwing	Achab	Ae Cualand	Aru
19, ✛	Ohn/Furze	Odoroscrach/Cormorant	Oise	Odba	Eobul
20, ✛	Uhr/Heather	Uiseoc/Lark	Urith	Usney	Uissen
21, ✛	Eodha/Poplar	Ela/Swan	Essu	Navan	Erbus
22, ✛	Ioho/Yew	Illair/Eagle	Iachim	Islay	Indiurnn

8
Celtic Ogham

We tend to be uninspired about our script. Letters need to be written, preferably typed in black and white, in neat, ordered rows. We extend ourselves somewhat to accept as proper those letters written on stone or parchment, although we are more reluctant to accept calligraphy, relegating it to an art form. We also demand that our letters be strung into words to carry our thoughts.

Older spells were far more flexible. They might appear as tongues of flame or be written in the sands of time. Messages appeared in tea leaves or were carried by passing clouds. Older scholars could read the trees and understand the language of birds. The following script, Ogham, derives many of its symbols from their attributes in the natural world.

Ogham is a Celtic script of twenty stick symbols appearing in Ireland around 300 CE. Ogham undoubtedly existed as an oral tradition long before its physical appearance. A secretive code script, it was not used for general writing. Rather, it appears primarily on tombstones and boundary markers, suggesting the scribes knew of the alphabet's ancient promise of resurrection and travel between the worlds.

The letters are composed of groups of one to five lines arranged in a column and intersected by one to five cross lines at various angles. The shapes give no clue to their meaning. However, each ogham represents an object, and each Ogham series follows the same set order.*

---

*The term *ogham* (lowercase) denotes a generic letter in one of these scripts. The term *Ogham* (capitalized) denotes the proper name of one of these scripts (*Tree Ogham*).

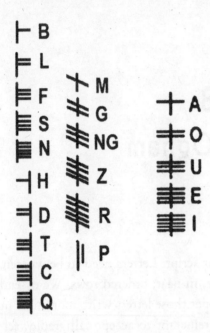

Fig. 18. These are the shapes used for all the Ogham series, with the letters named after trees, forts, et cetera, depending on the series.

Thus, we can study the myths associated with each ogham object and compare them to those of other ordered traditions. In doing so, I found either the first or second ogham must be skipped to keep the pattern consistent. I chose to skip the second. My reason will become clearer as we explore each letter in the second part of this book. (Spoiler alert: Second position is associated with Apollo, sacred to early Celts. The name of G-d cannot be spoken. As the oghams progress, I will also skip the fifteenth symbol, a position associated with the Devil in some traditions.)

The Tree Ogham, popularly known as the Celtic Tree Oracle, is the earliest known Ogham, with its "letters" primarily named after trees. Stories associated with each tree fit the same story we see unfolding through other alphabet symbols. That is, qualities associated with the twenty oghams mimic qualities associated with objects chosen for the same position in other alphabet patterns. There is some disagreement about which were the original trees of the Ogham, but all the choices seem to relate to the unfolding Creation myth of the original template.

After the Tree Ogham, several later series developed. Named for other collections of objects, such as assistants, birds, colors, arts and crafts, forts of Ireland, pools of water (Lin), and so on, each collection uses the same initials and symbols as the Tree script. The oghams of these later series seem to be simple schoolchild mnemonics, not containing the richer qualities inherent in the original tree symbols. The full ogham script is given in the charts at the start of this chapter. All collections begin with symbols whose names start with B and then L and end twenty letters later with a word starting with I.

BATTLE OF THE TREES

Another name for Ogham is Beth-Luis-Nion, the names of the oldest letters: Birch (Beth), Rowan (Luis), and Ash (Nion). All written Oghams, however, use Beth, Luis, and Fearn (Alder) as their first three symbols. At some point in time before Ogham became a written script, Ash (Nion) defeated Alder (Fearn) and assumed the sixth position belonging to the queen. Celtic kings could not rule without marriage to the queen of the land. Robert Graves, in his book *The White Goddess,* discusses this "battle of the trees'" and their fight for the coveted positions. (We will look at reasons for the battle when we discuss the fourth and sixth letters in part 2. Ash [(Nion)] was originally fourth and Alder [(Fearn)] sixth. Alder, as you will read, lost the battle and was demoted.)

THE ORIGINS OF OGHAM

History often ignores the convergence and divergence of peoples sharing and developing traditions to make them uniquely their own. The later Ogham series often refer to events and objects occurring around the Black Sea, a melting pot of traditions and cultures belonging to the goddess Asia. Here we find Troy, Miletus (settled by people from Crete), Germanic tribes, Scythians, and Celtic groups known as the Galatians. The first Bird Ogham symbol, for instance, is Besan, a pheasant. According to the *Oxford Universal Dictionary* the pheasant is also known as the phasian bird,* after the Phasis, a river of Colchis; Colchis hosted the adventures of the Golden Fleece, another story associated with golden mysteries, metallurgy, great goddesses, and astrological serpent-trees. Seventy-two languages were spoken in the land of Colchis. Note: Ancient Iberia, which carries the same name as Spanish Iberia, is a kingdom located next to Colchis.

Oghams constantly hint at shared mysteries and measurements. B and I, first and last letters bookending all Ogham scripts, are the initials of two masons, Boaz and Iachim. Myth tells us Boaz and Iachim were brought from Egypt by Phoenicians to build the Temple of Solomon in Jerusalem. Their initials were inscribed on the Temple's pillars flanking the door into its mysteries. According to the *Mabinogion,* a medieval collection of Welsh tales whose origins, in oral history, date back centuries earlier, Solomon, known for both his knowledge and material wealth, "obtained in Babel's Tower all the sciences of Asia's land."[1] Herodotus (c. 440 BCE), considered the lands of the fate goddess Asia to include Anatolia and the Near East. Among the many explanations for her name, the Greeks defined Asia as "resurrection."

The Spanish Origin Theory
In his 1596 tract *View of the Present State of Ireland,* English writer Edmund Spenser addresses the mystery of Ogham's origin: "It seemeth that they had [the letters] from the nation that came out of Spaine."[2]

Although no physical oghams have been found in Spain, they may have been taught as an oral tradition until after arriving in Ireland. Adding weight to the idea that Ogham came to Ireland from Spain, there are several Spanish scripts—including North and South Iberian, as well as Milesian, Etruscan, and Arcadian—that, like Ogham, drop the second and fifteenth letter symbols.[3] Using them as a template, I also skip the second and fifteenth when describing Ogham symbols. This keeps Ogham's myths congruent with those of the symbols from other traditions.

---

*Don't miss the use of *Asian* in this word. Puns are never far from meaning and connections when discussing mythology.

The Milesian Origin Theory

In some traditions, the Irish claim descent from the sons of Mil—
that is, Milesians. The Milesians were Gaels who sailed from Spain to
Ireland, a point in support of the Spanish origin theory. Milesians take
their name from their ancient home city of Miletus. Settled by people
from Crete, Miletus is located south of the Black Sea near Troy and
Colchis and claimed a lineage from Cadmus: "Milesian nobles traced
their descent back to the Phoenician or one of his companions," notes
an entry on Cadmus in the 1910 *Encyclopaedia Britannica*.

The city of Miletus was the first to use letters as numbers, an idea
that later came into play in the Greek practice of gematria. Discussing
ancient number conventions, Kieren Barry notes that the older, simpler
Milesian alphabetic system used every letter in the alphabet to represent
a number.[4]

According to the eleventh century CE book, *The Book of the Taking
of Ireland* (*Lebor Gabala Erenn*), after traveling the Earth for hundreds
of years, the Milesians arrived in Iberian Spain before sailing to Ireland
to conquer the Fairy race. Discussed later, the Sons of Mil and the cow
goddess Bue, also known as the Hag of Beare, sailed with the Egyptian
Israelite, Cae of the Fair Judgements.[5] The Kabbalah tradition linking alphabets, number magic, and other mysteries appeared about the
time of Ogham's appearance. It is thought to have first appeared in the
twelfth century in Provence and Catalonia in Northern Iberia.

The Hercules Theory

Another tradition tells that honey-tongued Hercules as Ogmios, a giant
laboring like Orion through the sky, invented Ogham. Hercules is the
Greek name for the Phoenician god Melquart, King of the City. Cadiz
in southwestern Spain was one of the many trade cities established
(c. 1100 BCE) by Phoenicia's seagoing sailors. Pillars being a mark of
Phoenician temples, the pillars of Hercules once stood in his temple
of Cadiz. The historian Herodotus (c. 450 BCE) traveled to the city
of Tyre in Phoenicia to visit a temple of Hercules where he saw the
temple's two pillars. One was made of gold; the second was of green
emerald. The pillars of Hercules in Cadiz were bronze as were those of

the Temple of Solomon in Israel. Their temples are long gone, but two rocks marking the passage from the sheltered Mediterranean into the wild Atlantic still bear Hercules' name.

The Scythian Theory

A variant tradition about the creation of Ogham attributes the script to Scythians, warriors traveling between the Black Sea, India, and China. According to medieval Irish texts, Ogham was first invented soon after the fall of the Tower of Babel by the Scythian king, Fenius Farsa. Fenius and his son journeyed with a retinue of seventy-two scholars to study the confused languages at Nimrod's tower. Fenius created the Irish language out of the confusion and the Beithe-luis-nuin (Ogham) to write his new language.[6] Fenius's name, also written as Phoeniusa, hints at his connection with the Phoenicians. His wife, Belait, recalls Baalat, the feminine form of Phoenicia's Baal. In this version of the story, his stepson was Hercules; in another, Fenius's son married Scotia, the daughter of a pharaoh, also known as Bue (cow, like Balaat and Egypt's Hathor) and as the Hag of Beare. The majority of Ireland's ogham stones are found in Beare's home in Ireland's Munster.

Nimrod, builder of the Tower of Babel, was also known for his knowledge of astrology and measurements. This ties him to the legends of Masons, another group inheriting the hidden secrets of measurement. According to an early Masonic manuscript: "At ye making of ye toure of Babell there was a Masonrie first much esteemed of, and the King of Babilon yt called Nimrod was a Mason himself and loved well Masons."[7] (And Nimrod is yet another name for Orion, the measurer god who lost control of his astrological circle with the implacable precession of fixed stars.)

Fenius Farsa, king of Scythia, was a grandson of Magog, himself the grandson of biblical Noah and mythic ancestor of Germanic tribes and the Celts. The homeland of the wandering Scythians was north of the Black Sea and extended toward China, another source of patterns bequeathed by bull-headed serpent gods (see chapter 11). Archaeologist Renate Rolle notes, "These drinking, hemp-inhaling lords of the steppes north of the Hellespont . . . had been well known [to the Greeks] since

Fig. 19. Grave shapes with soles, from a Paleolithic painting
found in the Cave of da Pasiega, Monte Castillo, Spain

Drawing by Henri Breuil, 1913

the fifth century BCE."*[8] A Scythian priest of Apollo, Abaris, studied
with Pythagoras around 500 BCE.

One final note about Ogham's script hinting at a return after death:
when a person dies, the soul remains. The letter A shapes seen in figure
19 show an ancient image of alpha's cow head. This is equally the shape
of a woman's womb and a shape used for ancient graves (see the description of the first letter in part 2). Next to it are the prints of a prince
who has left his sole behind as he stepped off the Earth.

The necessity for a new prince (and his prints) to be able to fill his
father's shoes is ancient. Last returning as first determines the choice of
Islay as the final Fort Ogham. Islay is a small island northeast of Ireland,
one of Scotland's Western Isles. Beginning in the fourteenth century, the
chiefs of the various isles would meet on Council Island, a tiny island
in a loch on Islay. When it came time to elect a new Lord of the Isles,
a ceremony took place involving a large rock whose surface bore a time-
worn depression in the shape of a human foot. The new lord would set
his foot into that mold, in the same manner as had all the chiefs before
him, thereby "denoting that he should walk in the footsteps and upright-
ness of his predecessors," as author John Michell put it.[9] Islay also has a
stone circle, the Stones of Cultoon, aligned to the winter solstice, the day
the sun dies and then is reborn as days once again grow longer.

---

*Magog is also the mythic ancestor to a Jewish warrior kingdom of Huns, Khazaria
(c. 600–1200 CE), near the Black Sea. Descendants of Attila the Hun, they converted to
Judaism.

ELDER FUTHARK RUNES

Letter Position	Shape	Rune Name	Symbolic Representation
1	ᚠ	Fehu, Feoh, Fe	Cattle or money
2	ᚢ	Uruz, Ur	Aurochs, ore, dross, or shower
3	ᚦ	Thurisaz, Thurs	Thorn or giant
4	ᚨ	Ansus, Os	High god or mouth
5	ᚱ	Raido, Rad or Reidh	Wheel or ride
6	ᚲ	Kenaz, Ken, or Kaun	Torch or canker
7	ᚷ	Gyfu or Gebo	Gift
8	ᚹ	Wynn	Joy or white
9	ᚺ	Hagalaz	Hag god, Hail, or Heal
10	ᚾ	Naudiz, Nyd	Need
11	ᛁ	Isaz	Ice
12	ᛃ	Jera, Ger, or Ar	Harvest or year
13	ᛇ	Ihwaz	Yew tree
14	ᛈ	Perth or Peorth	Lot or dice box for casting lots
15	ᛉ	Algiz	Elk (horned deity) or elk sedge (protection)
16	ᛋ	Sig or Sigel	Sun or victory
17	ᛏ	Tir or Tiuwaz	God of the North Star; associated with Mars
18	ᛒ	Berkana	Birch
19	ᛖ	Ehwaz	Horse
20	ᛗ	Mannaz	Man
21	ᛚ	Laguz or Logr	Lake or leek
22	◇ᛜ	Ingwaz (also Ingvi-Frey)	In alchemy, used as a symbol for lead.*
23	ᛞ	Dagaz	Day (this is sometimes placed last)
24	ᛟ	Othala	Homeland or inheritance

*Like Saturn (lead), Ingvi was responsible for fertility. Like Orion/Saturnus, he went "east over the waves."

9
Germanic Runes

The country east of the Tana Kvisl [River Don] in Asia
was called Asaland [God's Land] and the chief city in that
land was called Asagaard [God's Garden]. In that city was
a chief called Odin.

SNORRI STURLUSON, *YNGLINGA SAGA*

(TRANS. SAMUEL LAING)

The River of the goddess Don, running into the north end of the Black Sea, separates the lands of the goddesses Asia and Europa, after whom the continents took their names. Asia in the ancient world included Anatolia and the Near East.

The Germanic script known as runes or Futhark began appearing early in the Common Era. It provides further clues uncovering the secrets hiding in our alphabet. Among the definitions of *rune* is "mystery." Odin, a warrior aspect of Mercury, learned these mysteries from a dead god while he hung on a tree by a well near the Black Sea.

A blend of the Roman gods Mercury/Hermes and Mars, Odin is also known as Irmin, Jormunr, or Hermann. As Hermann, he is patron of both war and trade. As Mercury/Hermes, he has been associated with the treelike pillars known as herms. Thousands of years after the vulture goddesses of ancient Anatolia carried their dead to Heaven, Odin's band of bird women, the Valkyries, performed the deed. Arriving as swans or ravens or riding on flying horses, they carried away warriors slain in battle.

Odin did not acquire a mason's skill along with the runes. He hired a giant to build the great walls of his city Asagaard, building with massive stones, Cyclopean masonry being one of the skills of the older Earth giants (Cyclops). After learning the runes, and after killing his mason to avoid paying his wages, Odin traveled north from Anatolia with the gods known as the Vanir (wagons), the captured Earth gods, including Frey and his sister Freya.

Like many ancient goddesses, Freya owned a necklace of stars. Known as the Brisingamen (jewel of flame), it was forged by four dwarves—the same number as the corners of the year (solstices and equinoxes). A goddess from a much earthier era, she slept with each of the dwarves as payment.

FUTHARK FAMILIES

The runic alphabet's name, Futhark, derives from the first six letters F-U-Th-A-R-K: the Hex (meaning both six and a magic spell). The Elder Futhark of twenty-four letters appeared around 150 CE. Other Futharks (including the Younger Futhark and Anglo-Saxon/Old English runes) developed after 650 CE. These later traditions have varying numbers of letters and shapes. Like other alphabets, each rune represents the initial sound of an object—e.g., the sound of F from the word *fehu,* meaning "cattle" or "wealth."

Various traditions (Norwegian, Icelandic, etc.) use variant names and spellings for the runes, but through all the versions, the order and symbolism of the pattern is similar. Because I am only interested in uncovering the attributes underlying each letter, I do not emphasize the source of various rune traditions. Although the stories unfolding through runes follow closely the magic hidden in Phoenician, the shapes and sounds of most runes derive from Germanic sources. Each group adapted the pattern to suit their own culture. To repeat the important caveat, when comparing mythic alphabets, one must consider the story, *not* the shape or sound of each letter. This is not the tale of an epigrapher. My interest is in why the symbols were chosen to represent the orderly number position of each letter.

Featuring the hallmark of all circular scripts, in the Futhark script, the first and last symbols reflect a promise of return. The last of the twenty-four runes is the cow-shaped, womb-shaped Othala (ᛟ), meaning Earth, inheritance, or homeland. The first is Fehu, offering the promise of Earth's wealth. As is true for Ogham, runes were not used for general writing; rather they were primarily inscribed on boundary markers or tombstones (another boundary) or used to work magic. But like other ancient alphabets, runes, if properly spelled, embody the promise of resurrection, the power to return the dead to life.

The twenty-four runes are arranged in three families of eight (or *aettir,* a Germanic word meaning both "eight" and "compass direction"): the families of the fertile Earth god Frey, the Underworld goddess Hel, and the Sky god Tir. (This division mirrors the three separate families of the ancestor Phoenician alphabet.)

The first family of eight symbols reflects a cycle of fertility, growth, harvest, and then, a rising up into a new light. In the north, these powers belong to the generous Frey. Under his golden reign, Earth knew peace and good harvests.

The second family begins with Hel, goddess of the Underworld. Her eight runes, like the letters of other alphabets, describe a soul's journey after death and emergence once more into the light of day, symbolized by the sun of the sixteenth rune. This parallels the sixteenth letter in the Phoenician/Old Hebrew alphabet, whose symbol is the eye. The Phoenician/Old Hebrew alphabet begins Hel's family with the ninth letter Teth, translated "coil," which marks the entrance into the watery labyrinth of the goddess Tethys. Like the goddess Hel, all rivers emanate from her womb.

The third rune family begins with the sky god Tir as the seventeenth rune. Tir's family seems to include astronomical data and is associated with the command of stars spinning around the North Star. In parallel, the Greek seventeenth letter, pi (π), commands the area of this circle, and the Hebrew pe (meaning "mouth" or "commandment") also appears as a seventeenth letter.

In my search for runic attributes, I found several ancient poems to be helpful: the Old English Rune Poem, also known as the Anglo-Saxon

Rune Poem (twenty-nine staves, c. tenth century); the Norwegian Rune Poem (sixteen staves, c. thirteenth century); and the Old Icelandic Rune Poem (sixteen staves, c. fifteenth century). The Old Icelandic poem is especially helpful since its riddles are answered with glosses beneath each verse.

There are other briefer mnemonic poems and magic spells in the sagas. The *Volsunga saga* "tells of the origin of Runes and seems to contain another fragment relating to the signs of the Heavens and the mysterious characters which they trace on the black vault of a moonless night, a fancy which the Jewish cabalists shared," relate scholars Gudbrand Vigfusson and F. York Powell in their collection of the *Eddas* and sagas.[1] The study of astrology was, of course, linked both to divination and to alphabetic calendars.

In *Grímnismál* (Grimner's lay), a mythological poem of the *Poetic Edda* "whose subject is Celestial Geometry," according to Vigfusson and Powell, Odin describes twelve halls, each occupied by a god.[2] As we shall explore, the attributes of these numbered symbols illuminate those of other traditions. In the *Hávamál* (High One's words), a text from the thirteenth century, Odin taunts a dying dragon with his knowledge of eighteen charms. The dragon, once commander of the pole stars, lost control to the wagon stars due to the precession.

There have been numerous attempts to understand the meaning of the cryptic rune poems, curses, and less frequent blessings appearing in Norse poetry and sagas. I find the empowerment of each rune derives from the number magic present from its earliest Phoenician appearance. It may be that runes once included the deeper soul journey still present among the twenty-two letters of the Phoenician/Old Hebrew alphabet, but if so, they were not passed on. I have found only a simple practical magic present in the rune charms available to us. We shall unravel those charms in the second part of this book.

The *Second Lay of Helgi Hundingsbane* (c. 900 CE) declares: "It was the belief in former days that people were reborn after death; but this is now called an old wives' tale."[3] By the time of this saga, the last rune was no longer a welcoming womb-shaped Othala (homeland), hinting at rebirth. It had become a grave. By 800 CE, the Old English Rune Poem

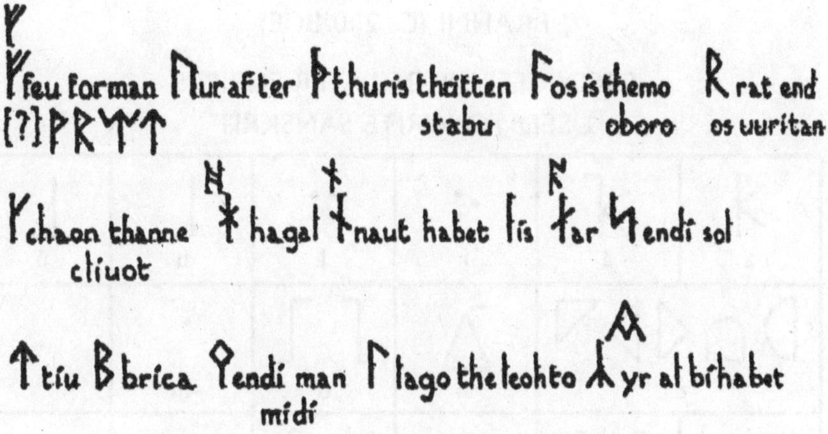

ᚨ
ᚠ feu forman ᚢ ur after ᚦ thuris theitten ᚠ os is themo ᚱ rat end
[?] ᚹᚱᚤᛏ   stabu   oboro   os uuritan

ᚺ   ᛈ   ᚱ
ᚲ chaon thanne   ✳ hagal ᛏ naut habet ᛁ is ᛏ ar ᛋ endi sol
  cliuot

                                                             ᚨ
ᛏ tiu ᛒ brica ᛈ endi man ᛚ lago the leohto ᛉ yr al bi habet
      midi

Fig. 20. A version of the Younger Futhark,
the Abecedarium Nordmanicum, c. 825 CE

Image reproduced from R. Derolez, *Runica Manuscripta*, 78

declares "Grave is hateful to every man when the flesh, the pallid body, begins inexorably to grow cold, to choose the Earth as its consort."[4]

The Abecedarium Nordmanicum (c. 825 CE), a version of the Younger Futhark, glossed the last rune with the letter A, perhaps hinting at the older return into the circle. The first rune is glossed Earth and Tir (arrow), the arrow that will fertilize Earth with the third charm. The last rune has been flipped over and translated as "yew." Intensely poisonous, the yew, which also represents the last Tree Ogham, was planted by graveyards. "Yew holds all," as the old saying goes. Yew vats once held the blood of the Vine King: wine. In this shape, it usually indicated death rather than rebirth. The king dying for his land, it eventually came to represent our peace symbol.

BRAHMI (C. 200 BCE)

PREDECESSOR OF LATER SCRIPTS USED TO WRITE SANSKRIT

a	ā	i	ī	u	ū
e		ai	o	-ṃ	
ka	kha	ga	gha		
ča	čha	ja	jha	ña	
ṭa	ṭha	ḍa	ḍha	ṇa	
ta	tha	da	dha	ná	
pa	pha	ba	bha	ma	
ya	ra	la	ḷa	va	
sa, ṣa	ṣa	śa	sa	ha	

10
India's Brahmi, Sanskrit, and Chakras

There are said to be shrines in Southern India where the same secrets are taught under binding pledges as are communicated to us in the Craft [Masonic tradition].

C. W. LEDBETTER,
FREEMASONRY AND ITS ANCIENT MYSTIC RITES

In India, by 2500 BCE, the cosmopolitan cities of Mohenjo Daro and Harappa were trading with Mesopotamia. Their script-like symbols may have represented an early writing system, but like those of the ancient Black Sea cities of Asia Minor, they are not in an order, nor do we know the names associated with the symbols. Therefore, we cannot include them in this comparison of mythic journeys.

Although many symbols used for later Indian scripts undoubtedly came from these early indigenous images, some letters—and possibly the very concept of the alphabet—came from Phoenicians. The earliest documented true alphabet in India was Brahmi (c. 300 BCE), which eventually became the fifty letters of Sanskrit.[1]

Although the Sanskrit language is dated to around 3,500 years ago, the various stories and teachings (the Vedas) were transmitted orally for hundreds of years. Eventually inheritors of the Sanskrit stories began writing them in their own various languages

67

and scripts.* In North India, Sanskrit appears in the Devanagari script, developed around 700 CE. In Sanskrit, letters have been scientifically divided into groups of fives by the sound's formation in the mouth.

Because we have not (yet) discovered an object named by each letter, we are unable to include this ordered script in our investigation of alphabet patterns. But it is important to note that the Sanskrit alphabet begins with potent A (or ah) as the first vowel and K (or ka) as the first consonant. The last letter is H (or ha).

Religion scholar Madhu Kanna notes, "First letter 'A' represents Siva. When the letter A is aspirated . . . it sounds Ha, the letter symbol of Sakti [Kali] (female energy) as well as the last letter of the Sanskrit alphabet. . . . The two letters embrace the entire range of the Sanskrit alphabet . . . the whole of creation in its subtle aspect as sound."[2] Shiva, like Hermes, is represented by a pillar, a herm, a lingam, a number I. Note that the first letter can be black or white, male or female. Shiva often appears painted white with the ashes of cremation. Kali is the black form of India's mother goddess.

Mother Kali and her consort Shiva create and destroy each world. After he dances his own destruction, she takes his seed into her womb to deliver each new generation. The ultimate form of the Creatrix, she too dances, wearing a necklace of skulls known as the *mundamala* when she wears it in her fierce aspect. The skulls, said to be from human heads, are counted as fifty (or sometimes fifty-one), each representing a letter (*varna*) of the Sanskrit alphabet known as the *Varnamala*, meaning literally "a garland of alphabet letters." Dressed this way, she is generally seen as the mother of language and all mantras (sounds).[3]

We will discuss Sanskit's vowel, A, and the first consonant, K, with the profile of the first letter in part 2. For now, consider the sound "ma." In India, the cow is said to be the mother of all. The Brahmi letter ma ষ appears as the same cow head as the early aleph ᛕ.

---

*The first known appearance of Sanskrit in writing was found in Vietnam, dated to the third century CE. See Daniels and Bright, *The World's Writing Systems,* 445.

CHAKRAS

The serpent resting at the end of the twenty-four letters of the hiero-glyph alphabet from Egypt mimics the serpent energy of India's Black Goddess, Kali. In the form of a sleeping serpent, Kali resides at the base of each human spine. A Hindu seeker of enlightenment is directed to awaken that power, or kundalini, by drawing it up the spine along the path of the seven chakras, or wheels of energy, paralleling the stages of manifestation that guide a soul on the path toward enlightenment.

Awakened, Kali as kundalini ascends along the twenty-four ver-tebrae of the spine, passing through and activating each of the seven chakras, until she emerges from the crown. Guiding the serpent along her ascent are the sounding of the fifty alphabet letters scattered among the petals of each chakra.

Qualities of the seven chakras mirror those of the first seven let-ters of our alphabet. Each chakra is associated with deities, colors, and sounds to aid the unfolding stages of a soul journey toward the light. When exploring and comparing these chakra attributes to those of the alphabet, we will rely on the wisdom of an ancient text, *Shat-chakra Nirupana*, "Description of the Seven Chakras" (compiled in 1577 CE by the pundit Purananda).

Sir John Woodroffe (writing as Arthur Avalon), who translated *Shat-chakra Nirupana* into English, tells us that Tantra, an esoteric mystical tradition of India, "correlates sound, form and colour. Sound produces form, and form is associated with colour. . . . Kundali . . . is the source from which all sound or energy, whether as ideas or speech, manifests. That sound . . . when uttered in human speech assumes the forms of letters. . . . The same energy which produces these letters mani-festing as Mantras produces the gross universe."[4] That is, Tantra, like Kabbalah, is another tradition using alphabet letters to produce a color-ful Spell of Creation.

India's astrology dates back thousands of years. The Vedic zodiac of twelve constellations is further divided into twenty-seven or twenty-eight "mansions" visited by the moon. The mansion located in Scorpio/Sagittarius is Mula, the root (*mula*) of all life, the foundation, and the recognized womb of our cosmos. This is our galactic center that we can equate to our Cosmic Mother which still gives birth to new stars. Although we constantly underestimate the intelligence and sophistication of ancient scientists, I find it utterly amazing that early skywatchers could identify this insignificant-looking dark area of the sky, our galactic center, as the womb of the Great Mother.

Kali resides in the Mula. Like other Black Goddesses of fate, she is associated both with the origins of writing and the measurements of time and chance. At the end of time, Kali takes the seed of her spouse, Shiva (associated with time and death, and colored white with the ashes from the cremation ground), into her womb.

> At the end of each cycle, during which one creation lasts,
> [Kali] gathers up . . . the seeds of the universe that is
> extinct, out of which a fresh creation is started.
>
> IMPERIAL RECORD DEPARTMENT,
> AN ALPHABETICAL LIST OF THE FEASTS AND HOLIDAYS
> OF THE HINDUS AND MUHAMMADAN (1914)

Kali is sometimes said to be "the game of dice personified."[5] As a "throw of a dice," she is sometimes illustrated riding a horse, the dice attached to her saddle. Sixty-four fairies (dakinis) attend her. This won't be the last time the number sixty-four makes an appearance. In fact, it's an important part of the next chapter.

11
China's I Ching
and Tao Te Ching

"It is significant that [North Central China] is where
the trade routes across Central Asia from the West enter
China." There is [a] theory, attempting to find in Central
Asia the common source of both the earliest Mesopotamian
and the earliest Chinese civilization, but positive proof
is wanting.

DAVID DIRINGER, THE ALPHABET,
QUOTING KENNETH SCOTT LATOURETTE,
THE DEVELOPMENT OF CHINA

Chinese culture arose in what is now north-central China. While early
pictograms were in use by around 4000 BCE, the first known Chinese
script written on oracle bones appeared around 1500 BCE. The thousands of characters, representing sounds and syllables, needed to write
Chinese left it in the hands of a trained elite. As far as I have been able
to determine, the symbols were never placed in order like the ABCs.

Chinese history equates writing with images derived from observing
the changing Heaven and Earth. The invention of writing is attributed
to the first of China's mythic Three Sovereigns, Fu Hsi (c. twenty-
ninth century BCE). Possessing a bull's head, like the first Phoenician
letter, aleph, or like the Bull of Heaven as Orion or Mercury, he also

71

has been depicted twining like a revolving DNA strand (sixty-four codons on three bases) around his spouse, the serpent Nu Kua. Anne Goodrich, in her review of the hundreds of temple gods found in the Temple of the Eastern Peak in Beijing, describes Fu Hsi: "His mother was Lao-Mu, Old Mother, who conceived him on seeing a falling star. He instituted the calendar, invented musical instruments . . . and is one of those given credit for the invention of writing."[1]

Fu Hsi and Nu Kua, a musician like Cadmus's wife Harmonia, stretch between Earth and the North Star. Because they measured the world after the Great Flood, they carry a compass and T-square. (The same symbols identify modern Masons, another group associated with measurements and ancient Mysteries.) "Fu Hsi and Nu Kua, i.e., the craftsman god and his paredra . . . measure the 'squareness of the earth' and the 'roundness of the heaven.' . . . The intertwined serpent-like bodies of the deities indicate clearly . . . circular orbits intersecting each other at regular intervals."[2]

Fig. 21. Fu Hsi and Nu Kua
as serpents spinning among
the stars, silk hanging
scroll, China, Tang Dynasty,
c. 200 BCE

THE I CHING

The I Ching (Book of Changes) is the earliest known book of divination. It first appeared in written form in the sixth century BCE, though it is attributed to much earlier origins. Its oracles are based on hexagrams. Each hexagram is composed by stacking two sets of trigrams, one above the other. Each trigram is itself three stacked lines, broken or unbroken, representing yin and yang. There are eight possible trigrams (the *pa kua*); each has a name, a compass direction, and a season. When ordered into pairs, the eight trigrams can form sixty-four different hexagrams.*

> *The number 64 is always related in some way or another to play and fate.*
> ANNE MARIE SCHIMMEL, *MYSTERY OF NUMBERS*

Like divination by a hex of Germanic runes or a throw of a six-sided dice, a hexagram was traditionally made by choosing, in a ritualistic but random manner, from among fifty "arrows" (yarrow wands). The selection determined each of the six lines of the hexagram. The I Ching then offers commentary on the hexagram. The casting of arrows evolved from earlier oracle traditions in China, such as reading the cracks that formed when turtle shells or bones were heated over a fire.

Tod Harris tells us, "Some scholars assert that the I Ching originated as a dictionary of the Chou variant of the Chinese script."[3] That is, the I Ching, like Germanic runes or the Kabbalah, provides another link between divination and alphabet "spells."

---

*Another Chinese game involving the number sixty-four is chess, which is laid out on sixty-four light and dark squares. According to Nigel Pennick, "Chess has a far greater symbolic significance than a mere pastime. . . . It has been connected with mental training, military strategy, complex mathematics, divination, astronomy, and astrology. . . . There is a close affinity between the layout of the gameboard and ancient Chinese diviners' boards. . . . Unlike Chess, this game was played with the aid of dice." (See Pennick, *Secret Games of the Gods*, 186–87.)

The trigrams can be laid out in an Early Heaven (Fu Hsi) sequence or a Later Heaven (modern) sequence. I use the Early Heaven sequence, which denotes the ideal world of harmony. The Later Heaven Sequence depicts the less-than-perfect world of reality.

Early Heaven Sequence

The Early Heaven Sequence represents the world in perfect balance:

Heaven/Chien (1) balanced against Earth/K'un (8)

Lake/Tui (2) balanced against Mountain/Ken (7)

Fire/Li (3) balanced against Water/K'an (6)

Thunder/Chen (4) balanced against Wind/Sun (5)

1. Chien (Heaven): the Creative; south ☰
2. Tui (Lake): the Joyous; southeast ☱
3. Li (Lightning/Fire): the Clinging; east ☲
4. Chen (Thunder): the Arousing; northeast ☳
5. Sun (Wind): the Gentle; southwest ☴
6. K'an (Water): the Abysmal; west ☵
7. Ken (Mountain): Keeping Still; northwest ☶
8. K'un (Earth): the Receptive; north ☷

The trigrams correspond to the unfolding story hidden in our alphabet symbols and to the Creation as described in Genesis. The sequence begins with a yet undivided Heaven (☰) and ends with the totally receptive female Earth (☷). Like the Sheela Na Gig and Kali described in earlier chapters, receptive Earth takes the seed of a dying land into her open womb to create another generation. In their introduction to James Legge's 1889 translation of the I Ching, scholars Chu'u Chai and Winberg Chai explain, "The objects or attributes . . . symbolized by the Eight Trigrams are made [from] the constituents of the universe. . . . The Eight Trigrams, together with the Sixty-Four Hexagrams formed by their combinations, therefore, represent all the possible situations

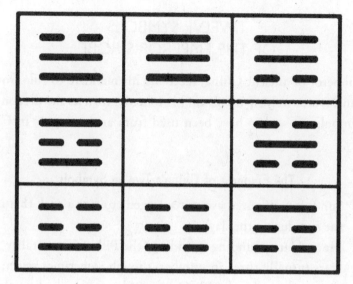

Fig. 22. Trigrams

and mutations of creation, a universe in miniature."[4] Again, we see here a recognition that symbols can re-create the world.

The similarity of themes from China to Scandinavia is clear and supports the idea that the patterns developed far back in prehistory. Whether true history or myth, "casting rods by which the diagrams of the I-Ching are calculated was known to the Greeks as a Scythian practice, suggesting that the art may have been introduced into China by Mongol seers."[5]

I include the above quote to show a recognized kinship, not to suggest the historical origins of writing and divination. My exploration is simply to show that there exists an ancient and widespread pattern of unfolding Earth magic, and those hermetic mystics recognized a kinship between their various traditions. Appearing in history around 800 BCE, the Scythians rode their horses on the north plains between China and the Black Sea. The earliest version of China's oracle script, written on turtle shells and bones, preceded the wandering Scythians by a thousand years, but the Scythians may have suggested the use of sticks (arrows) for casting. Both the Celts and Germanic tribes have cultural and physical ties with the Scythians.

TWELVE SYMBOLS
OF THE EMPEROR'S ROBE

The emperor of ancient China, receiving his mandate to rule from the Heavens, wore twelve symbols on his robe. Known as the dragon robe, the symbols are said to have been used from ancient times in China's history.[6]

The Emperor of China's Twelve Symbols

1. Sun (often pictured as a three-legged crow or a cock that carries the sun during the day)
2. Moon Hare pounding (grinding) the Pill of Immortality*
3. Stars (usually three in number, though sometimes seven; three stars are associated with Orion, and seven with the pole stars spun by Orion's north-pointing arrow)
4. Mountains
5. Dragon (symbol of the emperor)
6. Pheasant (symbol of the empress)
7. Two cups†
8. Spray of pond weed
9. Fire
10. Grains of rice
11. Axe
12. Textile design (possibly the *fu* symbol of good luck)

These twelve symbols form an ordered system, and each has attributes fitting our ancient pattern. We will discuss these symbols as we proceed through the stories of the alphabet letters in part 2.

---

*Moon Hare is a traditional character in East Asian mythology. The Pill of Immortality is said to be an elixir prepared for the gods by the husband of the moon goddess, whom the Moon Hare serves.

†In regard to the seventh symbol, Whitlock and Ehrmann write: "The meaning is very obscure." Number seven's obscurity offers an interesting parallel to Mother Goose: "Seven's a secret."

TAO TE CHING

Another Chinese source associated with our Mysteries is an alchemical text, the Tao Te Ching (c. 550 BCE). Containing eighty-one verses, the book, like our own alphabet, hides a guide to the path (Tao) through life. At various times in its history, it was outlawed for being too earthy.* The meaning described in the first seven verses fits closely with those of the alphabet symbols, as we'll see in part 2.

The author of the Tao was Lao-tzu, "Old Baby." By tradition, he was born in 604 BCE, thirteen incarnations after Fu Hsi. Reborn old, he was one of Three Pure Ones, beings who descended from the stars of Orion to remind a corrupt world of the proper way to rule.[7] Recalling Orion's ancient role as Bull of Heaven, Lao-tzu is often depicted riding a bull (an ox or buffalo) and is associated with a tiger and a dragon. The serpentine Milky Way runs past Orion's feet, the Dragon once holding the North Star by his head.

---

*The definition of *earthy* being direct and uninhibited, especially about sexual subjects or bodily functions.

PART TWO

The Three Groups of
Alphabet Letters

Letters of the Earth,
Letters of the Underworld,
and Letters of the Heavens

INTRODUCTION TO PART TWO

Now we will explore the qualities attached to each letter by its position. The first eight letters (belonging to Earth) tell a story of readying Earth for planting, the birth of her children, the sharing of their harvest, another planting, and a final harvest. Then, on the eighth day, we see a rising up. I think this section of eight letters was the original "Spell" of the alphabet. A later tradition may have added letters to guide a soul journeying through the Underworld, represented by the next eight letters (the letters of the Underworld), offering a return through the eye of the sixteenth: ain/eye. The last few letters (the letters of the Heavens) reflect astronomical knowledge. These last letters in all the patterns imply a return that was ultimately judged a heresy and its believers to be heretics.

In these discussions, I juxtapose quotations from various ancient traditions to show the similarity of the underlying pattern. Again, I must emphasize I do not mean to trivialize the numerous traditions of luminous soul journeys that emerged from the original Spell. I am mixing and matching vastly different cultures simply to demonstrate that there *is* a pattern. To do so, I must simplify or ignore deeper mysteries. This is a journey over the surface of deeper waters.

First Family:
Letters of the Earth

Introduction to the First Family

Our oldest alphabet, the Phoenician (c. 1050 BCE), gave its order and letter names directly to Hebrew. We began this book by looking into the mythology of the symbols representing each Phoenician/Old Hebrew letter. Then we began comparing traditions with a reputation for magic, including Germanic runes (c. 150 CE), Celtic Ogham (c. 300 CE), and a twenty-four-hieroglyph "alphabet" from Egypt. Realizing their histories are broken traditions, their meanings hidden, we also explored other ordered patterns that are not true alphabets.

All follow the same hermetic pattern, and when we expand our search to include such diverse traditions as palmistry (each finger named for a god representing certain qualities), astrology, the path of the Tao Te Ching, the I Ching, Tarot cards, and alchemy, among others, the story hidden in the alphabet letters begins to clearly reveal itself. Each letter/symbol/verse has several related attributes determined by the placement in the order. I will try to act as the pathfinder to guide us through these multiple traditions. We begin with an undivided One leading the letters of the Earth.

First Letter

A Guide at the Gateway

Phoenician/Old Hebrew	Aleph (ox)
Greek	Alpha
Ogham	Beth (Birch)
Runes	Fehu, Feoh, or Fe (cattle, money)
Hieroglyph	Vulture
Tarot	The Magician
Palmistry	Little finger, Mercury's finger

A GUIDE AT THE GATEWAY

> *A way can be a guide, but not a fixed path. . . . Nonbeing*
> *is called the beginning of heaven and earth; being is called*
> *the mother of all things. . . . These two come from the same*
> *source but differ in name; both are considered mysteries.*
> *The mystery of mysteries is the gateway of marvels.*
>
> FIRST VERSE OF THE TAO TE CHING,
> IN *THE ESSENTIAL TAO*, TRANS. THOMAS CLEARY

The first and last symbols of all early scripts (using the word loosely)
promise a come-around-home. Our tale begins with a gateway, a

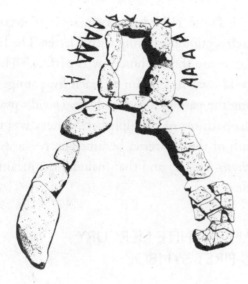

Fig. 23. Grave in form
of letter A, Yugoslavia,
c. 6000 BCE

Image from Marija Gimbutas,
Language of the Goddess, 156

promised entrance into the world of time. It ends by marking the path of return after each rest. The alphabet starts its journey with A. Written ⼪ in Phoenician and ancient Hebrew, this bull's head is also the shape of a woman's birth-giving womb and the shape of ancient graves to which the dead return. Tav (mark) as the last letter was once written with either the × of multiplication or the + of addition, signs promising a good return after each gravid pause.

Symbols representing a thousand words, the letters of our oldest alphabets hide multiple themes. First letters include such characters as a guide standing by a gate, a pathfinder, a psychopomp traveling between the worlds of light and dark. Promising the wealth of the material world, he helps travelers, merchants, and thieves along their journey, marking boundaries along the journey. He also bestows the measurements of an ordered—that is, properly spelled—alphabet to help Earth's people along their path. He then guides them home at the end of time. The Old Norse poem *Svipdagsmál* (c. 1500) offers: "The first charm I chant thee. . . . Let thyself be thy guide."[1] In the *Hávamál*, Odin chants eighteen rune poems to a defeated dragon, Loddfáfnir:

> *"Those songs I know. . . .*
> *The first is Help which will bring thee help*
> *in all woes and in sorrow and strife."*[2]

One key to our Mystery is Psalm 119, which organizes itself according to the alphabet, with each section beginning with a letter. The first stanza, aleph, declares: "Happy are those whose way is perfect." There is a tradition that King David used this psalm to teach his young son Solomon the alphabet hiding the path of a spiritual life. David's psalm suggests that in his time the pathway of the alphabet Mystery was not yet hidden. In time, the path of the Mysteries became heresy—a word derived from the Greek *hairesis* (choice) and that includes the meaning "to choose one's own path."

BLACK AND WHITE MERCURY
AS FIRST SYMBOL

My [left] hand has founded the earth, and My right hand has spread out the heavens.

ISAIAH 48:13

Around 250 BCE, moving away from the Baals of their ancestors, the Hebrew alphabet replaced the bull of the Phoenician alphabet, ᛚ, representing aleph, with א. Like the Magician appearing thousands of years earlier, A's bull's head became a line arcing between two hands (compare fig. 24 with fig. 3 and 4, page 12 and 13). One hand reaches toward the sky, the other touches Earth. We will encounter this shape,

TAURUS   ✳ **Pleiades**

Fig. 24. Bulgaria, c. 5800 BCE. The constellation of Taurus as ᛚ. (Taurus is also sometimes depicted as an X shape.) Note: fifteen dashes on the reader's left may represent the seven Hyades and six stars of the Pleiades flying before Taurus.

Gimbutas, *Civilization of the Goddess*, 240

a shape recognizing events in Heaven reflected on Earth, multiple times on our journey through time. Eventually, the Magician-Guide indicating "As Above, So Below" will become a deity known as young Mercury.

The first symbol, as aleph, represented an ox. Numerous sky bulls and cows have been posited, not incorrectly, as the source of aleph's bull. They include the entire sky as the Sky Bull, the stars of Taurus, and Orion as Osiris, another Bull of Heaven.* Osiris is the first of the five gods chosen to help regulate the Egyptian calendar of 360 days. As the dying and rising pharaoh, his Mysteries included the path toward the dawn. Representing each deceased pharaoh of ancient Egypt, Osiris returns each day as the risen sun in the form of his son Horus. Described in the Book of the Dead and inscribed on coffin lids, pharaohs, and later common men, could follow the steps of the path and like Osiris return to the light.

The Magician as Mercury, first of the five wandering planets, must also be included. His astrological symbol is yet another bull (☿). The Magician Mercury, also known as Hermes, is "one of the younger gods in myth. In reality, he is probably one of the oldest and most . . . primitive in origin."[3] Although he will eventually mature, at this stage of creation, as our numeral one, he is yet undivided. As the quicksilver messenger of the gods, Mercury guides spirits between the worlds of dark and light. In time, the young Bull will mature, become potent, then grow old, but for now his circle through time is just beginning; his potential has not yet unfolded.

> *Alef never occurs as a suffix, while as a prefix, it indicates the first person future—"I will." God is the absolute "I," and the statement "I will" indicates His yet unrealized potential.*
> THE BAHIR (TWELFTH CENTURY),
> TRANS. ARYEH KAPLAN

Palmistry is another ordered tradition helping unravel our story. Of the five fingers of our hand, the first finger, little finger, belongs

---

*One of Orion's later origin stories had him born from a bull's hide that three gods had urinated on and then buried in the ground (that is, the womb of Earth).

to Mercury/Hermes. His name bestowed the word *hermaphrodite*. A ring worn on the little finger is a badge of gayness.[4] In this youthful form, our gay numeral 1 has not yet split apart. Sun and moon, Heaven and Earth, the waters of male and female have yet not separated nor matured; the potential of Creation has not yet been realized.

Continuing this theme, the first Germanic rune, Fe, meaning "cattle" or "wealth of the material world," is related to the word *fairy*. Combining both sexualities, he/she is at this stage of manifestation still fey, still able to travel between spirit and material worlds. In palmistry, the rare line of fey intuition runs from the palm toward the mercurial little finger. In his *Book of Palmistry*, William Benham states, "I have noted this mark in the hands of celebrated spirit mediums."[5]

Old traditions allowed deities to change form, and the One God once wore many masks. He can appear in multiple places at one and the same time and can acquire different aspects with passing time and cultures. Like Gaia's Earth changing her face with the seasons, aleph's shining young Bull will divide and evolve into all the other letters of the alphabet. Passing from undifferentiated child into adolescent, he will marry his land, father his people, and finally, age black into dark Saturn (Cronus). In her female aspect, after birthing a new generation, she will ultimately become a black Hag, a Crone, a Dying Moon. Renewing after each menopause (moon pause), the fey bull/cow will return to shine again.

The element mercury painted behind glass forms a mirror—the mirror reflecting a mercurial double image. Like Mercury, the mirror darkens as it ages and like Mercury, mirrors stand at entrances to the Otherworld. At death they must be covered to prevent the dead soul from losing its way on the journey to the stars. (Although I must introduce it here, with Mercury, the quality of duality's mirror-like wisdom does not actually appear until the second charm.)

HERMS AND SUNDIALS

Tarot is yet another tradition helping our exploration. As the Magician of the first Tarot card, mercurial Hermes gave his name to hermetic traditions hiding secrets. Given my assumption that alphabets reflect the measured stars moving over their Earth, the Guide-as-Magician

Fig. 25. The Magician
Rider-Waite Tarot

should also mark the passage of time. As the marker of boundaries, he may appear as a tower, a tor, a herm, a sundial, or a pillar in the shape of our numeral one (1).

Hermes began his journey through time as a simple pillar, a herm. At first, ancient gods had no feet. As simple herms, they were bound to their land. Eventually gaining feet, they began to wander away, necessitating that they be chained to their temples. Norse tradition, chasing the wealth of their wandering cattle (Fe, first rune), agreed: "Without bounds, Fe wanders off, aimlessly dissipating wealth."[6]

This early stability was a somewhat mixed blessing. Early gods were bound to their land, so travelers had to adapt to the gods of each new land they passed through. Each Canaanite Baal, "lord," was simply the lord of that town, each Baal being a different lord. The lord's secret name was not spoken. In time, pioneered by wandering Jews, the One God could eventually be found in his Word and was no longer bound in place.

As the Hermes of Siphnos (fig. 26), Mercury's coming role in his land's fertility is obvious. The earliest herms housing gods (Beth El) were simple standing stones.

Fig. 26. Hermes of Siphnos,
c. 520 BCE, Greece
Photo by Ricardo André Frantz, CC BY-SA 3.0

The illustration of the Tarot's Magician depicts the symbol of infinity, ∞, above his head. When Hermes, as a herm, a standing stone, or a taur/tor as the pillar representing our numeral 1, mirrors the shining sun's black shadow over a year, he marks out the figure-eight of infinity. In patterns ending with the seventh symbol, the eighth charm sings a rising up into a new octave.

The herm's shadow, dark twin of a white sun, moves from a north position in the sky, crossing the zenith (highest point) at midsummer, then continues south toward winter. Returning after the winter solstice, it moves north toward summer once again.

Multiple calendars have been created in the thousands of years over which this story developed. I don't suggest any specific calendar, only that the owner of the first place stands at the gate between the old year and the new, between the day and night. He looks forward as well as back. As an example, January, our first month, is named after two-faced Janus. A gatekeeper like Hermes, Janus was the god of Roman doors. Western calendar celebrations matching the

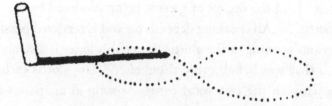

Fig. 27. Sundial tracing a year's shadow
Illustrator Unknown

alphabet's seasonal pattern, I include them as our letters evolve with the seasons.

BULL GODS OF CHINA

Like Mercury is credited with inventing alphabet letters, a bull as First Mythic Emperor of China is credited with gifting the I Ching, or Book of Changes, and its eight trigrams. The first of these is Chien, "Heaven." In this stage of evolving creation, Heaven, like aleph and fey young Mercury, has only potential. It has not yet begun to divide. Active movement cannot occur until coming duality supplies two points to travel between. The I Ching notes, "Heaven represents yang energy as a whole and cannot be sub-categorized."[7]

INDIA'S ELEPH AS ALEPH

India's gatekeeper associated with new ventures, wealth, and literature is elephant-headed Ganesh. Harold Bayley, a student of Mystery traditions, explains, "The Hebrew aleph is identical with the eleph of elephant."[8] Ganesh rides a rat, first animal of the Chinese zodiac (which does not correspond to the Western zodiac). Like Hermes, rats and Lord Ganesh are associated with both merchants and thieves of the material world. It's said that when Ganesh was first born, people became so interested in wealth they stopped going on pilgrimages.

In the sacred Sanskrit script of India, the first vowel is A. Describing the letter, an 1881 Tibetan-English dictionary noted, " [It] is formed in the lowest . . . of the organs of speech, being produced by the opening of the glottis. . . . All speaking depends on and is rendered possible only by a previous opening of the glottis; hence this letter is a symbol of the deity . . . that was before every thing else."[9] The glottis includes the opening between the two vocal cords. As soon as air passes through their duality, sound occurs.

Jewish tradition agrees: "Why is the letter *Alef* at the beginning? Because it was before everything, even the Torah."[10] Because this tradition worships the One God, whose name is not spoken, aleph is a silent sound. (Ogham's contrasting tradition hides the Deus as deuce.) Jewish tradition, therefore, begins the Torah's Genesis with the blessing of B.

MAGIC CROWS MARKING TIME

Sanskrit is divided into groups of consonants and vowels. The first consonant is ka, which is also the sound made by a crow. The Brahmi script, a syllabic alphabet (c. 300 BCE), ancestor to written Sanskrit, writes ka with the plus sign (see the chart on page 66).[11] Plus implies addition, a return on both profits and souls. Ancient images of crows stand, like the Tarot's Magician and Hebrew's aleph (א), with one wing toward Heaven and one toward Earth.

Calendars and alphabets can begin either with the dark shadows of evening or with the rising of the white sun. The first symbol can

Fig. 28. Crow, Crete, c. 1500 BCE. Ancient symbols being very specific, there may be an occult reason that some magicians raise the right arm, others the left.

Image from Marija Gimbutas, *Civilization of the Goddess*, 240

therefore be black, white, or, like the mothering vulture of the Egyptian alphabet, black and white. As the numeral 1, the Sanskrit ka is another herm, tor, or pillar. According to that same 1881 Tibetan-English dictionary, ka represents the "letter K, excrement, crow, pillar, one as a number."[12] For those calendars that begin at night, ka will be purified by the dawn of the second charm. (See the profile of the eleventh letter, K, for further information about the twin 1-1 ka as the dark shadow soul.)

Magic crows are white when young. In China, a white three-legged crow once carried the sun across the sky. The heat burning him black, each sunset he entered the womb of night to heal and brighten before the next day's journey. The first of the twelve symbols worn by the ancient emperor of China was a three-legged crow. Though I have emphasized the bull as a common first symbol, the mercurial sun with its black shadow (ka) is yet another white/black symbol associated with the first position: Bright Sun-day initiates the first day of our seven-day week, ending with a blackened Saturn's day.

DARK AND LIGHT REVOLUTIONS

Alchemy's hermetic tradition transmutes black earth to gold. It follows the promise of ancient alphabets returning the dark toward a golden day and guiding the blackened soul toward enlightenment. *The Six Keys of Eudoxus of Cnidus* (c. 400 BCE) opens with a black bird needing to be polished shining white: "The first key is that which opens the dark prisons. . . . What is born of the Crow is the beginning of this art. He must cut off the raven's head, whiten the black, and vivify the white."[13]

The first Creation story of Genesis, closely following an older Spell, echoes this theme of black and white separating out from Chaos. On the first day of creation, only dark and light appear. The sun and moon have not yet appeared, nor the waters separated. Yin and Yang still circle each other. Although I discuss the separation of the dark from the light, when the first thread of light appears that act of creation itself implies the beginning of duality and the ensuing cascade toward material formation.

OGHAM

Beth (Birch) is the first character of the Tree Ogham. Like the god Mercury, birch is a black and white tree. Young trees are intensely white against the shadows of the dark woods. As they age, white birches darken. Like Hermes, the tree contains both sexes, not needing a partner to propagate. Like wandering quicksilver, birch is a pioneer, moving into foreign territory before other trees. Mercury being considered one of the inventors of writing, the first Ogham message was written on birch, further tightening the connection between the symbols for a scribe basing their Ogham "letters" on an ancient alphabet Mystery.

ILLUSIONS OF THE MATERIAL WORLD AND DEATH

One for Sorrow
MOTHER GOOSE

When potential energy begins moving, creation begins: energy becomes material. The world of the Mater (mother) is a world of form, of material wealth. But entering this world, one also enters the world of Time, and Time's fey measurements always include fatality. Fe (first rune) is the name of a ruler measuring the Irish dead for their coffins; fey is one who travels beyond the illusions, the maya, of this world.

The mother of Mercury/Hermes is Maya, a name implying illusion and magic. In India she is the mother of Buddhi (Mercury in a female form), wife of elephant-headed Ganesh. India's Maya wed the Bull of Death, Yama. Her name written in the Brahmi script is Ma-Ya (ᚼↆ). Her spouse is Ya-Ma (ↆᚼ). That is, the world of life (Maya) and death (Yama) mirror each other." Entering the world of time and illusion, of maya, the Mother, brings life. In time, it also brings death.

India's Maya, taking the form of a serpent, sleeps at the base of the spine in the first of the seven chakras ascending the Twenty-four vertebrae. The *Shat-chakra Nirupana* says: "Over Shiva Linga shines the sleeping Kundalinī. She is Māyā (the bewilderer) in this world."[14] A linga is a pillar, a herm, like the number one. As aleph-phant, elephant-headed Ganesh also resides here. The seed sound of this chakra is "lam," denoting the path on which we now initiate our journey.*

RUNES—ONE FOR THE MONEY

*They worship as their divinity Mercury in particular . . .
and regard him as the inventor of all arts; they consider
him the guide of their journeys and marches, and believe
him to have very great influence over the acquisition of
gain and mercantile transactions.*

CAESAR, *COMMENTARII DE BELLO GALLICO*
(*COMMENTARY ON THE GALLIC WARS*)

Germanic runes (c. 150 CE) have Fe (symbolizing money or cattle) in place of Mercury as the first symbol. The rune tradition has mnemonic poems for each position. In addition to offering help along the path, the first rune represents the promise of wealth in a material world. The phrase "Feoh id est pecunia" recalls Mother Goose's "One for the Money." Like Fe and black-white Mercury, Ogham's (black and white) Birch also promises money: "Birch . . . if he be laid low, promises abiding fortune."[15]

Cattle represented money among ancient herders. Mercury, whose symbol is a bull, guides both hermetic traditions and traders seeking

Fig. 29. Cash cow as aleph to tav
(alpha to tau per Bayley)
From Bayley, *Lost Language of Symbolism*, 102

*The muladhara chakra is the first chakra and the gateway to the remaining six chakras.

gold. As archaeologist Miranda Green notes, "In the Celtic world, Mercury was first and foremost a deity of commercial prosperity and success."[16] A trickster, he also helps thieves. The first character of the Assistant Ogham is Babel, described as the man who brought cattle to Ireland on May Day. In the *Lebor Gabála Érenn: The Book of the Takings of Ireland,* "Babal was one of two merchants, the other being Bibal. . . . Babal is described as 'the white.' Babal brought cattle to Ireland, and Bibal brought gold."[17]

Although it is associated with wealth, I believe the first symbol originally possessed a far more luminous meaning than that of mere cold metal. The cow is not any cow but the womb of Earth: the Bottomless Pit as black fertile source of life returning after each death. She will be kissed awake each spring by the warmth of her white sun.

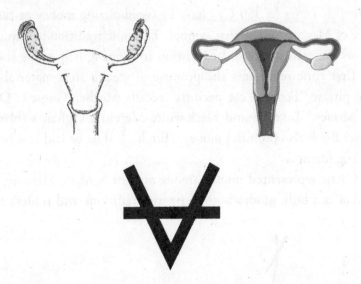

Fig. 30. Woman's womb in the shape of cow-headed aleph (when rotated)

(Left) From Gimbutas, *Civilization of the Goddess,* 245; (Right) Illustration by Laboratoires Servier, CC BY-SA 3.0

◁ Second Letter

Adolescence and the Purification of the Virgin Spring

Phoenician/Old Hebrew	Beth (house)
Greek	Beta
Ogham	Unspoken
Runes	Uruz (aurochs/wild bull) or Ur (ore, dross, shower)
Hieroglyph	Reed (from which houses were built; this is a twin letter, appearing sometimes as one reed and sometimes as two)
Tarot	The Priestess
Palmistry	Ring finger, Apollo's finger; in Chinese palmistry, this finger is the "unnamed" finger—like the second ogham, its name is not to be spoken

The pathfinding hermaphrodite of the first symbol now evolves into the frenzy of male and female adolescence with the coming of duality. After maturing and mating with the fertile third letter's magic, they will give birth to a new world through the delta of the fourth. With the virtuous fifth magic, Earth will share her laws as well as her harvest. As six's king, he will marry his land, once again storing his seed in Earth's welcoming womb before dying south toward the dark

ADOLESCENCE AND THE VIRGIN SPRING

Symbols representing the second stage of manifestation contain such stories as the budding adolescence of a Virgin Spring, purification, initiation rites, and duality arising with the onset of adolescence. They also describe an opening Underworld, an opening with both sexual and mystical connotations. Because of the association with the opening Underworld, the number two's magic is associated with spirits and prophecy. This entrance to the spirit world will close after adolescent Earth matures. Healing and divinatory powers also emerge during this virginal adolescent stage. They weaken with the onset of sexual activity, not returning until haggard old age and the cessation of menses.

Like the bovine second rune, Uruz (aurochs, the wild bull), Earth is an Earth cow. In Greece, Gaia is Mother Earth. In India, *gai* is the cow that is *ma,* our mother. As mother, the sound "ma" in India's ancient Brahmi was written with a cow's head. But the owners of the second position are not yet a mother nor yet a patriarch of the people. Returning young with each springtide, they are now young virgins.

Ireland's sacred cow is the Cailleach Beare, the black Hag of winter who once transformed into the Bride each year. Ireland, having never forgotten, still celebrates the Return of the Bride each February. A poem dedicated to Cailleach Beare, written in the eighth century when old traditions were being forgotten or outlawed, laments how she no longer returned young to her lovers. "I am Buí [cow], the Old Woman of Beare; I used to wear a smock that was ever-renewed."[1] Her festival, still celebrated by virgins seeking their lovers, now belongs to her Christian successor, St. Bridget.

As described in chapter 8, Ireland claims ancestry through the Sons of Mil (from the Anatolian city of Miletus, by way of Spain) and an Egyptian princess. Mythic heredity evokes transmission of wisdom rather than true genealogy. Milesians, after wandering for hundreds of years, are said to have sailed from Spain to conquer Ireland's fairies. Before setting sail, the king married a pharaoh's black daughter, Scotia, who was later identified with the Cailleach Beare. The Cailleach is particularly associated with the Irish land of Munster. I hope that, by now, you begin to recognize the numbers associated with this description: "Munster is associated with the dead. . . . Five-sixths of the ogam inscriptions on memorial stones in Ireland are located in the three south-western counties of Waterford, Cork, and Kerry [in Munster]. . . . Munster is pre-eminently the province of female supernatural personages. . . . The Cailleach . . . had fifty foster-children in Beare. She passed into seven periods of youth, so that every husband used to pass from her to death of old age."[2]

As Cailleach, her name is cognate with India's Maya-Kali dancing her dance of death and renewal with fifty alphabet letters in the form of skulls around her neck. As Beare, her name recalls Greek Artemis as both a nurturing mother and a hunter-virgin (artio, "bear"). In her aged aspect, Artemis is black Nemesis, that Fate awaiting everyone at the end. But again, we are getting ahead of our story. With the second charm, the Virgin Spring has just renewed herself.

In comparing various alphabet patterns, Ogham's symbols do not fit unless we skip either the first or second letter of the series. This will become clearer when we reach the third letter. As noted in chapter 8, several other alphabets—Milesian (western Anatolia), Etruscan, Faliscan (Italy), Arcadian (Greece, home of Pan), and northern and southern Iberian (Spain)—also hide the second letter. I suspect there was a religious reason. Perhaps Deus as deuce—like G-d's name or the deity of the "unnamed finger," second finger of Chinese palmistry—was not pronounced. The Tao elaborates: "I do not know its name. I am forced to call it Tao" (second of twenty-four verses by Tai Shang Lao Chun c. 200–589 CE).*[3]

---

*Tai Shang Lao Chun is one of the Three Pure Ones descending to Earth from the stars of Orion to reform a corrupt world. Appearing in many avatars, his most important incarnation was as Lao Tzu.

TWINS AND DUALITY

With the magic of the number two, the duality of twins arrives. Each young bride has her mate: the young sun opposite the crescent moon. Apollo, the sun god, and Artemis, the reflective moon, make one such set of young twins. The moon is one of many faces worn by the owner of the second position (Moon Day, Monday being our second day). The maiden moon cow grows horns as a young crescent. At full moon, she relates to the fertility of the third symbol, and then horns reappear as she wanes into number seven's dying Crone. After each menopause (her moon pause), the new born moon rises, young again.

The Great Mother of Artemis and Apollo wore many aspects, including that of a bird goddess. The shape of our numeral 2 would seem to suggest her aspect seduced by a swan. Turning into a goose, she laid an egg, giving birth to the Gemini, youthful twins traveling between the light and the dark. The astrological symbol for Gemini's twins is the Roman numeral two: II.

Mother Goose, whose son is Jack Orion, is another aspect of these ancient bird goddesses. Fourteen thousand years ago, she appeared on a rock wall in France (fig. 31). Across her egg is tav's X of promise of fertile multiplication. The aimed arrow (a prick as third symbol) will eventually impregnate her egg with the third month of March's arrow magic.

By astrological tradition, Mercury rules Gemini's twins. Mercury, Venus, and the moon are three lights orbiting between the sun and Earth. Each has both an evening and morning aspect, sometimes rising just before the morning sun, other times in the late afternoon. All three grow horns as they wax out of Earth's shadow, then after becoming full, assume horns again as they fade into the shadow. They disappear twice in their cycle as seen from Earth: when they pass in front of the sun, and again when passing behind.

Rising near sunset, the evening star of Mercury was known as Hermes. When rising with the morning sun, he was known as Apollo and associated with the second position. Apollo, like young Mercury (Hermes), is always depicted as a youth. Originally a god of forests and

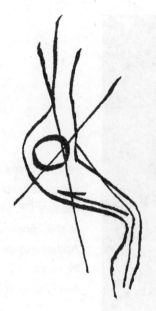

Fig. 31. Bird goddess, from a rock wall in France. Dates for this image vary.

From Johnson, *Lady of the Beasts*, 17 (c. 18,000 BCE) and Gimbutas, *Language of the Goddess*, 168 (c. 11,000–9000 BCE)

animals, Apollo became a sun god and twin to his reflection, the virginal moon as Artemis (Diana).

In the hopeless tangle of ancient myths, shape-changer Nemesis, fateful mother of the healer Apollo and the midwife Artemis, was a wolf as well as a bird goddess. Wolves mate "in January or February . . . after 63 days of gestation, the birth takes place from mid-March to mid-April."[*4] Romans held their wolf's festival, the Lupercalia, in February.[†] Our second month of February, the month when wolves, birds, and virginal valentines choose their mates, celebrates the estrus (*februa*) of the wolf. When winter's Hag turns young with the year, her red waters, her menses, her adolescent moon measurements, begin to flow.

Nemesis gave birth to her twins under a palm. Also known as Diana, Artemis has been depicted as a many-breasted palm tree (Diana of Ephesus; see fig. 32). She wears a necklace of the zodiac around her neck and the nourishing dates of the new year on her chest. The breasts have

---

*Caras's count of sixty-three days is very close to sixty-four, a number associated with deities of fate and games of chance.

†The entry for Lupercalia in the *Oxford Classical Dictionary*, 2nd ed. (1972), notes, "The name suggests . . . propitiation of a wolf god."

Fig. 32. Diana of
Ephesus, second
century CE,
at the Ephesus
Archaeological
Museum
Photo by Blckspt, CC BY-SA 4.0

been described as testicles, but young Inanna, another form of the Great
Goddess manifesting as the Storehouse for the date harvest, is dressed with
her dates.*⁵ Reflecting the resurrection promised by ancient Earth mothers, the "'scientific'" name for the date palm genus is *Phoenix.* The center
medallion of her necklace depicts Scorpio, location of the galactic womb,
which mothered the stars of our universe (see chapter 2).

BETH AS "HOUSE"

The second letter of the Phoenician alphabet is beth, "house." Because
of the sacredness of early writing, this dwelling is not just any house

---

*This goddess comes from Mesopotamia.

Fig. 33. Goddess as
a house, Macedonia,
c. 6000–5800 BCE

Image from Marija Gimbutas,
Civilization of the Goddess, 257

but rather a special dwelling, an altar, a temple. Ultimately, it is the storehouse of Mother Earth. With the second charm, the storehouse of the maturing adolescent will be purified, anointed, and prepared for her coming wedding.

Earth is now awakening. She is renewed in the spring of her youth, and her home will now be swept clean and purified. Her temple will be readied for her to receive her king. If he makes her happy, the fertility of the land ensues.

In Rome, the Vestal Virgins tending the sacred flames of the goddess were young virgins, their festival celebrated in February. Their goddess Vesta derives her name from the Indo-European *Heus,* meaning "hearth" or "house." The young Bride of Ireland, Brigit, also kept a flame within her sacred enclosure. Her February festival, like those of Rome's virgins, is celebrated by the hearth as she trades places with the Hag of winter.

SERPENT ENERGY AND SAPIENCE

Gods as well as historical figures enact old stories. Ancient bull gods could also appear as serpents. With the changing of the world's ages, dragons/serpents often lost their position as rulers of Earth. Apollo took rule of the oracle of Delphi after defeating a python. Phoenician Cadmus founded his city in Greece after killing a dragon by a sacred

Fig. 34. English miniature of a serpent in the shape of the letter B listening to his tail

spring. Jacob's angel is sometimes identified as the archangel Samael. He is (or rides) a serpent-camel associated with the north star of crooked Draco (Dragon). After 3000 BCE, Draco lost his position as ruler of the pole stars of Heaven.

Despite their celestial defeat, serpents still appear during our second month. In China, the dragon, revered as a symbol of the emperor, returns each February to dance in the New Year's parade. Scottish serpents, like Chinese dragons, also arrive in February. "In Scotland, a serpent was supposed to emerge from the hills on Imbolc, the Day of the Bride."[6]

> *With wisdom the house [beth] is built, with understanding it is established, [and with knowledge are its chambers filled.]*
>
> THE BAHIR (TWELFTH CENTURY),
> TRANS. ARYEH KAPLAN

A serpent whispered sapience into the ears of a shadowy young Eve, convincing her to eat from the Tree of Knowledge. This began the cascade of time leading to the birth of her children. Evolving into sexual beings, red Adam and dark Eve mate, seeding Earth with the third charm. Entering the world of time, a world leading to death, Eve will give birth to the world of man.

Serpents reflect a budding male sexuality, as do stone pillars and rising sap dripping from trees in early spring. In Judaism, February signals the New Year of the Trees (Tu B'Shevat). In India, the Shivaratri, worship of the rising pillar of the male (linga) and the female yoni (a ring as vulva), is also held in February or early March. The trees whose milky sap also produce hallucinogenic drinks are "the most appropriate timber source for making wood *lingas* . . . then the complex iconography sacred trees, Cosmic Pillars that are temple thresholds, and ambivalent notions of sexuality, ascetic meditations, and the warrior's vanquishing power may all be readily connected."[7]

The Old English Rune Poem links the initiation rites of male adolescents to the second rune, Aurochs, which describes the great bull as a very savage beast. According to Julius Caesar's *Commentarii de Bello Gallico* (*Commentary on the Gallic Wars*), aurochs were hunted during the initiation of Germanic youths.[8]

SEPARATION OF WATERS, PURIFICATION, AND PLOWING

The Second Key dissolves the compound of the Stone, and begins the separation of the Elements.

SIX KEYS OF EUDOXUS

Separation of Earth's waters occurs in this second stage of our Spell. With adolescence, the red salty waters of the female and the sweet white waters of the male appear as the young child of the first letter matures with puberty. "And God said, 'Let there be a vault between the waters to separate water from water. . . . And there was evening, and there was morning—the second day" (Genesis 1:6–8).

In the young spring of the now adolescent Earth, sap rises and trees drip their milky dew. Young animals also produce their first red or white waters. Following the appearance of these emissions, many cultures mandate purification. The letter B (beth) leading the second verse

Fig. 35. Inanna's symbol,
ring posts on the
Warka vase

Detail extracted from a photo by Osama
Shukir Muhammed Amin FRCP (Glasg),
CC BY-SA 4.0

of the alphabet (Psalm 119), questions: "Wherewithal shall a young man cleanse his way?"

February is, according to the dictionary, the "month of purification." As the letter aleph is not just any bull, so beth (house) is not just any house, but rather the house of Earth as sacred space. After the death of winter, dark Earth is now renewed. Her womb must be purified and prepared for marriage, her furrows swept clean with a new broom. The Virgin Spring is readied for her plowing. The rising pillar of her youthful consort stands ready:

> *"As for me, Inanna,*
> *Who will plow my vulva?*
> *Who will plow my high field?*
> *Who will plow my wet ground?"*
>
> . . .
>
> *"Great Lady, the king will plow your vulva.*
> *I, Dumuzi the King, will plow your vulva."*[9]

The symbol depicting this Great Goddess (also known as Istar, Astarte, and Venus) is a doorpost ring made of reeds to her storehouse. To ensure the fertility of her Bottomless Pit, to fill her storehouse with food for her people, a sacred marriage was celebrated every spring between the Lady and the Sumerian king. Physical union in her marriage bed was during the spring equinox, our third charm.*[10]

Our alphabet hides multiple traditions. A brewer, an alchemist, a mason, or a maker of iron might use different mnemonic poems than would a farmer, sailor, or herdsman to recall the pattern. For farming people, after Earth is purified, her furrows must be opened, made ready to receive the seed arriving with the alphabet's next charm. Ireland's February Festival of the Bride marks the official day of plowing.

China's Second Mythic Emperor is Shen Nung, the Divine Farmer. Wearing the head of a bull, like the aurochs of the second rune, he was said to have invented the plow. Educated in the Mysteries, he knew the secrets of immortality and making gold. He was also a healer; Anne Goodrich tells us, "There is little doubt that Shen-nung is considered to be the Founder of Birth of Medicine . . . he is credited with being the first to discover medicinal herbs."[11] And, in ancient China, the Moon Hare pounding the Pill of Immortality is the second of the twelve symbols worn on the emperor's gown.

HEALING, BREWING, AND MEDICINE

A second I know, which the son of men
must sing, who would heal the sick.[12]

Healing belongs among the powers of the second symbol. Young Artemis and Apollo are healers. The virginal High Priestess, Tarot's second card, is "a wise woman . . . she heals the body, knows fertility potions . . . [and is] a midwife."[13] Brigit, the February Bride of Ireland, is associated with springs of water, healing wells, poetry, medicine,

---

*Twin to the Phoenician beth is the eleventh hieroglyph, a reed house. For more details, see the profile of the eleventh letter.

brewing, and blacksmithing. She was said to have midwifed the Christ child and is now the saint of childbirth and midwives, "though some scholars have doubted her existence altogether."[14]

Apollo is associated with prophecy and oracles. His son is Asclepius, god of medicine, whose symbol is a snake wand. Apollo's finger is our second finger, which a twelfth-century bestiary tells us is "the ring finger because the ring is worn on it. This finger is also medicinal because the common eye-salves are applied with it by doctors." Also called the leechman, ringman, or lickpan, the second finger was used for tasting medicines. There is said to be an artery that runs up the palm to this finger, connecting it directly with the heart. Thus, the taster could immediately sense the presence of poison.[15]

The horn of the great aurochs of the second rune, sometimes confused with a unicorn horn, was said to possess this same power to detect poison. This would have been of immense use to the Vikings, given the lethal habits of their drinking partners. "Most important among its powers was that of neutralizing poison and protecting one using the vessel from any contaminated drink."[16] If ale runes were inscribed on it, the drinking horn was reputed to shatter when poison was present

In February, Hermes, the conductor of awakening spirits, was evoked in Greece to release them from the wine jars.[17] Their shades were harvested in fall from the blood of the dying Vine King, whose grapes

Fig. 36. Hermes releasing spirits from a wine jar

Illustration from Harrison, *Prolegomena to the Study of Greek Religion*, 43, first published by Dr. Paul Schadow, *Eine Attische Grablekythos*, Jena, 1897

were then fermented. In spring, the jars were opened, releasing the spirits of wine for enjoyment. Alchemy's second key of Eudoxus notes: "The vine of the Wise becomes their Wine, which, by the operations of Art, produces their rectified Water of Life."[18]

METALLURGY

Although the pattern of a farming year is relatively easy to decipher in the alphabet, other traditions also hid their secrets within the alphabet's order: alchemy and the chemistry of metallurgy, for instance. Brigit, young Bride of Ireland, midwife, and brewer of ale, was also a smith—a metalworker. Traditionally, the fires of the smith were blessed during her February festival.

A frenzied Earth now spills out red flowing ore (Ur, second rune) from her maturing womb. It will now be mined and purified. Because there are multiple overlapping meanings to words in a language developed before the fall of Babel's Tower, the second rune, Ur, can refer to the aurochs (aur ox); Ur can also mean ore, light, fire, and water. Primal Ur is not limited to these definitions. The Norwegian Rune Poem notes: "Slag (Ur) comes from bad iron; the reindeer often races over the frozen snow." That is, when ore (Ur) is purified by fire (Ur) and water (Ur), slag, the dross (Ur) remains.[19] Like the tradition of Alchemy, the making of good steel from iron includes the transformation of black earth (carbon). If the slag (ur) is not totally removed, the steel shatters. (See letter thirteen describing death resulting from brittle weapons.)

Alchemical secrets of our alphabet include metallurgy, masonry, medicine, and wine. The word *alchemy* comes from a word meaning "black earth," as does *alcohol* (*al kohl*). Fire is married to Water to ultimately produce their auras. For some, the aura is blue. Writing on shamanism and other healing traditions, Holger Kalweit notes, "There are also a multitude of reports that healing energy can manifest visibly, through blue emanations, tongues of blue color and lights. . . . It is clear that blue light emanations, shamanism, and altered states of consciousness are somehow connected. Blue light and healing energy are perhaps one thing."[20]

DIVINATION AND BLUE SPIRITS

It will be recalled that the sacred white cow, Io of Argos, who also manifested as the goddess Isis, is recorded to have paid visits to India.

ROBERT GRAVES,
THE WHITE GODDESS, 411

On the second day, a white light, the purified element of water, will shine, and . . . [a Buddha] will appear before you from the blue eastern Realm of Complete Joy.

TIBETAN BOOK OF THE DEAD
(FOURTEENTH CENTURY),
TRANS. FRANCESCA FREMANTLE
AND CHOGYAM TRUNGPA

In Tibet, the Buddha Family of Mirrorlike Wisdom from the blue land of Joy arrives on the second day after death. The I Ching's second trigram is Tui, "the Joyous." Mother Goose sings a similar song: After One for Sorrow, now comes Two for Joy.

The joys of wine and other aqua vitae (waters of life) are associated with blue burning spirits that awaken in early spring. The *Shatchakra Nirupana,* describing deities that reside in the second chakra, tells us, "Within this lotus is . . . Varuna, in the shape of a crescent. . . . Hari (Vishnu) . . . is in the pride of early youth. . . . the young goddess Rākinī . . . is of the color of a blue lotus. . . Her mind is exalted with the drinking of ambrosia."[21]

THE MOIST SHADOWS OF SPRING

Moist early spring, out of which cloud dragons, blue burning shades, and awakening serpents emerge, is when winter's black Hag transforms into the Bride of Spring. The word *hag* can mean "enclosure," and indeed the Hag keeps the seasons confined within her Great Round of the year. *Hag* equally means a boggy marsh where methane spirits flit while reforming into returning shades.*

In spring, the shadows of winter coalesce into a foggy world of rainy showers. The second verse of the Old Icelandic Rune Poem states: "Drizzle (Ur) is the weeping of clouds."[22] Under the poem is the gloss umbre/shadow. These moist clouds are linked to the goddess Skade (whose name means "shadow"). Giving her name to her land of Scandinavia, this bride traveled on skies. Like the wolfish goddess Nemesis, wolves ran at her side.

China's I Ching, fashioned from observations of Heaven and Earth, describes Tui (the Joyous): "When the airs of spring begin to blow, from the collections of water on the earth the moistening vapors rise up (and descend again)."[23] As the second trigram, Tui represents marsh water or a lake. It also represents spring. When the moist areas, the swampy areas embodied by the Hag, warm up after winter, the ghostly blue spirits of will-o'-the-wisps appear to commune with men. Tui itself can mean "spiritual medium between men and the gods."[24]

In China's divinatory trigrams, the first symbol is three unbroken lines of male yang representing the potential of Heaven (☰). The trigram representing the female yin of Earth is formed by three broken lines (☷). With the opening created by duality, shades and spirits now reenter the world.

Moist, dark yin represents female Earth and is associated with water, shadows, and the direction north. The pictogram for yin means "shady side of the hill." Like yin and Skade, the shadow of Scandinavia, shadowy Eve of Genesis descended from a much older aspect of the goddess, also from the north. The twelfth-century *Bahir* says, "This is the reason why the Serpent followed Eve. He said, 'Her soul comes from the north.'"[25]

OATH TAKING AS ATTRIBUTE OF SECOND LETTER

One last aspect of the second magic concerns rings and oaths. The ring finger, obviously, recalls one oath. The ring is placed on the second

*The *Oxford Universal Dictionary* defines *hag* as "witch," "enclosed field, hedge," or "marsh or bog."

finger when our maturing virgins betroth. Var (Truth), a northern goddess of oaths and pledges, is, like Nemesis, a wolf. Another name for Skade, the Bride of Scandinavia, is "bow-string-Var."[26]

Skade/Var is associated with another god, Uller. According to the *Grímnismál,* the glorious Uller (Wuldor) was given ownership of the rainy second hall of the Gods. He was keeper of the temple rings on which Vikings swore their oaths: "by the southing sun, the Great God's rock, the lintels of the bed-chamber, and the ring of Wuldor."[27]

Uller possessed nine healing twigs (wuldortanas) borrowed by Odin: "Then took Woden [Odin] nine magic twigs [and] then smote the serpent that he in nine [bits] dispersed."[28] (See the profile of letter nine for other deities associated with nine healing twigs.)

In most traditions, the keeper of oaths and rings is some form of the Hag, the wolfish goddess Var who gave us that word Beware the saturnine ruler. We continue her discussion at the seventh charm. But be aware, reentry into the world under the watching eye of Fate is here at the opening gate of duality. The undivided One God offers no opening for returning spirits.

One final note about the white first symbol and blue second symbol: various traditions place the One God as primal; others prefer the deuce as Deus. A Kabbalah commentary from the Zohar (c. second century CE) values both: "Nothing is aroused above before it is aroused below. Before the blue flame of the candle is aroused, it does not hold the white flame. But as soon as the blue flame is aroused, the white flame immediately rests upon it."[29]

1

Third Letter

Impregnation and the Bonds of Time

Phoenician/Old Hebrew	GML or Gimel (camel or rope)
Greek	Gamma
Ogham	Luis (Rowan)
Runes	Thurisaz or Thurs (thorn or foolish giant)
Hieroglyph	Forearm
Tarot	The (pregnant) Empress
Palmistry	Fool's finger, Saturn's finger, middle finger

With the magic of the third charm, the red and white rivers that began flowing in the youth of spring's adolescence are now bound. Dry land appears with the binding, while an expectant Earth awaits delivery by the fourth charm. With impregnation, death and time have entered the world.

IMPREGNATION AND THE BONDS OF TIME

> *The intimate union of the soul with its body . . . [is] the essential point of the Operation of the [third] Key, "which terminate at the generation of a new substance."*
>
> SIX KEYS OF EUDOXUS

Her womb plowed, his rising pillar purified during the second stage of manifestation, it is time to plant the seed. According to Mother Goose, after Two for Joy, it's Three for a Wedding followed by Four for a Boy. Returning life will emerge out of Earth's opening door, our fourth letter, D (◁). With the third charm, the sweet waters of serpentine rivers join the salty waters of the red sea. With the fourth, new land will emerge from her delta.

The third letter's story, like much of life, contains both a blessing and a curse. Its magic is one of red knots, binding, knitting, and overt sexuality. It is not until an undivided universe has sung herself apart, the red waters of the female separated from the white waters of the male by the second charm, that they could mate. Signified by such expressions as "Three's the charm" and "Three on a match," waters flowing from the letter C's fertile crescent are now bound. They cease to flow while expectant Earth carries her lover's seed.

The third finger, fool's finger, cursing finger, f-k-ing finger, belongs to earthy Saturn. The reader need only consider the middle finger while folding the others to recall its powers of re-creation. This is not an aged aspect of Saturn retiring at fifty, nor Old Father Time turned upside down on Twelfth Night. Third position belongs to the potent sower of the seed in his prime.

The three stars of the Fool, another name for Orion, now pleasure his Earth. But sex makes a fool of us all. "The third is the middle finger, by means of which the pursuit of dishonour is indicated," notes a bestiary from the Middle Ages[1]—a time that was, apparently, far more puritanical than that of the exultant goddess of the previous chapter rejoicing in the plowing of her vulva. A kinder memory recalls: "To wear a ring on the fool's finger naturally expressed a hope of resurrection."[2]

Romani charms from as late as the 1880s invoked the Fool on the Hill to bind the red flood flowing from a woman's womb. This charm, hopefully resulting in a swelling tummy, was chanted for an angry (sterile) womb:

> *Tumbo (dumm or stupid) sat in the hill*
> *with a stupid child in arms,*
> *Dumb (stupid) the hill was called*

Dumb was called the child,
The holy Tumbo (or dumb),
Heal (bless) this wound!

Thorn, a "prick," is the third rune. The thorn rune (Þ) borrowed the shape of twentieth Phoenician letter ros (head, ◀). "Head" has a sly double meaning, with both upper and lower aspects.* Leading with the lower head provides the world with new children as well as fools.

Tree Ogham, having hidden the deuce, places Rowan, also known as the quicken tree, in this position. A quickened womb is a pregnant womb, a gravid womb. According to a Finnish creation myth, "Earth was barren and devoid of all plants when [the goddess Rauni] came down from heaven and took the form of a Rowan tree. After Rauni ("Rowan?") had intercourse with Ukko, the God of Thunder, the result of their union was the creation of all the plants of the earth. According to this ancient creation myth, then, all plants and trees are descended from the Rowan tree as a result of it having been struck by a mighty bolt of magical lightning."[4] And lest we feel too superior about ancient creation myths, lightning troubling the waters of Earth is our "scientific" explanation for life emerging on our fertile planet.

Gamma (Γ), the third letter of the Greek alphabet, writes "gamete," a word derived from *gamos,* "marriage," now represents a male or female cell capable of producing a third after their conjugation; the English letter C is the shape of Earth's (and a woman's) fertile crescent at the entrance of her womb. Seeding Earth by this potent third charm will result in a birth. With Earth's deliverance through the door of the fourth charm, the wealth of the material world emerges.

Deal bountifully with thy servant
PSALM 119, THIRD STANZA,
BEGINNING WITH THE LETTER GIMEL

---

*This may explain the Greek myth of Baubo the Fool. Depicted only as a head with a vagina, she made a sorrowing Isis laugh. With her laugher, Earth began to bloom again. Renewed fertility is one role of three's Fool. Lomna (Lumneach), the third character in Lin Ogham, was Fionn Maccumhail's Fool.

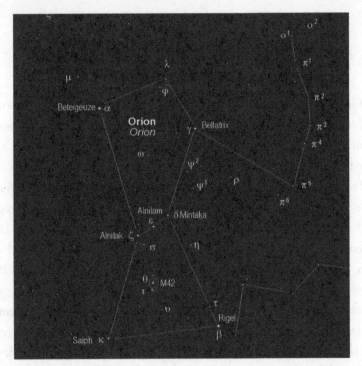

Fig. 37. The El-wand in Orion's belt. The three stars rising
toward the north and the star directly below the highest
form the L shape. The fuzzy area below represents
his sword as a euphemism for a more potent weapon.

Greek's gamma is written Γ, the shape of Orion's El-wand. In
time, the owner of the third charm will age and die, his letter upended as
the twelfth letter, L. Tarot places an (upside-down) Hanged Man as the
twelfth card; Ogham employs Vine in this position. The harvest of
the vine has its own association with rising spirits and Mystery traditions. In third position, the ruler will measure and fertilize his land.
Twelve's ruler is a dying king, his seed awaiting a new dawn. But for
now, he is still young and virile. It is time to celebrate his marriage.

Gimel acquired a thorn's prick by the time of square Hebrew, moving from ᴦ to ג. "Gimel draws from above through its head, and dis-
perses through its tail," says the *Bahir*.[5] Like other owners of three's

charm, the actions of this potent tail once dried a red flood. With impregnation, the waters of the womb are bound. The God of Genesis, closely following an older Spell, also dries Earth's waters. Fertile plants now appear. "Let dry ground appear. . . . Let the land produce vegetation: seed-bearing plants and trees on the land that bear fruit with seed in it. . . . And there was evening, and there was morning—the third day" (Genesis 1:9–13).

CAMEL-SERPENTS AND BLIND FOOLS

Male symbols seeding dark Earth can be serpents, bulls, arrow-shooting deities, or one-eyed Fools. The third rune, Thurisaz, is a one-eyed (cyclopean) giant. These giants are "marked by their stupidity. Thurses, too, are of great age."[6] The sexual symbolism of the foolish one-eyed "heads" should be as obvious as that of thorns, rampant bulls, and lightning-serpents striking a moist, receptive Earth.

Mother Eve, whose name means "life," is also connected "with Semitic words for serpent, a possibility that is especially interesting in light of the fact that the hieroglyph for woman was also the hieroglyph for snake."[7] Eve and her serpent descend from far older deities than the personae they wear in Genesis.

> This is the reason why the Serpent followed Eve. He said, 'Her soul comes from the north, and I will therefore quickly seduce her.' And how did he seduce her? He had intercourse with her . . . [Samael] descended with all his host, and sought a suitable companion of earth. He finally found the serpent, which looked like a camel, and he rode on it.
>
> THE BAHIR, TRANS. ARYEH KAPLAN

The third Phoenician letter is gimel (camel). A blind or one-eyed devil known as Samael has been identified either as Eve's serpent or as a deity come a-riding the serpent. His name translates as "blind." Serpents, renewed by shedding their skin, become briefly blind in the process. A Devilish archangel in Jewish legend, the serpent's actions

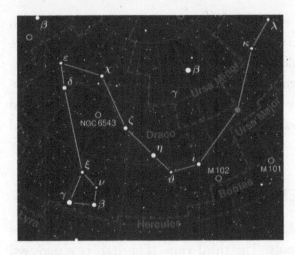

Fig. 38. Drawing of Horned Draco as a humpbacked serpent

Illustration by Tonatiuth0212, CC BY-SA 4.0

resulted in the introduction of both free will and the birth of genera-tions following dark Eve into a new day. The serpent's actions begin the formation of our material world. Neither time, death, nor children existed in the heavenly stasis of Eden.

In the ancient Phoenician alphabet composed of twenty-two let-ters, the serpent returns out of the floodwaters of the thirteenth letter (mem/water) as the fourteenth letter ⟨ (nun/serpent-fish). Stories can be read on multiple levels, from the simplest, most literal interpretation to consideration of their most secret meanings "that offer insight into the structure of the universe," as Rabbi D. Cooper puts it.[8] I am discuss-ing only surface patterns. But for every simple reading, there are eons of deep thinkers who have used the stories in this map of letters to guide souls toward illumination.

BINDING RED WATERS: THE DROUGHT OF MARCH AND BONDS OF ORION

In Norse legend, an elderly witch, called from her grave, enchants her magic: "The third I chant thee: if great waters threaten to overwhelm thee, may flood and foam turn back to Hell, the while and dry up before thee."[9] The witch, Groa (whose name means "growing"), is wife to Aurgelmir, yet another name for Orion/Saturn, owner of the bonds

Fig. 39. The Empress
Rider-Waite Tarot

of Orion. Like Samael, Greek Orion became blind before being healed by the returning dawn.

Hebrew words being composed of three letters, GML is the third letter object. Usually translated as camel (gimel), GML can also translate as rope. The Syriac word meaning "camel" is *gamlo*. However, *gamlo* has other meanings as well, one of which was given by the tenth-century Syriac lexicographer Hasan Bar Bahlul as "a thick rope which is used to bind ships."* Greek also has one word, *kamilos*, meaning both "camel" and "rope."

Young Eve's belly grows fuller as her waters dry with the binding of her womb. A pregnant Empress sits as the third Tarot card. A symbol being worth a thousand words, three's charm allows multiple uses of these bonds. According to legend, the rowan, or quicken tree, representing a pregnant (quickened) womb, once saved Thor, male owner of the third rune (thorn), from a flood peed by a giantess. The peaceful Golden Age having passed, Thor, hanging on to a rowan, threw a boulder at the giantess, crying: "Floods must be dammed at their head."[10]

---

*As explained in "The Syriac Bible" on the Syriac Orthodox Resources website. Syriac is an ancient variant of Aramaic, which is related to Phoenician and Hebrew.

This third symbol clearly shows the overlapping and changing myths as arrow-shooting hunters, warriors on horseback, and sky gods throwing lightning bolts mixed with the traditions of farming and hunting communities several thousand years ago. Runes belonged to a later culture, a sea-traveling warrior culture. They used the magic differently from farmers seeking abundant grain or women seeking full wombs.

Odin, who claimed to have learned his runes in the lands of Asia, possessed a triple knot, the Valknut,* a "sign of Woden, showing his craft of binding and loosening and his might over the knots of Wyrd."[11] In the *Hávamál*, Odin, also known as Woden, sings:

> *A third I know, if need be,*
> *that can fetter any foe.*[12]

That is, the magic bonds that knotted a quickening woman's womb in pregnancy eventually morphed into the fetters of war.

Egypt's storm god Set also owned locking bolts and fetters. The third of the five extra days regulating the Egyptian calendar belonged to Set (Seth). A red serpent-bull eventually associated with the Devil, he could also appear as a phallus, the head capable of seeding a new generation. The Papyrus of Ani (c. 1250 BCE) contains this line: "The bonds of Seth which restricted my mouth have been loosened."†[13] Loosened, he will be able to speak through the mouth of the fourth charm. By Hebrew tradition Seth was the third child of Adam and Eve. In this manifestation, he is the ancestor of man, Abel being killed and Cain exiled.

FIERY OWNER OF THE THIRD SYMBOL AND MORE KNOTS AND BONDS OF TIME

China's third trigram is Li, meaning lightning or fire. Li, also known as "The Clinging," taught an emperor the art of knots. As James Legge in

---

*Three triangles linked: three three-sided shapes.

†The fifteenth hieroglyph in the Egyptian pattern is a bolt, the number fifteen also being associated with devils.

his translation of the thirtieth hexagram (named Clinging Like Fire) in the I Ching explains, "(Fu Hsi) knotted cords to make nets and baskets, for both hunting and fishing. The idea of this was taken, probably, from *Li* . . . meaning 'attached to.'"[14]

Recalling Orion's manifestation as the Fool, "the Fool's French name, Le Fou, [is] cognate with the word 'fire.'"[15] Gods taking multiple forms, the Bull of Heaven can equally project the fire of serpent-striking lightning. Red-haired Thor, whose wife is a rowan, is a thunder and lightning god, as is Egypt's stormy-red Set. Arrow-shooting Mars, fiery ruler of the third month of March and the third planet seen from Earth, also belongs to this charm. The astrological symbol for red Mars is another prick (♂).

In India, the third of the seven chakras is the navel chakra. An archer, who won his wife Sita (meaning "furrow") by shooting a winning arrow, resides here. The *Shat-chakra Nirupana* tells us, "At the root of the navel . . . [is] the region of Fire, triangular in form and shining like the rising sun. . . . Within [is] the Bīja of Vahni (i.e. the seed-mantra of Fire, 'Ram') himself. . . . Meditate upon him seated on a ram. . . . He is of an ancient aspect and three-eyed."*[16]

Ram's giant bow of stone lies in the jungles of southern Nepal, near Sita's home in Janakpur. We meet Sita again at the ninth charm, when she is stolen away to a labyrinth in the fall. The Ram of Aries, ruled by Mars, replaced the Bull of Taurus as the ages of the world changed with the precession.

Three's primary magic includes seeding the dark moist furrows of Earth, which binds red rivers flowing from her womb. The ancient sowers, including serpents and lightning gods, were later demonized as silver-tongued devils. With impregnation, death and time entered the world. Harold Bayley writes, "The serpent in the form of the mystical figure 3 represented in the Pythagorean philosophical system, TIME—Past, Present and Future."[17]

The world of time begins with the bonds of the third charm. The

---

*A *bīja* is a seed sound; Vahni is another name for Fire as god. Thurs, the Foolish Giants of the third rune, can have one, two, or three eyes.

Spinner of Time spins the stars circling the North Star, creating a clock in the sky. One can tell the time of night or season by the directional position of the handles of the Dippers. In winter the handle points north, in spring it points east, in summer it points south, and in fall it points west.[18] Preceding these stars, a Dragon ruled the circle.

Tuesday, our third day, is named for red Mars (in Latin, *Martis diem* is the Day of Mars, which became *Mardi* in French). The Great Spinner of the pole stars is associated with Mars (though probably not as the planet). The Norse god Tir, another name for Mars, is represented by an arrow (↑), which still indicates north on maps and marks out the hours on a clock. Tuesday is the day of Tiuwaz, or Tir. Time measured by the spinning stars begins when the seed has been planted and the womb quickened. March, the third month ruled by Mars, begins time for the Western zodiac. Each zodiac year starts on March 21, when Aries, ruled by Mars, rises on the spring equinox.

CHINA

The Sage's way of governing begins by emptying the heart of desires, filling the belly with food.

LAO-TZU, *TAO TE CHING*, THIRD VERSE,
TRANS. JOHN WU

Like all wise rulers, the Tao, an alchemical tradition adhering to the ancient Mystery pattern, fills an empty belly with the magic of the third charm.

The third of China's zodiac animals is a black and white tiger whose stars correspond to those of our Sagittarius (Arrow). In his book on the Chinese practice of geomancy, Derek Walters tells us, "Tigris the Tiger gets his name from his speedy pace; for the Persians, Greeks, and Medes used to call an arrow 'tygris.'"[19] That is, Mars with his arrow of time is not unlike the Arrow's tiger of the East. The tiger's black and white stripes mark it as a symbol of revolving time. In addition to belonging to the stars of the Arrow, the Tiger also represents the stars of Orion: "The Goddess of the Wind rides a tiger, and the animal represents Orion in Chinese astrology."[*][20] Bound by ropes of wind to the celestial pole, circling stars mark out the hours of each night and the seasons of the year.

Through the actions of characters associated with the third charm, the world of human time begins. The Third Mythic Emperor of China, Huang-Ti, was the first human emperor. The previous two emperors had bull's heads. Huang-Ti introduced the horoscope, a measurement of circling time. Pricks and thorns being aspects of the third magic, he also invented acupuncture. Unfortunately, his smith introduced the art of war. War and death entered the world along with time with the iron arrows belonging to Mars (σ). The symbol for the Middle Kingdom as China is an arrow piercing the square land.

A verse from the Tai Hsuan Ching, a variant of the I Ching, describing Li (lightning), is especially fascinating when comparing it to the image of a far-dreaming shaman painted on the walls of a cave in Lascaux, France, during the Paleolithic period (see fig. 40, next page). In the cave image, an arrow pierces the womb/balls of a giant bull, while a rhinoceros, potent with deep symbolism, drops a hex (six) from his rear. That this is symbolic is evident in the unnaturally paired droppings. In real life, stools come out in a ribbon, not marching two by two. The verse describing Li states: "In the South-East, shooting forth; the she-rhinoceros. In the Northwest, an arrow. . . . Killing and begetting are mutual arrows. Central Harmony is the way."[21]

The Tai Hsuan Ching oracle being firmly connected to astronomy, the sunrise in the southeast each winter solstice begins a new year. Six months later (the number dropping from the tail of the above rhinoceros), the sun sets in the northwest, at midsummer, falling toward the death of the year. In winter, the sun has reached its most southern position before reversing. The oracle, using a variant sequence of trigrams, places Li sixth (see the profile of the sixth letter for midsummer myths of killing and begetting).

---

*Orion's constellation has also been depicted as an arrow pointing north or as the Norse goddess Frigga spinning the stars.

Fig. 40. Cave painting from Lascaux, Dordogne, France, c. 15,000 BCE

Image from Robert Wallis, "Art and Shamanism: From Cave Painting to the White Cube," *Religions* 10, no. 1 (2019): 54

THE FOOL OF TIME

The Fool of Time as Orion was ultimately replaced by martial Aries as ruler of the year. He became a cipher, a zero, a hidden mystery. The oldest use of a zero as a mathematical symbol was in Babylon (c. 500 BCE) in a "table of squares [with] four cases of a 'zero' written exactly like 30."[22] Thirty is the number of years the Fool as planet Saturn needs to circle the zodiac. The lunatic moon travels his circle in thirty days.

The spinning Fool lost his place as leader of the zodiac, but he was too important to be forgotten. Instead, as cipher and secret, the no-account Zero still wanders the sky, his faithful dog star at his heels. But each time he returns, he increases Earth's harvest tenfold: 1, 10, 100, and onward.

MEASUREMENTS AND MATH

I have been concentrating on seasonal or farming magic. But other technical secrets are hidden in the alphabet pattern, such as measurements needed to build temples and lay out boundaries after floods recede and the land dries. Once you have three points, triangulation is possible. The square corner of a pyramid can be determined with three knots on a rope spaced 3, 4, and 5 equal measurements apart. Adding up to a proper ruler's 12, bending the ropes at the knots to form a triangle will always produce a right angle shaped like Orion's El-wand.

There are other measured secrets as well. The Tao Te Ching notes, "Tao gave birth to One, One gave birth to Two, Two gave birth to Three, Three gave birth to all the myriad things."[23] In other words, $1 + 1 = 2; 1 + 2 = 3; 1 + 3 = 4; 4 + 1 = 5$, and onward.

The measurements of El can also represent a cubit, an el, a unit of measure between the elbow and the tip of the Fool's finger. This may explain "forearm" as the third hieroglyph (⟍⎯⎤). Egypt was so concerned with exact measurement that stone arms, elbow to Saturn's finger, were carved so there would be no variation of cubit measurements due to body size.

The third charm is a charm of bonds, fetters, and drying of floods. Male aspects owning third position include Set, Mars, Saturn, Orion, and devilish Samael, also known as Samekh-Mem.[24] Devils, dragons, and great serpents of the Deep of the third charm reappear at letters five and fifteen (samekh/"fish" or "prop"). Because the connection is important for understanding these later letters, I digress to explain. The association between 3, 5, and 15 may derive from the use of magic squares. In the magic square of Saturn, potent Fool of the third charm, the numbers one through nine are placed in groups of three, with the number five at the center. Every row adds up to fifteen. Note that every fifteen years of his thirty-year cycle around the sky, Saturn shines most brightly in the sky.

Saturn's square is associated with the ability of three's charm to bind floods. First mentioned in Chinese literature around 650 BCE, this square was undoubtedly known in an earlier age. The Chinese version of the square of Saturn (called the Lo Sho square) appeared when King Yu (c. 2200 BCE) confronted a great flood. Of especial relevance to the drying action of the third charm, this pattern was used by the people in controlling the river. King Yu is known to have instituted flood control using dikes and canals. He also divided China into nine provinces, the number of positions in a Saturn square.

4	9	2
3	5	7
8	1	6

Fig. 41. Saturn's square

Fourth Letter

Deliverance from Knots and Bonds

Phoenician/Old Hebrew	Dalet (door)
Greek	Delta
Ogham	Fearn (Alder)*
Runes	Ansus (high god) or Os (mouth)
Hieroglyph	Quail
Tarot	The Emperor
Palmistry	Jupiter's finger, fourth finger, pointer

---

*Previously, the ogham for this fourth position was Nion (Ash), which conquered the sixth position belonging to the queen.

When that April with his showers sweet, the drought of March has pierced to the root.

CHAUCER,
CANTERBURY TALES FROM
THE HENGWRT MANUSCRIPT
(FIFTEENTH CENTURY)
IN MODERN ENGLISH

DELIVERANCE FROM KNOTS AND BONDS

The secrets hidden in our fourth charm are, perhaps, the most straight-forward and least tangled by the multiple cultures using the pattern. Four's charm frees three's magic of knots and bindings. This is Mother Goose's "Four for a Birth," as Earth bursts free in all her glory. A Fool bound the waters of Earth with three's arrow, but now her womb opens; birth waters moisten the land, and her children emerge through the generous door that marks the fourth symbol.

Although a calendar could begin with any month, I follow the Western (Gregorian) calendar, whose seasonal celebrations fit nicely with the alphabet pattern. The name of the fourth month, April, is thought to derive from the Latin *aperire,* meaning "open." Her womb opened, Earth's delta now pours forth life.

> *Canst thou bind the sweet influences of Pleiades, or loose the bands of Orion?*
>
> JOB 38:31

We must now loosen the fetters to release the seed that has been growing in the womb. Each mother's hair will be combed, her furrows groomed, to prevent any knots impeding delivery into the sprouting world. The fourth verse of the Tao Te Ching advises: "Untangle the knots."[1]

Rome's goddess Juno, wife of Jupiter, ruler of our fourth finger, was, like other Brides, a midwife. Knots were forbidden in her worship

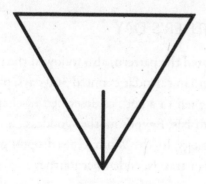

Fig. 42. Symbol for "woman," ancient Mesopotamia

Drawing for munus/woman as shown on the Omniglot website

Fig. 43. Comb charm of
a woman with the delta
symbol, Switzerland,
c. 4000 BCE

Image from Marija Gimbutas, *Language of
the Goddess*, 301

"because the presence of a belt, knot, or the like on any participant
could hinder the delivery."[2]

Alphabet magic was transmuted into rune magic in the far north, a
land possessing a climate unfriendly to peaceful farming life. Here, four's
magic of release was adapted for a warrior's need, more useful to a Viking
out pillaging. Odin, singing the High One's Words (*Hávamál*) declares:

> *A fourth I know: if warriors place links of chain on my
>   limbs;*
> *I can sing a charm that will make me free.*
> *Fetters fall from my feet and the hasp from my hands.*[3]

As the Vikings were seafaring people, another use of the fourth
rune of the Old Norwegian Rune Poem was for travel: "Os [estuary] is
the way of most journeys."[4] An estuary is the mouth of a river where it
meets the sea. This of course forms a delta as land is deposited by the
sweet rivers meeting the salty mother sea. Os is equally the mouth of
Earth's now opening womb.

MOTHER'S DAY

Egypt, which may have originated the pattern, also followed the path of
the alphabet charms. The Egyptian calendar counted 360 days, plus five
"holidays," with each one assigned to a god, as described in chapter 4.
The fourth holiday belonged to Isis, Egypt's mother goddess.

According to Greek mythology, Io, the White Cow, dropping alphabet letters along the route of her travels, ended her journey in Egypt as

Isis. Set, having killed Isis's husband Osiris, also planned to kill her son Horus. She protected her young son in her delta until he grew more powerful, mirroring the increasing power of her sun-as-Horus as it moved toward midsummer. Continuing this theme, on the fourth day the god of Genesis also produced his sun and moon to rule.

Around 6000 BCE, Cancer rose with the sun in April or early May. Although she still rules the fourth house of astrology, she precessed into a midsummer rising by the time the Western zodiac was frozen. We will discuss her myths with the sixth charm, but know that Cancer is considered a mother sign. Among her stars is a sun king's manger.

The constellation of Cancer and the number four are interlinked with the symbol of a quail across ancient Mysteries. Cancer's constellation was seen as a quail in ancient China. The fourth hieroglyph of the Egyptian alphabet is a quail. Apollo (the sun god) and Artemis (the moon goddess) were born to their mother who once took the shape of a goose trying to escape Zeus. He seduced Nemesis in the form of a swan. As Robert Graves tells us, the twins were "born on Quail Island, off Delos."[5] The goddess Asteria, like Nemesis, also took many shapes trying to escape the lust of Zeus. She finally leapt from the Heavens in the shape of a quail and transformed into the island. Their father, Jupiter/Zeus, rules the fourth finger of the hand (the four-finger pointer).

Equally fitting, "A Quail in a cage was a symbol of the soul imprisoned in the body and longing to escape."[6] Manifestation, the "terrification" of the soul into a physical body occurring with four's birth, is echoed by an alchemist in the *Six Keys of Eudoxus*: "The terrification of the Spirit is the only operation of this work."

Ancient bird goddesses' colorful eggs still appear at Easter on the full moon four weeks after the spring equinox. The eggs, fresh from the womb, symbolize the release of the sun from the grave. They are eaten with salt, itself a square (four-sided) crystal, at Passover, which is "the Season of Our Freedom. Its central theme is release."*[7] The parting of the Red Sea preceded that escape.

---

*The correct translation of the sea Moses parted, the Yam Suph, is a Sea of Reeds. I believe that the firm characterization of the sea being parted as "red" relates to mythic rather than historical memory.

In the Western calendar, this season encompasses mid-April to mid-May, during which time we celebrate Mother's Day. The precession of the Bull/Cow as Taurus through these months has left his shadow on the myths. I won't further confuse the reader, but someone with an interest in astrology can easily uncover ghosts left by earlier stars. Just to start, note that the Brahmi script of ancient India used the mothering cow's head (𐀈) for the number four. As a consonant, this shape symbolizes the sound "ma," the mother now birthing her returning sun.

MERCURY AND THE FOURTH CHARM

> *Such depth, something seems to exist there.*
> *I do not know whose child it is.*
> *It seems to have existed before the Ancestor.*
>
> FOURTH VERSE, TAO TE CHING,
> TRANS. TAM C. GIBBS

The Tao ("path"), like the Spell hidden in our alphabet, implies a continuous return into the Great Round of Time.

The returning sun is associated with the magic of four. But recall, ancient deities assumed numerous names and forms, often at one and the same time. It was only late in history that magic solidified. Each charm also contains both male and female aspects.

The fourth day of our week is named after various incarnations of Mercury. Wednesday is Woden's day (with Woden, a.k.a. Odin, as Mercury). Budhvar, or Mercredi, is one of the mercurial names for the fourth day.

Mercury's mother is Maia, now one of the stars in the Pleiades. A magician, magi, and illusionary (maya) goddess, she also is said to have birthed India's Budh (Mercury). The mother of the historical Buddha (Gautama), who was born in early May, is known as Maha-maya. Fitting with (the planet) Mercury's attributes, when the historical Buddha was born, he took seven steps in each of the four directions.*

---

*As a planet, Mercury spends just a little over seven days in each of the zodiac houses during his eighty-eight-day cycle around Earth. During a lunar year, each cycle is in a different quarter (4 × 88 = 352).

Fig. 44. Chinese Buddha as a magician speaking the First Word. Note the similarity to the shape of the letter aleph.

Image from Alice Getty, *Gods of Northern Buddhism*, 10

CREATION BY THE WORD

Give me life according to your word.

PSALM 119, FOURTH STANZA,

BEGINNING WITH LETTER DALET

If we turn our attention to etymology, we find that the "root of 'four' in Semitic is built on *rab*, found also in words for 'lord,' 'captain,' and 'lookout, sentinel.'"[8] As a rabbi, four is a great lord of the Word.

At some point in history, creation moved away from the Mother's delta and became the Word, spoken from the mouth (Os/fourth rune) of a royal god. Tarot placed an Emperor as its fourth card. Having learned the Word, he is "an embodiment of the Logos."[9] Like Jupiter, Tarot's Emperor is a warlord and sits on a square (four-sided) throne to rule. In Brahmi, the shape of the square throne (❑) stands for the sound "ba" (father).

Jupiter/Zeus, ruler of the Roman/Greek gods, fathered his children on every possible form of maiden, beast, or plant. His astrological symbol is our numeral four (♃—old magic endures). In palmistry, the line of the heart begins under the fourth finger, the forefinger, Jupiter's finger, and a prominent Jupiter's finger implies ambition and a strong

Fig. 45. Jehovah creating Adam with his pointer, the "four-finger"

Painting by Michaelangelo, Sistine Chapel, 1508–1512 CE

desire to rule. As late as the Renaissance, thousands of years after the origin of the alphabet's numbered Mystery, Michelangelo depicted Jehovah creating Adam with his fourth finger.

A thunder god, Jupiter speaks after the lightning flash of the third letter. The Early Heaven Sequence of China's I Ching also decrees the sound of thunder as its fourth trigram, following Li (lightning or fire) as the third.

"Ase [Odin] is the olden-father and Asgard's chieftain and leader of Valhall."[10] Underneath the stanza of the Old Icelandic Rune Poem for the fourth rune are the glosses "Jupiter" and "point leader," reiterating the attributes of the fourth finger, Jupiter's finger, as the creative pointer.

Germanic Odin plays a role in the transition from the sower of the seed to the Creator by the Word as it replaced the mother magic of four's delta. The fourth Germanic rune is Ansus (supreme god) or Os (mouth), and "the element of Odin . . . is behind this rune . . . the esoteric feature . . . [includes] sound as a medium of communication."[11] Odin shares the fourth of twelve halls of the northern gods (Grimner's Lay) with Saga (story).

The fourth chakra is the heart chakra (also known as Anahata, the unstruck sound). India's *Shat-chakra Nirupana* says that the fourth chakra is the abode of Shiva; "he who meditates on this Heart Lotus [i.e., chakra] becomes like the Lord of Speech."[12] Shiva once traveled to Tibet. As that Buddhist country did not need a Hindu king, Shiva remained as the doorkeeper (dalet/door) for the Buddha. His wife, the Black Goddess Kali, became an oracle speaking to the Dalai Lama.

In time, kings fought for rule over the fourth or sixth positions. Although warlords came to rule Mother Maya's magic, "ritual is always tenacious. So too at Delphi, Apollo may seat himself on the [throne], but he is still forced to utter his oracles through the mouth of the priestess of Gaia."[13]

OGHAM AND THE BATTLE OF THE TREES

Ogham scripts are known as Beth-Luis-Nion after the original three trees: Beth (Birch), Luis (Rowan), and Nion (Ash). As noted in chapter 8, we skip the traditional second Ogham character (the unspoken name of the Deuce), so now the sequence places Beth as first, Luis as third, and Nion as fourth. However, all existing written scripts place Fearn (Alder) in the fourth position (Beth-Luis-Fearn). In *The White Goddess,* Robert Graves discusses a "battle of the trees" in which the red Alder (Fearn) is defeated by the white Ash (Nion), a battle-ready spear tree. Nion/Ash then moved from the fourth to the sixth position in the Ogham, while Fearn/Alder was demoted to fourth.

An Irish tradition may explain why the victorious Ash might have left this important fourth position associated with the word of kings and emperors. A Celtic king could not rule by power alone. He must marry the land herself after proving his ability to make her fertile. Mounting her throne occurs among the honeymoon myths of the sixth letter.

The victorious Ash once fit nicely on four's emperor's throne, his original position. In harmony with Os, the fourth rune, Ash (Old English *aesc*) derives its name from the Indo-European *os*. In Norse mythology, the first man was formed from an ash, befitting Mother Goose's "four for a boy." Ash and his wife, an Elm tree, were said to have birthed the first humans after the Deluge. Genesis, however, doesn't create man (*aish,* in Hebrew) until the sixth day, the position Ogham's Ash commandeered after his victory over the red Alder.

No ancient symbol was ever lightly chosen. Elm, Ash's wife, is a jug-shaped tree whose bark is a nourishing food. The Mother constellation of Cancer contains a jug-shaped, Y-shaped group of stars. These stars are also known as the Manger. "It is the most inconspicuous figure in the zodiac," writes Richard Allen in his 1899 *Star Names.* "Yet few heavenly signs have been subjects of more attention."[14] Having migrated with the precession, Cancer and her Y shape will rejoin us at the sixth letter, along with the Ash tree.

Fearn, the red alder tree, is associated with a giant named Bran. *Bran* can mean alder, grain, or raven. The word *alder* itself ultimately derives from Proto-Indo-European *el.* We have already met giant El several times. Most of Bran's stories come from the Welsh, since the Irish, having killed this giant, erased his memory. In the medieval Welsh epic, the *Mabinogion,* Bran is killed in a war with an Irish king. His head is cut off but remains singing and storytelling as it is carried around the land. Ultimately Bran's head is buried under the Tower of London, where his rooks (ravens) still circle, protecting the tower.

In Fort Ogham, the fourth character is Femen. The Hag of Beare, whom we met with the second letter, laments: "I envy no one old, excepting only Feimen: as for me, I have worn an old person's garb; Feimen's crop is still yellow. The Stone of the Kings [is] in Feimen."[15]

MATHEMATICS

With three seeding all later numbers, four represents material manifestation: the spirit made flesh, the terrification of the soul. Four contains the first complete round of numbers: $1 + 2 + 3 + 4 = 10$. After the decimations of 10, numbers, like returning souls, "fin-again"—begin again—on their orderly path through the world: $1 + 10 = 11$, $1 + 11 = 12$, toward infinity.

Another mathematical connection to the number 4 comes from the concept of the tetrad, attributed to Pythagoras, a student in Egypt and

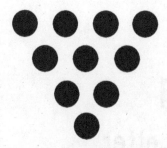

Fig. 46. Pythagoras's tetrad

a descendent of the Phoenicians. A tetrad is a set of four. Pythagorus's tetrad is a set of four lines of dots, totaling ten, in the shape of an isosceles triangle: 1 + 2 + 3 + 4 (see fig. 46). The triangle is, of course, the shape of the Greek fourth letter, delta (Δ), carrying its generative capacity: "Solid space . . . is 4. . . . Since all material things exist only in space, they too are number, and the tetrad generates them all"[16]

Like Irish Ogham, a gift of Fenius Farsa, the mysteries of mathematics have links to Phoenician spells. Some accounts have Pythagoras, son of Apollo and a Phoenician mother, studying twenty-two years in Egypt. "Others have him wandering . . . all over Egypt, Mesopotamia, Phoenicia, India, and even Gaul . . . [absorbing] all the knowledge and wisdom of the Hebrews, the Persians, the Arabs, and the blue Druids of Britain."[17] I include this quote to emphasize recognition of a widely shared Mystery tradition associated with wandering Phoenicians. In the next stage of manifestation, both sprouted seed and wisdom will be harvested, shared, and transmitted.

Fifth Letter

Teachings, Pupils, and a Gift of Tongues

Phoenician/Old Hebrew	Hey (aspirated H or window)
Greek	Epsilon (the quintessence)
Ogham	Saille (Willow)
Runes	Raido or Rad (wheel or ride)
Hieroglyph	Leg
Tarot	The Pope
Palmistry	Thumb (around which other fingers circle)

Through the magic of the fifth charm, a harvest of grain and law is shared. Words now radiate, wheeling out from the centering heart. With the breath of the lungs enclosing our hearts, the still soft voice of the wind is also part of five's magic.

Too many words are exhausting; Hold fast to the center.

FIFTH VERSE, TAO TE CHING,

HAMILL TRANS., 7

TEACHING, PUPILS, AND A GIFT OF TONGUES

I believe the pattern of soul journey described by numerous widespread traditions indicates the path was present in the symbols from their earliest ordering: that each symbol encompasses an unfolding stage along a journey. The letters of Old Hebrew appeared on the stone tablets of the Law (Torah) given to Moses on Mount Sinai. When the Torah was finalized (dates vary from 539 to 164 BCE), the Jewish scholars placing the Five Books of Moses into its final order were undoubtedly aware of the number magic inherent in their alphabet. Not a single letter can be changed or deleted without invalidating the entire Torah scroll.

The first and last letters of the Torah spell "heart" (LV). This fifth charm includes both heart symbolism and the transmission of laws. By enclosing the teachings of the Five Books within a heart, they echo an ancient tradition linking the wisdom of the centering heart, number five, and teaching of the Law: "Teach me Lord the way of your decrees," says the fifth (hey) stanza of Psalm 119. As wisdom was once located in the heart, we find heart symbolism associated with this letter. We also find a radiant sun and eye symbolism.

Five's clear eye belongs to the young pupil centering each round eye. In this early summer season, pupils sit (in a circle) around the teacher, who may appear as a bald priest-king. Shearing of both hair and wheat conjunct in this charm with priest-kings and gods transmitting laws. In the fifty days leading up to the day celebrating the gift of the Torah, observant Jews do not cut their hair until 49 days have passed and the festival begins.

Both learning and law giving are associated with the fifth symbol. In Iceland, the Althing, an assembly for recitation of the laws dating

Fig. 47. Astronomy's symbol for the sun
Convention used by NASA

from the tenth century, opened on a Thursday, the fifth day; India's Thursday is "teacher day" (Guru-var).

The pure wisdom inherent in this position was so important that of all the twenty-two possible letters of the alphabet, the God of the Hebrews bestowed the fifth letter (hey) to their names. Sara and Abram then became Abraham and Sarah. They then produced nations more numerous than the stars. In Hebrew, hey as a prefix meaning 'the' makes the character special; as a suffix, it denotes a fruitful female. The fifth letter is literally the quintessence, the fifth essence, the purest, most perfect manifestation of a being. After their perfection, Sarah and Abraham went on to bear the Children of the Book. The *Bahir* states, "When God added this Heh to Abraham's name, He gave him dominance over the final five parts of his body, namely, the two eyes, two ears, and the sexual organ."[1]

Five's pure green magic follows a world set free by four's. The stone has been rolled back for a resurrection. The Angel of Death has passed over. The pronouncements of spring have once again thrown off the shackles and bonds of death. Worlds and words having been reborn, the fifth letter's attributes include sharing the bounty delivered by the preceding charms.

The harvest may be carried in baskets made of willow, Tree Ogham's fifth symbol. Another name for a basket is *riddle,* this also being a puzzling question that was used for teaching: "A riddle, a riddle, as I suppose. A hundred eyes and never a nose." Mother Goose's answer, "a sieve," was a willow basket long before it was made from metal. In many traditions, a basket delivered bards and teachers, including Moses, across the water into a new life.

A CHASTE RISING UP AND PILGRIMAGE TRAVEL

God then said: "Let the waters bring forth swarms of living creatures, and let the birds fly over the earth, across the face of the expanse of the sky."

THE TORAH, A WOMEN'S COMMENTARY,
GENESIS 1:20, DESCRIBING THE FIFTH DAY

Following the Western calendar, it is now late May or early June. This is the season of rising up, the season of dispersal. The fifth key of Eudoxus concerns itself with the leavening, the rising up, of bread. Pupils are set free from school.

Hummingbees (having their own wisdom) begin to swarm, although their honeymoon is not until the sixth month. Our fifth charm contains a rather chaste transmission of teachings and laws. Celibacy is inherent in this season's radiating magic. If the buzzing bees now preparing to fly leave their hive instead of waiting until the kinder, more fertile sixth month, there would be no offspring. Wise Mother Goose is aware that "A swarm of bees in May is worth a load of hay. A swarm of bees in June is worth a silver spoon."

At Pentecost, occurring this season, King Arthur's knights set off on their quests, and pilgrims went traveling to Canterbury. "Make me go in the path of your commandments," continues the fifth (hey) stanza of Psalm 119.

Shavuot, the festival of the giving of the Torah, contains a fascinating association with the fifth Egyptian hieroglyph, Leg (𓏤). The festival is one of three mandated pilgrimage festivals. Unlike other festivals, these are, rather obscurely, known as "Legs" (ReGaLim; RGL in Hebrew). As a pilgrimage festival, the leg is an appropriate symbol for people who primarily traveled by foot.

The Jewish festival of Pentecost, Shavuot—celebrated fifty days after Passover—celebrates both the early summer harvest and the transmission of the Five Books of the Law in the hills of Egypt. The festival is associated with chastity: "Shavuos, the time of the giving of the Torah on Har Sinai, represents the rejection of unchanneled lust. . . . Inappropriate sexual thoughts fill the heads of those empty of wisdom. The solution is to engage oneself and one's thoughts in Torah. It is noteworthy, therefore, that in preparation for the receipt of the Torah, the Jews were required to separate from their wives."[2]

Although the chasteness associated with the virtuous pupils and priest-kings is an attribute of this charm, there is a conflicting quality of sexuality held in reserve. "The most important finger is the thumb, which among other things, is strong in virtue and power."[3] The earthy thumb (fifth finger), around which the other fingers circle, is a phallic symbol. As always, there is a constant tangling of mythic attributes. The thumb protruding from the fist protects against an evil eye, as do phalluses and five-fingered amulet hands. The gesture of a thumb fist is a ficus (a fig). While the fig's plump fruit is graphically sexual, the fig's leaves modestly cover the privates of shy statues.

FIVE'S VIRTUOUS SYMBOLS AS STUDIOUS GODDESSES

Earth goddesses were not usually known for their virtue or celibacy, but the chaste virtue of this fifth symbol is so widespread it must be an ancient attribute. Both male and female symbols associated with numeral five are modest. Perhaps earthy Nature is meditating (another centering fifth association) until her summertime marriage at the sixth charm. Or perhaps in her roles as teacher and pupil, she is now more interested in the dissemination of knowledge than the insemination of seed.

India's restless goddess of fortune, Lakshmi, is a goddess of writing and intellect. Her siblings are Sarasvati, goddess of crafts and writing, and Ganesh, the lord of writing we met in our discussion of the first letter. Worshiped in the form of a basket of grain, Lakshmi is literally five, being known as Shri Panch (Lady Five). Her worship was on Thursdays (the fifth day) or on the fifth lunar day like Greek Minerva (Athena), and like Minerva, she is associated with a great-eyed owl. We will meet her owl again at the eighth charm.

Robert Graves tells us that the celibate "Roman Goddess of Wisdom, Minerva, had 5 (written V) as her sacred numeral."[4] She is the patron of handicrafts, and possibly the reason the Crafts Ogham chose *sairsi* (handicrafts) as its fifth ogham. Minerva's festival, like the Lakshmi puja, lasted five days.

Of the five holy days regulating Egypt's calendar, the fifth day belongs to Nephthys, another goddess associated with writing and wisdom. As Lady of the Books, her fetish symbol (like Lakshmi as Lady Five) was a wicker basket. Married to red Set of the third charm, she never had children. This sterility may underlie her being known as a

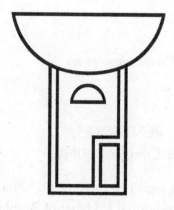

Fig. 48. The symbol for Nephthys—a basket over a house. Nephthys always appears with her basket crown.

goddess with no vagina—perhaps the ultimate characterization of chastity.

Venial Venus, although not a chaste goddess, is another deity associated with the number five. We will explore her astronomical pentacle below.

MALE OWNERS OF GREEN FIVE: TRANSMISSION OF LAW AND WISDOM

Note: Though I am separating the male and female aspects of the deities, the earliest gods could appear in either male or female forms.

The green emerald, upon which the first book of alchemy was written, belongs among this season's symbols of celibacy. The alchemist's Green Lion must first tame himself in order to produce gold with his potent stone. Emeralds must never be worn while making love. Compelling their owner to chastity, they shatter with indignation if worn during intercourse. According to Albertus Magnus, philosopher-scientist-saint of the thirteenth century, "If [emerald] is good and genuine it will not endure sexual intercourse."[5] The emerald was considered, however, good for improving eyesight, eyes being another association of this radiant fifth charm.

Although most of the Norse rune poems for the fifth position refer to ill-tempered voyagers and their radiating travels (Rad as ride or wheel), the *Hávamál* refers to the clear sight of this position:

A fifth I know: if I see hurled
Arrows hard at my horde;
Though rapid their flight I arrest them in air
If I see them clearly.[6]

LITERARY LIONS, PENTACLES, AND CIRCULATION OF LEARNING

The Green Lion as the constellation of regal Leo rules the fifth house of astrology. Deep within his stars lies the beating red heart of Regulus. A fire sign ruled by the sun, symbolized by a circle with an iota, a dot, jot, a pupil in its center, Leo may have bequeathed his shape to our numeral five.

Concerned with law and knowledge, literary lions still guard our library steps and courts of law. Instead of lions, the great library of Alexandria across from the island of Pharos* embedded five-sided figures—pentagons—in the pavement. It was here that seventy-two scholars translated the Five Books of the Torah (transmitted at Pentecost, fifty days after Exodus) into Greek. As Graves notes, "Since pentagons are inconvenient figures . . . , compared with squares and hexagons, the number five must have had some important religious significance."[7]

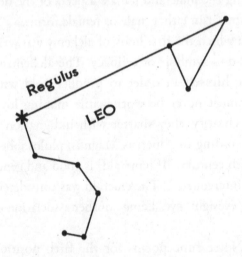

Fig. 49. The constellation of Leo

---

*The island of Pharos by Egypt's delta housed a great harbor, now submerged, where Phoenician ships docked when trading with Egypt.

This might be the place to teach the pentacle's astronomy. The numbers five and eight are both associated with the planet Venus's path through the sky.* Each time she rises, she appears in a different zodiac sign. It takes 1.6 years between each heliacal rising. The entire cycle returning her to the original zodiac position takes eight years (8 / 1.6 = 5). During her journey, she has five morning risings. Each appearance is in a different zodiac sign, tracing out a five-pointed star, a pentacle (☆) in the sky (360 / 5 = 72; that is, each arc is seventy-two degrees, and seventy-two, as we've seen, is a number that repeats throughout the alphabet Mysteries).

Venus's five-pointed star of law, order, and learning manifests in many ways even today. The star still graces the breasts of U.S. Marshals. An apple, traditionally given to a teacher, when sliced open, reveals a five-pointed star. The Egyptian hieroglyph for "star" is always written with five points. This is the hieroglyph "which indicates a journey across water, . . . the pilot who guides the ship . . . and, above all, . . . the verb 'instruct, teach.'"[8]

GREEN FIRES OF THE FIFTH SYMBOL

The planet Venus, circling between Earth and her sun, has both morning and evening appearances. As an evening star, she is the bright fertile female Venus. She spends 263 days as an evening star, the length of a human pregnancy. Then she disappears from the sky. Dying in the West, like all circling stars, Venus must travel the dark before returning with the light of day. When she returns, rising just before the morning sun, she is known as Lucifer the Light Bearer, who was thrown from Heaven for his presumptive brilliance.

The twelfth-century *Bahir* says: "The fifth is the great fire of the Blessed Holy One."[9] Another name for Lucifer is Phosphorus. Growing on rotten wood, it glows dark green in the same swamps that are home to the green willow tree (the fifth Tree Ogham). According to *The Concise*

---

*Venus orbits Earth thirteen times on that journey, also linking her with the number thirteen.

Oxford Dictionary of English Etymology, Phosphorus is the "morning star; phosphorescent substance; highly inflammable non-metallic element luminous in the dark.—L. *phōsphorus*—Gr. *phōsphóros* light-bringing." In keeping with the celibacy associated with the fifth position, the 1913 *Compendia of Materia Medica* states that phosphorus was a treatment for "impotence . . . no remedy [is] more efficient."[10] Being extremely poisonous, phosphorus was probably not the most useful remedy for this affliction.

KEYS TO THE KINGDOM

> *And the fifth angel sounded, and I saw a star fall from heaven unto the earth; and to him was given the key to the bottomless pit. . . . They had a king over them, which is the angel of the bottomless pit, . . . [who] in the Greek tongue hath his name Apollyon.*
>
> REVELATION 9:1–11

In Apollo's Temple of Delphi, a large letter E (our fifth letter) was inscribed over the door. As the second vowel in the alphabet (A-E-I-O-U), it was associated with Apollo as the deuce. As the fifth letter it is associated with learning.

A pope now owns the keys of the kingdom, which explains Sodath (meaning "primrose") as the choice for Color Ogham. This (five-petaled) flower is also known as Our Lady's Keys and Keys of the Kingdom. Tarot places a pope, the Hierophant, as its fifth card. This is not the Christian pope but rather a much older patriarch, once the papal Bull of his people. The Rider-Waite Tarot card, designed by followers of a Mystery tradition, put the cross of the patriarch in the Hierophant's hand. This same symbol represents the Phoenician fifteenth letter, samekh, which Tarot equates with the Devil. The South Iberian script from Spain, which like Ogham skips the second letter, uses the patriarch's cross as its fifth letter.[11] As described in the third letter, there are both symbolic and mathematical connections between the owners of the third, fifth, and fifteenth letters.

Fig. 50a. Samekh, fifteenth letter. Fig. 50b. Tarot Pope as fifth card.

Rider-Waite Tarot

SINGING WILLOWS AS THE FIFTH SYMBOL

Each symbol in the Phoenician alphabet represents a sound needed for the spoken language. Conforming to the hidden Mysteries, each later tradition, choosing their own symbols, must also reflect the stories determined by its placement in the series. Tree Ogham chose Willow (Saille) as its fifth character. Chaste teacher-priests shaved their heads to preserve their potency for wisdom; likewise, willow seed constrains potency: "If anyone drinks it, . . . he does not have children and it makes women unfruitful."[11]

Willow is a green tree. But, like the constellation of Leo, it has a red core at its heartwood. A mother needing a husband might wed a willow, but she shouldn't place her affection on a green willow tree, for his red heart belongs only to his goddess. There can only be unrequited love for one who wears the willow. The folk song "All around my hat, I will wear the green willow," commemorates the Willow's ancient significance as a symbol of the rejected or disappointed lover. It was originally intended as a charm and invocation to the Goddess.

Connecting the saille-go-round willow's green magic to many of the above stories, its branches once were used in a witch's broom to draw circles within which witches meditated on Thursdays, our fifth day. As scholar Judy Grahn notes, "The most important . . . day, to the Fairies and the witches alike, was Thursday." When I was young, one never wore green on Thursdays. On this day, the color was only for fairies.[13]

Multiple traditions associated green circles and law with the fifth position. I include this one from Tibet: When a person dies, it is said, his migrating spirit meets each of five Buddha families* on his travels through the dark. "On the fifth day there is the karma family, which is the pure quality of air or wind. It is a green light."[14] The symbol for the laws of karma is a wheel (mirroring the fifth Germanic rune, Rad, a wheel). Transmission of the laws of this circling karma wheel are spoken by gods and priest-kings and carried by the wind. "(Wheel or Ride) at the end is written mouth."[15]

The fifth Phoenician letter, hey, is usually translated as "aspirated H," meaning the sound of rough breathing. Hey has also been translated as "window," which derives from Anglo-Saxon "vindr eage": the "wind's eye." The I Ching places Wind as the fifth trigram in its Early Heaven Sequence. Continuing the theme of air movement and the resounding breath of God, square Hebrew (c. 250 BCE) changed the Phoenician shape of the fifth letter, ∄, to give it a window, letting the letter breathe: ה. Likewise, the fifth verse of the Tao Te Ching notes: "Between heaven and earth is a space like a bellows."[16] Bellows, of course, are used to move air.

The green willow is the slough tree, the sigh tree, known for the sound of the wind whispering through her hair. Poets touched willows for eloquence, but one should never tell secrets to a willow, for she is a transmitter, not a keeper, of the Mysteries.

---

*The previous four Buddha families also follow our alphabet pattern. Each family is associated with a color and symbol.

THE SPEAKING GIFT OF TONGUES

*God then formed the great sea monsters, and every living
creature that creeps, with which the waters swarm—God
then blessed them, saying "Be fruitful and multiply."*
THE TORAH, A WOMEN'S COMMENTARY,
GENESIS 1:21, DESCRIBING THE FIFTH DAY

Now this may seem opaque, but the Creation of Genesis closely follows
the ancient Spell. The swarms appearing on the fifth day of Genesis
mesh nicely with this symbol of going forth, rising up, and radiating
words or roads. The fish of the sea, the great monsters, and the birds
of the air fit with the gift of tongues received at Pentecost with five's
thumb, and with wisdom once possessed by a silver-tongued devil.

In his book on the mythology of Ireland, Michael Dames writes, "In
many Indo-European languages, the final part of several words meaning
tongue also serves as terms for fish. This fish-tongue amalgam can be
assigned to a very early date with tongue being derived from fish."[17] I
have no academic explanation for the association, but thinking poeti-
cally, both fish and tongue live in a moist environment, darting about
as they go about their business. If the fish-tongue is removed from its
moist home, speech (and fish) dies.

In Ireland, the wisdom inherent in the fifth charm was transmitted by five fish: According to legend, there is a well where the hazels of
wisdom drop slowly into the water. "And then the five salmon that were
waiting there would eat the nuts . . . and any person that would eat one
of those salmon would know all wisdom and all poetry."[18]

The fifth finger, the thumb, also can transmit this wisdom. Celtic
hero Finn gained his wisdom when he burned his thumb while cook-
ing the magical fish. He popped his thumb into his mouth, and "that
is what gave knowledge to Finn, when he used to put his thumb into
his mouth."[19]

The Old Norwegian Rune Poem also refers to five's thumb magic
and a gift of tongues. The verse for the fifth rune reads, "Riding is the
worst for horses. Reginn forged the best sword."[20] The verse refers to

Fig. 51. This twelfth-century carving of Sigurd (Siegfreid) in the Hylestad stave church of Setesdal, Norway, shows him sucking his thumb while roasting the dragon heart, carved into five steaks. Regin sleeps nearby with the sword.

Photo by Maraieke Kuijer, CC BY-SA 2.0

the story of Siegfried, who killed a great serpent-dragon with a sword forged by the smith Regin. While roasting the heart of the dragon, he burned his thumb and so popped it into his mouth, thereupon gaining the ability to understand the speech of birds. After eating, he loaded the heavy dragon's gold onto his weary horse.

Continuing the association of five with rulers and the great sea monsters created on the fifth day of Genesis, in China, five-toed dragons, the dragon kings, were associated with water and symbolized the emperor. A dragon is the fifth zodiac animal in the Chinese horoscope, and the fifth of the twelve symbols worn by the ancient emperor of China on his robe. Remembering the virtue inherent in this quintessential position, the dragon is a "symbol of imperial power. It is symbolic of virtue in a ruler."[21]

Today, the five-fingered hand, the hamsa with its watching eye, is a common symbol to wear or hang in the house. Traditionally, it is said to protect against the evil eye. It also promotes fertility which arrives with the sixth letter. After sharing the harvest and receiving the wisdom of the law in the chaste fifth position, we move toward the magic of midsummer's night. A sun king will now marry his land and plant another seed before dying south toward winter.

Fig. 52. The five-fingered
hand protects against the
evil eye and promotes
fertility.
Photo by Carles VA

*And there was evening and there was morning, a fifth day.
. . . God saw how good it was. God now said, "Let us make
human beings in our image, after our likeness."*

THE TORAH, A WOMEN'S COMMENTARY,

GENESIS 1:23, 26

Y
Sixth Letter

Marriage of Heaven and Earth
and the Throne of God

Phoenician/Old Hebrew	Vav (hook or nail)
Greek	Vau or digamma ("di"-gamma = two gammas mated = F)*
Ogham	Nion (Ash)† or Nin (forked branch)
Runes	Kenaz, Ken (torch), or Kaun (canker)‡
Hieroglyph	Seat (or throne, as the lap of a goddess)
Tarot	The Lovers

---

*This letter disappears from the Greek alphabet after Homer's time.
†Previously, the ogham for this sixth position was Fearn (the defeated Alder), which was demoted to fourth position.
‡The word *ken,* meaning "to know" in the biblical sense, produces kin (offspring) as well as kaun (canker, sore).

Myths of the sixth charm include the celebrations of a King mounting the throne of his land. There is an underlying sadness reflecting a Fall following the high point of summer.

Fig. 53. The Lovers
Rider-Waite Tarot

THE THRONE OF THE GODDESS

Studenthood is over. Now it's time for a king to wed his land, the midsummer sun to mate his moon, for they are in their prime, a word associated with six. The Tarot Lovers marry as well as kings, linking families to establish kin. In the honeymoon month of June, bees fly with their queen, their wedding flight producing children along with honey for their (six-sided) combs. But after their marriage, both king bee and sun king will die by year's end.

Midsummer's wedding represents a legal wedding. Legitimate kingship is invested in the one who quickened his land, the fertility of the partners proved by four's birth. The king must mount the queen's throne with the sixth charm if he is to claim his kingdom. My original assumption, that "Three for a Wedding" was Earth's only marriage, was ethnocentric. Among some country folk, it is only after fertility has been established that formal marriage takes place. The Lovers, the sixth Tarot card, now make their vows (a word similar to that of vau, the sixth Greek letter).

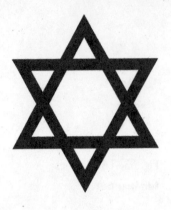

Fig. 54. The six-pointed star joins the male spirit with the female matter.

On the sixth day, Genesis creates humanity. Man (*aish*) is formed, as are his kin and kine. Genesis 2:23 states: "She shall be called woman [aishH], because she was taken out of man [aish]" (KJV). The Hebrew word *aish* hints at the ash tree from which northern people emerged.* King Ash is now the sixth (though formerly fourth) character in Tree Ogham.

Greek's digamma mates two gamma (Γ) symbols to form the sixth letter, F. Phoenician used a forked Y to represent their sixth letter, vav; *vav* means "hook" or "nail," which, of course, joins two objects. In Hebrew, this "vav of conjunction" joins two words with the sense of "and." Arabic also uses vav to join words and to declare a vow: W-Allah, meaning "I swear by Allah." (Arabic vav is pronounced with a w sound.)

Six's marriage vows now legalize the passion of mating. *Sex-* meaning "six," couples join with the spell magic of this charm. Our sixth day of the week belongs to passionate Venus. It is the time for the Friday night date, the night a good Jew is reminded not to neglect his marriage pleasures, the night when Israel's Bride is welcomed with candles at dusk. *Friday* is named after Norse Freya; India's Friday is *Shukravar* after sweet Venus; in Spanish, the word is *Viernes*.

---

*According to the *Prose Edda* book *Gylfaginning*, Odin and his two brothers found two trees (Ask/Ash and Embla/Elm) by the beach. He created man and woman from them.

Give me pleasure with your diamond scepter phallus. Look
at my three petaled lotus, its center adorned with a stamen.
It is a Buddha paradise. . . . Unite with my reclining form.
CANDAMAHAROSANA TANTRA (C. TENTH CENTURY),
VERSE FOR THE SIXTH CHAKRA,
AS TRANSLATED BY MIRANDA SHAW,
PASSIONATE ENLIGHTENMENT

China also places a Bride to rule as the sixth symbol. Sixth of the symbols the ancient emperors wore on their robes was a pheasant representing the empress; the virtuous dragon of the fifth charm is her consort, the emperor.

THE THRONE OF GLORY

The sixth one is the Throne of Glory, crowned, included,
praised and hailed. It is the house of the World to Come.
THE BAHIR (TWELFTH CENTURY),
TRANS. ARYEH KAPLAN

Several of six's symbols refer to thrones, the lap of the land goddess the king must formally mount to claim his kingdom. Isis, mother goddess of Egypt's black land, is represented by the hieroglyph 𓊨 for throne. "Seat" (□) is sixth of the twenty-four Egyptian hieroglyphs. Egypt had a long association with Canaanite Phoenicians and Hebrews. In Phoenician temples, the goddess was present as a simple throne, her spouse as a pillar.[1]

The name Isis "probably meant 'seat' or 'throne' and was written with a sign identical to the one which she wore on her head."[2] Note: Isis, as the star Sirius, rose with the June sun in Cancer around 2000 BCE to announce the Flood arriving with the seventh letter.

After Isis's spouse Osiris was killed, his coffin sailed to Byblos in Phoenicia. Faithful Isis, manifesting as the star Sirius, followed her Osiris/Orion. Finding his coffin, she returned him to Egypt where it was discovered by the red storm god Set and torn into fourteen pieces,

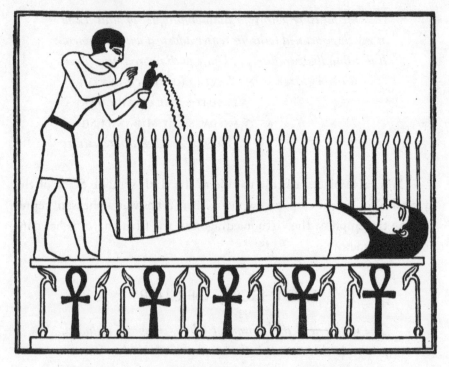

Fig. 55. Osiris as sprouting wheat, bas-relief at Philae

Illustration from Budge, *Osiris and the Egyptian Resurrection*, 58

but restored by Isis. His phallus being lost, Isis created one of gold and drew it into her to preserve his seed for the new creation promised after each flood. In Egypt, the rising of Sirius/Isis announced the annual Nile flood coming soon to deluge the land. When it retreats, the seed of Osiris will sprout again.

In time, Earth lost control of her Throne of Glory. "The outcome of the clash of Old European with alien Indo-European religious forms is visible in the dethronement of Old European goddesses," says Marija Gimbutas.[3] The □ shape in the Brahmi script denoted the sound "ba," meaning "father" rather than a "seat" as the goddess.

Myths overlaying alphabet symbols reflect the changing social scene of many mother goddesses losing authority to a king. But the king must still mount her sweetly to assume legitimate power. "One could say that there existed between the king and his divine spouse a contract. . . . He who ignored custom and seized the throne . . . courted the wrath of the gods."[4]

THE BATTLE BETWEEN
THE DARK AND LIGHT KINGS

Mother Nature accepting all her children as legitimate, it was possibly a concern for paternity that demanded a king legally marry his land to produce his kin.*[5]

> *I will tell of your decrees before kings.*
> PSALM 119, SIXTH STANZA,
> BEGINNING WITH THE LETTER VAV

Earth and her young lover first joined in the spring. As she prepares for June's honeymoon, a dark king and a light king compete for her favors. Although there have been other battles between the dark and light, in midsummer, the light loses the fight. The days now fall toward the dark, growing shorter.

Chapter 8 discussed the Ogham "battle of the trees," when the white spear tree Ash (Nion) left the emperor's fourth position after defeating the dark Alder (Fearn). Originally Alder (Fearn) occupied sixth place, and Nion (Ash) fourth place. I think the move among kings represented by ogham symbols was mandated by the powers associated with this sixth magic: possession of the Queen. Celtic kings could not rule without mating with the goddess of the land.

The following story hints at an earlier victory, before Fearn (Alder) lost the throne of the sixth position. All oghams in a series begin with the same letter. In Fort Ogham, where all the characters are named after forts, the fort is Femen. Located in Tipperary, Femen holds the Stone of Cashel,† where the kings of Munster were crowned. In Color

---

Konungr is the Old Norse word for king, a word which means, "descendant of good kin." The gloss is added to the sixth rune of the Old Icelandic Rune Poem.
†Cashel in early Irish described a ringfort, a circular structure for defense.

Ogham, the position was held by Flann. A history of Ireland tells us, "It was there [Femen], in 877, that Flann, High King of Ireland, sat nonchalantly after defeating King Loracan of Thomond in battle. To demonstrate the security of his superiority Flann disdainfully began a game of chess."[6]

The game of chess, which has the sixty-four black and white squares associated with fate, is won when the opponent's king is taken. As noted earlier, although the name for the Ogham alphabet is Beth-Luis-Nion, indicating Nion as the original holder of the fourth position, all written Ogham scripts place Nion in the sixth position, the F oghams now occupying the fourth position.

Both positions have been associated with emperors and kings, so the myths transferred smoothly. But as noted above, among the Irish, the king could not rule without the queen, the land herself. The mounting was not always consensual. A king seeking to impose rule over Munster raped Aine, sun goddess of that land. She bit off his ear, rendering him unable to rule (the kings of Ireland could have no deformities).

The ash tree (Fraxinus, not Rowan) whose ogham won the battle for sixth position is a white straight-grained wood. The saplings shoot up quickly, with little branching, which makes them suitable for spears. Ashwood was also suitable for making a queen's throne: "Ash when Green is fit for a Queen." As late as the 1500s, kingly Ash still pursued his Venus. In dowsing for copper, a metal associated with Venus, a forked stick of ash was used.[7]

VIRGO AND CANCER

The precession steadily moves the ruling stars backward through the sky. Virgo, once rising in the sixth month of midsummer, influenced some of six's myths. She carries her bright grain child (Spica) in her arms. Virgo still owns the sixth house of astrology, the house of contracts and housekeeping. The Golden Age of the mother goddesses ended when Virgo lost her throne.

Around 2000 BCE, Cancer, following kingly Leo, arrived this season. This was the period when Canaanite alphabet letters began appearing in the mines of Sinai. Among her other qualities, Cancer is a water sign. Likewise, K'an, representing water, is the sixth trigram of the Chinese I Ching. K'an, similar in name to a variant name for the Germanic sixth rune Kaun (ulcer), is also known as the Abysmal.

Cancer is a small, faint constellation in the shape of Phoenician vav: Υ. Between her legs is a faint collection of stars known as the Praesepe (Manger) or the Beehive Cluster. Mating honeybees supply the gold for six's honeymoon month of June, but the king will die after his flight with the queen.

The Beehive calls to mind, again, Ash as the victorious ogham winning the queen's throne. Many species of ash trees (*Fraxinus* spp.) exude a sugary substance that the ancient Greeks called *méli,* "honey." Some scholars have suggested that the sap was fermented to create the Norse Mead of Inspiration, which fits nicely with the saga and story associated with four, the position Ash (Os as the fourth Germanic rune) originally occupied.

LAMENTATIONS OF THE COMING DEATH

Six's marriage is to the land herself, both golden Sovereign and Housekeeper. As housekeeper, Earth expects the Children of Time to frolic at her party, but to clean up before they go home. At the end of their prime, the sun king and king bee begin to die as days grow shorter. New seed now rests in Earth's dark womb. The sun's yearly arrival in cankerous Cancer (♋) signals the coming of death of the year. Describing Kaun, the sixth rune, the Old Norwegian Rune Poem notes: "Ulcer [Kaun] is fatal to children; death makes a corpse pale."[8]

The sun in its travel through the sky moves from rising in the southeast at midwinter to rising in the northeast at Midsummer's Day. Then it slowly reverses, dying south once more. The Gate of Cancer, the Tropic of Cancer, is the furthest point the sun travels north along the horizon. The Gate of Capricorn, 180 degrees away, marks the southernmost rising of the sun at the winter solstice.

I believe there was always some melancholy following the exuberant mating, the jumping over the midsummer fires, when lovers meet and merry before growing old. But the darkness that now shadows this position's myths may also reflect the ending of the Golden Age of peace. War and warriors now control Earth's thrones. The pleasures of Venus have become venereal diseases and cancers, cankers, and sores.

> *Honey is sweet and so is he . . . he's married with a gay,*
> *gold ring . . . a gay, gold ring's a cankerous thing.*
> TRADITIONAL SONG, "ABOUT THE MERRY-MA-TANZIE,"
> FROM ROBIN SKELTON AND MARGARET BLACKWOOD,
> *EARTH, AIR, FIRE, WATER*

The land, however, remains a mothering presence. Death has entered the world, but the seed of kings and their kin, regardless of the ruling stars, will rest in her womb until called forth to rise again: "The Spirit of the Fountain dies not. It is called the Mysterious Feminine. The Doorway of the Mysterious Feminine is called the Root of Heaven-and-Earth."[9]

I
Seventh Letter
Floods, Apocalypses, and Pregnant Pauses

Phoenician/Old Hebrew	Zain (weapon)
Greek	Z
Ogham	Huath (Hawthorn)
Runes	Gyfu or Gebo (gift)
Hieroglyph	Cerastes, snake with horns
Tarot	The Chariot

How many miles to Babylon?
Three score miles and ten.
Can we get there by candlelight?
Yes, and back again.

Here comes the candle to light you to bed,
Here comes the chopper to chop off your head.

NURSERY RHYMES

FLOODS, APOCALYPSES, AND PREGNANT PAUSES

Two diverging stories are hidden in the seventh charm. One is a reflective pause, a quiet celebration and sharing of Sabbath gifts. *Grímnismál* describes the seventh hall of the gods as "the seventh Broad-Shining . . . A blessed place, the best of lands, where evil runes are rare."[1] The second, associated with endings, Deluges, and coming apocalypses, is more common. In this telling, the charm of seven usually represents the fierce aspect of the Great God and Goddess. Numeral seven (7), written with the sign of his El-wand, belongs to an aging Saturn, his name literally meaning "seven." Like the Black Goddesses of time, he eats his children.

Saturn (or, variously, El or Orion), the ancient Lord of the Rings, represents Time himself. Death and endings are among the aspects he wears here. But after each end is the promise of another turn on his Wheel: "The seventh Name from the Holy Names is the one known as El. . . . The attribute known as EL appears in order to show mercy so that the world will not be destroyed."[2]

Death lurks among Saturn's stories, along with secrets of alchemy and metallurgy. The adolescent second charm produced both red and white rivers. Hardened, the ores (second rune: Ur) were eventually forged into seven's weapons of slaughter (seventh Phoenician letter: zain/weapon). As users of the alphabet Mysteries moved shapes around to suit their own stories, the Z shape variant of the Phoenician seventh letter became the sleepy final letter of the English alphabet.

Earlier, we met Saturn/El as young Mercury glowing white, then as three's martial red cinnabar, a form of mercury. Now dulling with age, he appears as darkening lead, a metal attributed to Saturn. Shining quicksilver, mined from red cinnabar, grows leaden, becoming heavy with age. Black lead can, however, be transformed, creating a white (though intensely poisonous) paint.

Color Ogham uses Huath (purple) as code for this position. Purple is plum, the formal name for lead (*plumbum*). The origin of the word is from an unknown pre-Indo-European language, metallurgy originating in ancient Anatolia. It gives us the words *plumber* and *plumb bob,* a tool to measure the position of stars or to sound the depths of the watery abyss soon to engulf the land.

Huath, having many translations, also means "hawthorn," the seventh Tree Ogham. In this location it represents the Hag aspect of the Black Goddess. Seven being the number of endings and pregnant pauses, the witch of the hawthorn supplied the sleep thorn that caused swan-maidens and princesses to sleep. They will rise when their young lovers kiss them awake in the spring.

Huath, also translated as "horrible," appears in the Irish tale of Niall of the Nine Hostages. The five sons of the king became lost while out hunting, and made camp for the night. The eldest went in search of water and found an ugly old woman by a well. "You are horrible," said the lad. "Aye," said she. She told the boy that he could have water if he gave her a kiss, but he refused. Each brother in turn came to the well and made the same refusal, until the youngest, Niall. When he lay with her, she became "as fair a girl as any in the world." When Niall asks her identity, she replies, "I am Sovranty" and pledges that his "seed will be over every clan." The episode concludes, "As he had seen her, horrible at first and beautiful in the end, so also is sovranty, for it is most often won by war and slaughter, but is glorious in the end."[3]

We now await the rising flood. Although seven's letter became associated with death, I think an earlier association was with renewal rather than finality. Ireland's Crone, Cailleach Beare, lamented the change that kept her from growing young with her lovers and their kisses: "When my arms are seen, all bony and thin! . . . They used to be about glorious kings. . . . It is well for an island of the great sea: flood comes to it after its ebb; as for me, I expect no flood after ebb to come to me . . . what was in flood is all ebbing."[4]

DELUGES AND APOCALYPSES

Whatever the ultimate source for our alphabet pattern, various owners have left traces of their stories. Egypt's annual Nile flood begins in our seventh month of July. Signaled by the rising of Isis as the star Sirius, the Deluge covers her Black Land to restore its fertility. Hidden by her closeness to the bright sun, she is not visible for about seventy days between May and shortly after midsummer. Then she rises in the morning to announce the Nile flood.

In Ireland, a rainy Saint Swithin's Day (July 15) promises forty days of rain, and dry wells magically fill with water.[5] When the flood recedes, the carefully stored seed is again planted; new life re-emerges. The Cailleach Beare remembers, "My flood has guarded well that which was deposited with me."[6]

Myths and world ages change. Floods restoring the lands of farmers became a tale of blood. The Revelations of Saint John, written to seven churches of the people of Asia, declares that only the sacrificed (but rising) son can open the Book of the Seven Seals. By this black period, only a bloody sacrifice offered the chance of rebirth, not the watery womb of the Mother's blood. It was the Son of the Widow Woman who carried on the magic after the Virgin lost her throne and her arks and grails were stolen away.

With the opening of the Seventh Seal comes the Deluge. As always, pragmatic Vikings employ the charms to survive a harsh world.* Odin, the High One, uses the rising waters to put out fires:

> *A seventh I know: if I see a hall*
> *high o'er the bench-mates blazing,*
> *flame it ne'er so fiercely I still can save it—*
> *I know how to sing that song.*[7]

By the Western calendar, we have reached July and early August. These months in the Hebrew calendar are "Tammuz and Av . . . the low point of the cycle, marked by commemorations of tragedies that befell the Jewish people in several ages of their history. . . . This period . . . is marked by customs of grief."[8] In Babylon, Tammuz, another deity identified with Orion, is the dying and returning god of grain.

Egyptian hieroglyphic script places a deadly horned serpent, the horrible Cerastes ( ), as the seventh symbol. "Only the female has horns."[9] "The sacred adders . . . are not friendly snakes. Rather than suggesting trusty guardians of household treasure, they imply terror and swift death and recall the death-dealing side of the Goddess, in whose mystery cult one must die to be reborn."[10]

---

*Perhaps they had a deeper Mystery tradition, but if so, it has been lost to us. Only simple rune magic, curses, and charms remain.

The horned serpent is specifically linked, as is China's Old Mother living in a Purple Palace, to the circling pole stars. By this time, they numbered seven. "The 'Mother of the Measure' is an alternative name for the Queen of Heaven . . . she has her seat among the stars which form the Great Bear."[11] Recall that one of the stars of Draco was once (6,000 years ago) Earth's pole star, and that slowly the pole star position shifted to the North Star of the Great Bear.

Draco was the Dragon Lady until the precession cast her from her throne. Richard Proctor, in his 1877 *Myths and Marvels of Astronomy*, notes, "One might almost, if fancifully disposed, recognize the gradual displacement of the Dragon from his old place of honour, in certain traditions of the downfall of the great Dragon . . . alluded to in the Revelation xii, 4."[12]

Earth and sky change with the passage of time. Seven's magic promises a gift (seventh rune), but gifts became bloody, polluting an older Earth. The Phoenician alphabet uses "weapon" (zain) as its seventh letter; Ogham uses "horrible" (Huath). Stories on these themes are widespread. Ancient Jews circled the Temple of Jerusalem altar seven times with the blood of sacrificed animals, until, in the month of Av, both Temples were destroyed. Ancient labyrinths are said to have had seven walls that

Fig. 56. A map of the seven walls of Jericho, c. fourteenth century

Image from the Farhi Bible, compiled by Elisha ben Abraham Cresques must be toppled to reach the treasures hidden within. Jericho (c. 9000 BCE), possibly the oldest city in the world, had seven walls, as did Troy. The walls of Jericho were destroyed after Joshua's army circled the city seven times, blowing seven trumpets.

KEEPER OF THE RINGS, PLEDGES, HUGS AND KISSES (XXOO)

One wonders just how old our number magic is. Neanderthals performing the oldest known rituals in our world left their dead sprinkled with life-giving flowers, healing herbs, and blood-red ocher. Seventy thousand years ago, in a cave called Drachenloch (dragon's hole) high up in the Alps, they left a stone chest containing seven bear skulls "carefully piled on top of one another with muzzles pointing toward the cave's exit."[13]

As source of life after death, the Great Mother, who was also male, was called Guardian of Pledges and the Keeper of the Rings. Her cosmos contained a promise of return, a red revolution of time, for she had not yet become linear. Enclosed within the family, the clan, the village, her people had their own part to play in the wealth of their land. Although Earth owns the wheel of fortune grinding out wealth, it was the fulfillment of pledges and gifts between the land and her people that kept her green circle rolling.

> *That attribute known as El has mercy on those individuals*
> *who do not deserve it and bestows it . . . as a Gift.*
> RABBI GIKATILLA, *GATES OF LIGHT*

The seventh Germanic rune is Gyfu (gift), written X. Variant dictionary meanings of "gift" are "to lessen," "to give way," and, significantly for this letter of Deluges, "to make moist." Written with the promise of the mark of tav (X), the gift's power magically linked individuals to a wider circle. By their gifts, a person makes pledges with both fellow people and their gods.

Xs and Os came to represent our kisses and hugs. While X "marks

Fig. 57. Osiris as a sacrificed bull,
marked with X-O-X-O

Budge, *Osiris & The Egyptian Resurrection*, 327

Fig. 58. Sipenitsi pattern, Ukraine, c. 3800 BCE

From Marija Gimbutas, *Language of the Goddess*, 218

the spot" of various endings, tav's mark (X), seven's gift (X), and the "decimations" of Roman numeral ten (X) all promise the circle's continuation. Thousands of years after the symbols for our hugs and kisses appeared in ancient Europe, they still offer sticky-sweet promises of a returning spring's hot cross buns.

With the kiss of death, the soul flying from its worn host was gathered into the Hag's welcoming womb to await rebirth into the unbroken circle: the word *osculate* means to kiss. In mathematics, *osculate* means "to have contact with a higher order."

The Romani people, associated like the Scots with the Mysteries of Egypt, came to Europe from India, another home of Black Goddesses measuring out fate and time. As pragmatic as the Vikings, the Romani invoked a spell to charm their horses, painting X on one hoof, O on the other. Despite its great age, Earth's magic was still strong enough in the 1800s to keep unfettered horses from straying; the Romani invocation to do so went as follows: "Round, round, and round! . . . Be to (go not to) any other man. . . . Seven spirits of earth hear! I have seven chains, protect this animal, ever, ever!"[14]

Mother Goose says, "Seven's a secret n'ere to be told." At the same time, tradition holds that laying a finger alongside one's nose means "hush" or "a secret." We find these two tidbits of folk wisdom connected in the Mystery tradition of the Kabbalah, where each letter is a physical manifestation of part of God's body. Seven, the letter of oaths, promises, and mutual pledges, is God's nose.[15] The nose is said to be good for sniffing out secrets; a long nose is said to be a sign of a witch. It will also betray you if you tell a lie, as poor Pinocchio discovered. Seven demands the keeping of promises—and a double cross unlocks the oath, fingers X-crossed behind one's back.

THE PEDIGREE OF THE PRINCE

The eighth charm, which we'll discuss next, belongs to another aspect of Earth. As guardian of the circle, "the witch was . . . the ha-gazussa, a being that sat on the Hag, the fence, which . . . separated the village from the wilderness."[16] We shall meet her as the fence or gate (heth) of our eighth letter, through which the soul passes on the way to the Underworld.

Before a spirit passes through the opening gate of letter eight, they must first exit through Saturday's ending, after pausing to share their gifts. As the Old English Rune Poem says, "Gift is for every man a pride and praise, help and worthiness and for every homeless adventurer it is the estate and substance for those who have nothing else."[17]

The seventh charm contains both a pledge and a pregnant pause. A thirteenth-century text on Jewish mysticism notes: "The seventh day was ShaBaT (He rested)."[18] Harmonizing with this attribute, the seventh I Ching trigram is Ken (Mountain), or "Keeping Still."

Because this is such an important concept in understanding Earth

Fig. 59. Rock drawing
from Val Camonica, Spain,
c. 13,300–1800 BCE
From Fisher, *The Labyrinth,* 27

magic, I will try to elaborate for those who don't find it easy to think in bemusing images. Earth time is a mortal time, a measured time, and measured time eventually ends. The year, the span of life, the growing grain, all end with the harvest of souls. In time they rise again.

As Earth ages into a Crone, she becomes a vulturine Hag of a dying year: Ogham's "Horrible" is the "Seven for a Witch" of Mother Goose. Her child also ages, for he is Kronus, Saturn, aged Saturday, literally seven. Like his mother, Kronus/Chronos is subject to his biological clock. His era over, Earth's heir deposits his seed within her labyrinthine womb. There it will sleep until the pedigreed prince (from *ped-de-grus,* literally "crane foot") returns.

> *The clacking of cranes ascends. The self mounts the ancient*
> *stairway.*
> SEVENTH ORACLE, T'AI HSUAN CHING,*
> c. 50 BCE, FROM DEREK WALTERS,
> *ALTERNATIVE I CHING*

In figure 59, cranes and feathered birdmen dance over a giant resting within an ancient labyrinth. The square with a handle above

---

*This book of divination comprises eighty-one symbols, the same number as Lao-tzu's alchemical lessons. Each stems from a different tradition than the sixty-four hexagrams of the I Ching.

may represent a winnowing fan for grain used in Mystery traditions. Threshing floors being sacred places, the Temple of Jerusalem was built over a threshing floor of earlier Canaanites. Here the seed of the giant will sleep until life sprouts again.

The symbol for butterfly soul in Greek, psi, is Ѱ, the same crane foot (pedi-gru) used to represent the harvested and threshed barley (Ѱ). Harvested and hung upside down, it becomes a symbol for peace (☮). Further elaboration is outside the intent of this study, but triple crane goddesses were, like black Nemesis, ancient goddesses of fate.

After the apocalypses and Deluges following the opening of the seventh seal, a gate opens with the singing of the eighth charm. The eighth letter opens into a higher octave as the ascending scales begin anew.

> *The sage puts his person last and it comes first.*
> LAO-TZU, *TAO TE CHING*, SEVENTH VERSE,
> TRANS. D. C. LAU

Eighth Letter

Happy Gate of Heaven

Phoenician/Old Hebrew	Heth (gate or fence)
Greek	Eta
Ogham	Duir (Oak)
Runes	Wynn (joy or white)
Hieroglyph	Owl
Tarot	Justice*

---

*Justice is the traditional eighth card of Tarot. Sometimes justice is given the eleventh position due to the influence of the Rider-Waite deck.

> *Hail, Star of the sea, Blessed Mother of God, happy gate of heaven.*
>
> NOVENA TO OUR LADY PERPETUAL HELP

THE GATE OF HEAVEN

At the eighth charm there is a branching, a parting of the ways. One path ended with the seventh charm; another tradition continues the journey, traveling on to enter the coils of the Underworld. When feeling through the qualities associated with the alphabet charms, we find that the tale contained in the first seven letters flows smoothly. They seem to follow a seasonal ritual originating as a spelling of each new year.

In a ritual composed of seven stages, eight's charm has us rising with joy (Wynn, eighth rune) into the light of a bright new Sunday, a new octave, a new generation. After being judged and sorted, the soul returns through the opening provided by the duality of the second letter. Earth's treasure has reentered her storehouse (Beth) to begin another season under the sun. This eternal cycle is represented by the shape of numeral eight (8). Infinity is described in the first charm; numeral 8's symbol represents this eternal cycling into infinity: ∞.

The eighth charm straddling two stories includes either the promise of rising into a shining new world or the first stage of a journey through Earth's womb. The Norse poem known as *Grímnismál* (c. 1200 CE) hints at both possibilities: "Heavenmount is the eighth where Heimdal is said to rule the sanctuaries. The watcher of the gods with joy Quaffs good mead in this happy house."[1]

Wynn, the eighth rune, means not just "joy" but also "white." Heimdal, the "whitest" of the gods, owns the Gjallarhorn blown to signal Ragnarok, the end of the northern world. He also guards an ice bridge, the Rainbow Bridge (Bifrost) spanning the worlds of men and gods on the road to Heaven.

In 1836, Victor Hugo wrote, "G is the French horn."[2] The shape of the English seventh letter, G, suggests the horn blown to topple walls and worlds with the opening of the Seventh Seal. The horn that sounds

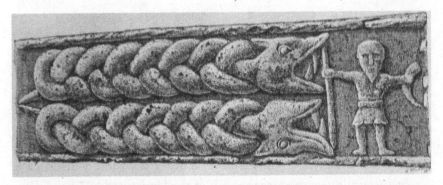

Fig. 60. Heimdal and his horn, Cosforth Cross, England, c. tenth century

Photo/reproduction by Finnur Jónsson, published in 1913

the Apocalypse signals the rising up on Judgment Day. It also signals the start of each new year; among Jews and Muslims, the New Year is timed by the first appearance of the crescent moon: "When this was sighted it was announced with the sounding of trumpets."*3 At the eighth charm, the horn has been blown. A new year is upon us. Seeking to make peace with each other, we now await a judgment.

The eighth verse of Psalm 119, devoted to the letter heth, remembers the joy of this symbol: "The earth, O' Lord is full of your love. . . . At midnight I will rise to give thanks because of your righteous judgments."

Described at the fifth charm, the numbers five and eight are both associated with Venus. These positions don't evoke a lighthearted Venus flitting from lover to lover. In those positions, she represents an older, more powerful goddess dispensing law and justice, but she still employs her winsome ways to resolve disputes. Justice traditionally is the eighth Tarot card. In Iceland, as noted earlier, the Althing, or law assembly, opened on a Thursday, the fifth day; the assembly was held mid-July to August, our eighth month. Folklorist H. R. Ellis Davidson tells us, "The purpose of the Althing was the recital of law . . . and judging of disputes."4 Inheriting Venus's tradition of peaceful settlements, "there was a ban on the carrying of arms."5

> The eighth I sing is for every one
> The most fortunate lore he can learn:
> When hatred is harbored by children of chiefs,
> This I can hastily heal.6

Duir (Oak) is the Tree Ogham for this eighth charm. Oak was the council tree where Druids held their summer courts. Robert Graves notes, "Its roots are believed to extend as deep underground as its branches rise in the air . . . which makes it emblematic of a god whose law runs both in Heaven and in the Underworld."7

Almost with the sense of taking a deep breath, our alphabet

---

*In Egypt, the New Year followed after the Nile flood, usually in the month of August (our eighth month).

continues. After getting past the diverging images of this eighth letter, the story becomes smooth for another eight letters. I will try to further separate the two possible paths.

THE GATE OF HEAVEN

With the eighth charm, the bodies of the dead are laid to rest in Earth's womb. If not immediately rising, the soul must travel the dark before emerging later in our expanded Spell. The eighth Phoenician letter is heth (gate). As an early symbol, heth appears as 𐤇, H, or the shape depicted on the womb of an ancient Anatolian goddess (fig. 61), Ħ.

Heth was the name of an ancient mother goddess. In her dark cave, the ancestors Abraham, Sarah, Isaac, and Jacob sleep. "The same is Hebron in the land of Canaan. And the field, and the cave that is therein were made sure unto Abraham for a possession of a burying-place, by the sons of Heth" (Genesis 23). This site, near the Oaks of Mamre where angels once came calling, was so important to Abraham that the Torah stresses he paid full price for it, rather than bargaining for a better fee. Although the Bible remembers Heth as a son of Canaan, as a goddess, she was Anna Heth or Anahita. Possessor of the

Fig. 61. Goddess figure, Anatolia, c. 2500 BCE
From Marija Gimbutas, *Language of the Goddess*, II

ultimate gate returning souls into the world, "she had the power to purify the seed of man."[8]

One child of Heth is an almost forgotten goddess of the Phoenician city of Sidon, named after the goddess Side. Side ("pomegranate") was one of Orion's many wives. Another goddess of the Underworld, she was placed there by a jealous Hera in Greek mythology.*[9] I suspect like other Earth goddesses, they were once known for their fierce protection of the dead sleeping in earthen tumuli, their tumescent wombs.

The eighth and last I Ching trigram is K'un, the Receptive Earth.† Depicted as fully feminine (☷), she offers no impediment to entrance into her womb. Her opposite is the yet undivided Heaven (Chien, ☰), whose potential initiated our journey. K'un also symbolizes the direction north, the direction of Earth's womb-tomb. North representing a welcoming Earth, the north side of the medieval churchyard was "appropriated for the internment of unbaptized infants, of persons excommunicated, or that have been executed, or that have laid violent hands upon themselves."[10] Earth, unlike later rulers, accepted all her children.

The eighth house of astrology includes death, inheritance, other people's money, and regeneration through sexuality. Its ruler is the (eight-legged) Scorpion associated with the fierce aspect of the goddess. Remember, Scorpio guards the star-producing womb of our galactic center.

That the fixed stars were slipping from their firm control of the Heavens became obvious to our star-watching ancestors. (Recall the number of legs of the scorpions flanking the womb in figure 6, p. 20.) These scorpions guarding Heaven's womb have nine rather than an anatomically correct eight legs. As no animal has an odd number of limbs, I believe this imagery was an attempt to reconcile the shifting of Scorpio as she precessed from a late summer rising into fall. No

---

*In Ireland, the women of the burial mounds are BanShee. In China, they are the Shi, also known as Thu.

†The website chinesethought.cn describes it like this: "The *kun* trigram symbolizes earth, and when it comes to society, it symbolizes the social roles played by the female, the mother . . . In this context, kun also means creating and nourishing all things under heaven."

matter when she appears, the womb of the Black Goddess lies among her stars. After passing through what is now our ninth month, the Western zodiac froze her into the Halloween skies of October, now our tenth month.*

OWLS AS SYMBOLS OF THE WISDOM AND POWER OF DARK GODDESSES

Venus as the Great Mother acquired multiple names and aspects during her long journey through time. In Mesopotamia, she was Inanna, Astarte, or Ishtar as goddess of the Morning Star (Venus). In Egypt, Ishtar was Neith, goddess of weaving and resurrection and, like Heth, a protector of the dead. Neith has been further identified (by Herodotus, c. 450 BCE) with Greek Athena. This brings us to the next image: the owl.

An owl (🦉) appears as the eighth character in the Egyptian hiero-glyphic alphabet, adding to my certainty that the twenty-four-character sequence was not a random pattern. The cycle of the planet Venus links the numbers five and eight; she appears in five morning risings, each in a different zodiac sign, marking out her pentacle. Traveling 1.6 years between each heliacal rising, the entire cycle returning her to the original zodiac position takes 8 years (8 / 1.6 = 5).

We first met several owl goddesses at the fifth charm. Those wise dispensers of the laws included Athena (Minerva), identified by the Roman numeral five (V) and by her owl, and Lakshmi, Lady Five (Shri Panch), who travels by owl. Astrology's eighth house including money among its attributes, Athena's coins (known as "owls") were the world's first international currency.

Ancient images do not come with nice little brass identification tags attached. I have seen the goddess in figure 63 identified as several bird goddesses, not just Inanna but also Ishtar, and Lilith (*lil* meaning "air," "wind," or possibly a night bird). Demonized like Ishtar as the whore

---

*Vedic (Indian) astrology continues to let the constellations move backward. Their zodiac stars fit the actual sky (sideral astrology) versus Western astrology, which froze with Aries in spring.

Fig. 62. Athena's owl on Greek coin, c. 500 BCE, at the Museum of Fine Arts in Lyon, France
Photo by Marie-Lan Nguyen, CC BY-SA 2.5

Fig. 63. Burney Relief, a Mesopotamian terracotta plaque showing Inanna flanked by two owls, c. 2300–2000 BCE, at the British Museum in London
Photo by BabelStone, CC0

of Babylon, Lilith was either first wife of Adam or that of the devil Samael. Becoming a queen of the demons, stories say she left Adam because she refused to be subservient.[11] Goddess of the night, she may have been an ancient aspect of the younger, more compliant Eve. "Seven for a Witch, Eight for a Whore" is another Mother Goose verse that doesn't appear in children's books.

FAR TRAVEL, DEATH, AND DRUIDS

Among Asiatic peoples the planet Venus excites unique
reverence as the shaman's source of prophetic inspiration.
NIKOLAI TOLSTOY, *THE QUEST FOR MERLIN*

Wherever the gates to the Underworld open, far travel and prophecy can occur. Although shamans and kings might sit on tombs opening to the Underworld to gain inspiration, this gate (heth), unlike the opening of the second charm, is a gate of exit, not entrance. With the eighth charm, late summer's harvest is carried into Earth's storehouse.

The eighth character of Bird Ogham is Droen, Wren. The wren was the symbol of the Druid: prophet, shaman, and lawgiver of the Celt. Irish historian P. W. Joyce writes, "The wren in particular was considered so great a prophet, that in an old Life of St. Moling, one of its Irish names, *drean,* is fancifully derived from *drui-en,* meaning the 'druid of birds.'"[12]

In Ireland, the wren, sacred to the oak king (Tree Ogham for this position), was traditionally hunted down and slain at midwinter. This ritual may have been an adaptation of a late summer festival celebrating a grain goddess's death at harvest time to reflect a sun king dying in midwinter.* I have come across multiple references to stories of kings dying in the eighth year of their reigns, and with other scholars asserting adamantly that no such evidence exists, I suspect that folk memory is at work.

Druids being female as well as male, the wren-as-ogham may refer to the nursery rhyme about Jenny Wren. She married red-breasted Cock Robin, who was slain by the "sparrow with my bow and arrow." The instigator of the battle resulting in Robin's death was the cuckoo, spring herald of Earth's new lover. "Who'll dig his grave? I, said the Owl, with my little trowel, I'll dig his grave."

A fascinating link showing myth slithering into dry historical "fact"

---

*Ireland's harvest festival, the Lughnasadh, was instituted by the sun god Lugh in honor of his mother who died of exhaustion after clearing her land for agriculture.

is the death of English king William Rufus. On Loaf Mass, in the eighth month of August, 1100 CE, an arrow killed this unpopular king. "Almost from the moment it happened . . . stories were circulating that William Rufus's death . . . was ritual regicide, in which he was compliant victim."*[13] His assassin, who stood by Tree Ogham's eighth symbol, an oak, was a man named Tirel, with the perfectly proper first name of Walter. Tir being a Germanic god symbolized by an arrow (↑), it may be that in the loose fashion of ancient names, Tirel acquired his name after his feat of archery. Loaf Mass, the Christian name for Lugnasadh, is a harvest festival that includes chopping off the neck of the last sheaf of wheat. Given that the eighth house of the Zodiac also includes the qualities of treasure and other people's money, note that Henry, Rufus's brother, "rode straight for Winchester [and] seized the treasury."[14]

SOWING HARMONY

Some of the other oghams in this position may refer to the not always virtuous qualities of Venus. The biblical King David, beloved of Jessie and his "eighth shoot," is Assistant Ogham's choice (Dabhid).† His role as a harper soothing to sleep a mad king, Saul, may have inspired the eighth choice of the Fort Ogham, Dinn Rig, where a slaughter occurred.

The Slaughter of Dinn Rig is not the usual quality associated with the winsome settlement of feuds inherent in the peaceful eighth charm. Digging deeper, I discovered that the inhabitants of the Irish fort were first lulled to sleep by the singing of a magic harp. Of the Dinn Rig harp, it was said, "It brought a death sleep on the host." And befitting a symbol of winsome Venus (Wynn), it also "sowed harmony between the lovers Moen and Moriath."

---

*We first met Tir as a prick in the third letter; we will meet him again in the seventeenth letter.

†David (whose name translates "beloved") is the eighth child of Jessie. Fourteen generations later, his descendent is Jesus. We will join the Piscean Messiah at the fourteenth symbol. A rather venial king, like Venus in the eighth position, he seduced Bathsheba, wife of one of his soldiers. For his adultery God would not let him build the Temple of Jerusalem. That honor was given to his son, Solomon.

Recalling the Venusian link between the fifth and eighth charms, the owner of the harp, Moen, had horse ears. Only his barber knew. The barber whispered the secret to a willow tree that was later carved into a harp. When played, the willow's harp sang out, revealing the king's hidden horse ears. Letter five's qualities included the transmission of knowledge. Willow, fifth Tree Ogham, is a transmitter, not a keeper, of secrets.

Second Family:
Letters of the Underworld

Introduction to the Second Family

Our story now begins to unravel as various peoples expanded the alphabet journey to encompass their own magical choices. In this section, we follow the next eight letters. The first eight told of the cycle of growing and harvesting. The eight letters examined here reflect an adaptation of a hero's journey through the Underworld.

Discussing a few of these letters, a historian writes: "While the majority of the names are very easy to explain, the names of the letters considered as additions present difficulties . . . heth [the eighth] means fence or barrier; teth [ninth] is explained . . . as ball or clew (for instance, of wool or cotton); lamed [twelfth] may indicate the rod of the teacher; samekh [fifteenth] is generally explained as fish."[1]

For those not ascending into the light of a new day with eight's new octave, the soul must journey the Underworld guided by an unwinding ball of thread received as the ninth letter, teth. It travels past new judgments and the decimations of the tenth. Crossing an ice bridge with the eleventh rune, hanging (upside down) with the ruler of the twelfth, the alphabet's extended journey continues toward the waters of the thirteenth letter (mem/water).

The Phoenician alphabet and its descendants including Runes, Ogham, and Hebrew scripts follow each other's stories closely. The twenty-four symbols of the Egyptian alphabet also suggest the same pattern through the first fifteen characters.* Other traditions begin to diverge or fall away. Palmistry has used up its five fingers; the eight I Ching trigrams no longer provide clues. The Tao Te Ching contains eighty-one verses that soon leave the alphabet's path. The fifty letters of Sanskrit, along with the sixty-four hexagrams of the I Ching, may include internal divisions that align them with our letters, but I haven't found a key.

The path provided by the alphabet symbols continues. After emerging from the waters of the thirteenth letter, mem (water), Earth's serpent-fish-messiah manifests as the fourteenth (nun/fish) and fifteenth letters (samekh/fish or prop). They may once have passed through the eye of the sixteenth letter, O (ain/eye), on their journey toward the sky. After O's opening eye, a final family begins: the Letters of the Heavens. This last family ends with the promised mark of resurrection, the cross of tav (mark).

---

*Although the twenty-four hieroglyphs appeared early in Egypt's history, Greek myth states they were returned to Egypt and now appear in scholarly books in their present order. I believe this is a case of an alphabet order's convergence.

Ninth Letter

Entering the Labyrinth

Phoenician/Old Hebrew	Teth (wheel or coil)
Greek	Theta
Ogham	Tinne (Holly) or Teine (Fire)
Runes	Hagalaz (Hag god, hail, or heal)
Hieroglyph	Water
Tarot	The Hermit

When work is completed, it is time to retire.

NINTH VERSE, TAO TE CHING,
HAMILL TRANS., 12

ENTERING THE LABYRINTH

The twenty-four Germanic runes are divided into three families, or *aettir* (eight or direction). The first family belongs to the god Frey, responsible for Earth's fertility. The second family is ruled by Hel, also known as Holle or Hulda, the goddess of the Underworld. An early symbol for the ninth rune, Hagalaz, is the same as shown on the womb of a goddess from Anatolia. We met Heth (gate or fence) at the eighth letter. Although the rune Hagalaz is usually translated as hail, Alaz is an Anatolian fire god, and like Anna-heth has the power to purify. The

Hag as Hel owns the ninth realm of the Northern cosmos, and like Eve, she comes from the north.

As noted above, the earlier soul/seed journey has branched into two paths. The first describes ascending into the light through the gate of the eighth charm. If not sung into the light by the octaves of eight, the soul must journey on through the Underworld. That journey begins with our ninth letter. According to Porphyry (232–305 C.E.), the Egyptians used an X within a circle as a symbol of the soul; it had a value of nine.[1] The secrets of mathematics are also hidden among the alphabet symbols; nine, like the pure soul, is considered a number of truth. Each appearance after multiplication of nine also equals nine: $9 \times 2 = 18, 1 + 8 = 9; 9 \times 3 = 27, 2 + 7 = 9; 9 \times 4 = 36, 3 + 6 = 9$, and so on.

One of the shapes used as the ninth Phoenician letter ⊗ is the symbol of a soul continuing its travels toward illumination. The ninth house of astrology, reflecting this, represents the house of long journeys. The Underworld representing death rather than life, in ancient Greece ballots used in voting for a sentence of death were inscribed with theta (Θ). It survives on ancient potsherds used for voting for the death sentence.*[2]

This second family of letters belongs to a darker period than that of an age enchanting a farmer's peaceful year. Droughts and apocalyptic floods have afflicted Eden. War and death appear in the stories as we move away from earlier traditions sung to keep a once fertile world turning in its seasons. The ninth charm tells a bleaker, more militant tale. Walls are stormed and battles are fought. According to Victor Hugo, i, our ninth letter, has become "a war machine launching its projectile."†[3]

In the ninth month of September, students reenter school to seek knowledge; Tarot's Hermit with his lantern sets off into the dark. Others prepare for war. In ancient India, kings turned loose a white horse in September–October, following it until it brought them to another king's territory. Then a war was fought for the rule of the kingdom, and the horse sacrificed.[4]

---

*Greek does not adapt the sixth letter of Phoenician (vav): theta, while keeping the value of nine, is physically the eighth letter in their script.
†The letter i replaced teth in the English alphabet.

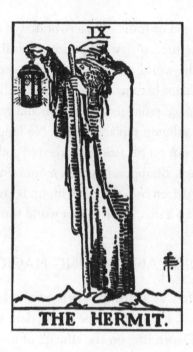

Fig. 64. The Hermit,
setting off through
the dark
Rider-Waite Tarot

In China, the emperor's proper actions ensured the turning of the seasons. In the ninth month, the ancient Li Chi (Book of Rites) says, "the son of Heaven . . . teaches how to use the five weapons of war, and the rules for the management of horses."* This being the season to travel through the Underworld, the emperor also "eats hemp seeds."[5]

Describing the nature of the Underworld, tradition offers various possibilities for the ninth charm. Some tell a dark story filled with monsters, dangers, and princesses stolen away to dark labyrinths. These attributes emerged from a bleaker time than the original Spell. There, a golden Storehouse was readied to gift her world with the bountiful harvests implied by the first family of letters. The first Spell, as an enchantment, might even predate agriculture, Earth's gifts being multitudes of animals as well as plants. (Recall fig. 8. on p. 20, where a Paleolithic hunter impregnates his goddess to produce plants and animals.)

Memories of this lost golden world remain. Once the dead were welcomed to the Dead Land, to eat rich food from golden plates in

*Horses were an important part of early wars.

beautiful surroundings. Yama, god of India's Underworld, was the first man to find the path to this afterlife. At first his palace was full of pleasures and had no sorrow. As the world and its stories changed, Yama became a figure of terror; his palace became an unpleasant Hell.

In the north, the old gods once promised protection and good harvests as land spirits, but a new religion replaced them. No longer worshiped, a Norse farmer looking out on his fields saw the old gods, dark, hunched, and covered with rags, disappearing into mountain caves.* The fairies of Ireland were also driven into the earth mounds after their conquest by the sons of Mil. Like Yama, their golden world was fading.

WATERS OF THE DEEP AND SAILING MAGIC

The Underworld might manifest as swirling waters of the Deep, in which case sailing magic is useful. It might also be a cold, dark world of Hel or the hot world of Hell. Depending on the climate of its owners, the Abyss may be either hot or cold, dry or moist.† The ninth charms represent both aspects depending on the culture. Symbols for teth (coil) have been used to represent salt, the rim between sky and sea, or simply Earth herself.

German psychologist Erich Neumann explains, "The Feminine is the belly-vessel as woman and also as earth. She is the vessel of doom, guiding the nocturnal course of the stars through the underworld; she is the belly of the "whale-dragon," which, as in the story of Jonah, swallows the sun hero every night."[6]

Teth being the ninth Phoenician letter, the name recalls the ancient Greek goddess Tethys. The rivers are born from her womb. Remembering the ninth Egyptian hieroglyph means "water," rivers flowing in the starry sky as well as on Earth emerged from Tethys's womb. When Egypt's pharaoh or sun died, the sky goddess swallowed

---

*For similar stories of the vanishing old ones, see Davidson, *Scandinavian Mythology*, 133–34.

†Ogham places Teine (fire) in the ninth position; the ninth Egyptian hieroglyph is a symbol for water. Ninth letter Teth may derive from Old Irish té, from Proto-Celtic teΦents, or from Proto-Indo-European tep- ("to be warm").

him. He then traveled by boat through her belly waters until reborn into another day.

"Tet is the belly." A medieval Hebrew tradition agrees. The twelfth-century *Bahir* comments that the Ten Commandments "contain all 22 letters except Tet, which is missing in them. . . . This teaches us that Tet is the belly—and it is not included among the Sefirot."[7]

Tethys may claim a kinship with the waters of the Babylonian goddess Tiamat. As the salty waters of a primeval world, she once mated with the sweet waters of Apsu (god of freshwater) to create men out of the resulting delta's silt.

Norsemen going a-viking used the magic of teth's coiled womb to keep their horses of the seas safe: "Brim-rúnar [sea runes] shalt thou grave, if thou wilt save the sailsteeds afloat. Grave them on the bow and on the rudder-blade, and mark Eld [fire] on thy oar."*[8] Like Tethys described above, the rivers of the North emanated from Hel's womb. This empowered the charm chanted by a witch to her son: "if in threatening waters thou fearest to find thy death: to Hel let fare both Hronn and Uth [wave], may dry the deeps for thee!"†[9]

The Norse god Brimir (Ymer), like Babylonian Tiamat whose dismembered body created a new world, was a giant killed by later gods. The *Vafthruhnir* describes, "From Ymer's flesh was the earth shaped, the barren hills of his bones; and of his skull the sky was shaped, of his blood the briny sea."[10] *Brimstone* is the fiery rock of dry Hell; *brine* is the salt from the ocean. One of the shapes representing Phoenician teth is an alchemical symbol for salt: Θ.

A variant form of teth's coiling symbol can represent the circling sun swallowed into Earth's belly: $\odot$. As a symbol, it also depicts Tethys's brother, the World Ocean circling Earth. Winds as well as rivers emerging from her belly, the goddess could recall storms when so invoked. In a Norse tradition, the *Hávamál* calls upon these powers:

---

*Teine, the ninth Tree Ogham Holly, can also represent fire.
†Hronn and Uth are possibly rivers flowing to Hel, according to Alexander Bugge (Norwegian scholar, 1870–1929). This chant was Groa's third: the binding of waters ensured a good pregnancy with the third charm.

> *A ninth I know: If need there be*
> *to guard a ship in a gale,*
> *the wind I calm, and the waves also,*
> *and wholly soothe the sea.*[11]

Greek sailors, like Vikings, invoked the goddess of the waters for safe voyages, throwing salt over their shoulders or drinking saltwater before sailing. The powers of a woman's womb mirror the magic of Tethys and Hel to bind wind and water. Pliny the Elder, around 50 CE, described the power of women in calming the sea, stating "out at sea, a storm may be lulled by a woman uncovering her body."[12] This is presumably a polite reference to exposing her powerful lower organ.

LABYRINTHS AND STOLEN MAIDENS

This brings us to another depiction of the Underworld. Along with great swirling waters, Earth could hide a coiled labyrinth within her belly. In Scandinavia, stone labyrinths kept the womb's power over the winds and sea. Fishermen walked through them in procession before setting off "in the hope of controlling the weather, obtaining a good catch, and ensuring a safe return. They would build a stone labyrinth if the weather was too rough to venture forth, in the hope of containing the force of the storm within the coils."[13]

Stories associated with this labyrinthine aspect of the ninth charm include heroes entering them to attack monsters and rescue maidens. Other traditions have a mother seeking her stolen child. Mother Earth as Demeter (Earth mother) is also known as Brimo, recalling the Earth goddess's womb full of healing brimstone and brine. Her child, Persephone, was among those maidens carried off to the Underworld. The Eleusinian Mysteries of ancient Greece enacted the descent and re-emergence of Persephone. According to the *Oxford Classical Dictionary*, at the end of the reenactment, the priest calls out: "Holy Brimo has born a sacred child, Brimos."

One translation for *teth* is "coil." Another is "clew," a variant spelling for the clues we have been following through the path hidden in the alphabet. A more relevant meaning for teth as clew is "ball of yarn." Several dictionaries I consulted specifically link this clew to the ball given the ancient Greek hero Theseus. Before he entered Crete's Labyrinth to slay the Minotaur, he was given a clew by the king's daughter to help find his way back. One definition of clew is a ball of yarn that guides the way.

Additional stories of labyrinths and clews, those balls of yarn spun by fate goddesses, come from the East. The mother goddess of India is known as Kali. Fleeing warring demons, Kali traveled north from a labyrinth in Ceylon (modern-day Sri Lanka) to Tibet where she became the oracle for the Dalai Lama. With her, she carried dice and a ball of thread: "On the rear flank of her mule hangs a ball of magic thread . . . made from rolled-up weapons."*[14]

The demon king of Ceylon's labyrinth kidnapped Sita (furrow), the earthborn wife of the god Ram. (We met Ram and Sita at the third charm when he won her in an archery contest.) After her kidnapping, in the ninth month of September, Ram woke the sleeping Durga-Kali, seeking her help. Durga, a fierce manifestation of Kali, was originally worshiped in spring. In memory of her aid to Ram, her festival, celebrated over nine days, was moved to the fall. She is represented in the form of a bundle of nine healing twigs.†[15]

HEALING MAGIC

You are good, and what you do is good.
PSALM 119, NINTH STANZA, BEGINNING WITH TETH‡

Healing magic is included among nine's powers. Hel, an aging Bride, is the cold Hag of the north and the ruler of the ninth world. Hail grew in her womb and snow flew when Frau Holle shook her feather bedding.

---

*Ceylon is where Buddha is said to have stepped off this world, leaving behind the marks of his foot, his sole.

†See the second letter for the story of nine healing twigs owned by Uller (the wuldortanas).

‡The first time *teth* appears in the Torah is in the word *good* (tov).

Although sometimes Norse mythology depicted Hel as a rotting corpse, in another aspect she welcomed small children and those who didn't die in battle. For those who couldn't sail, ride on horses, or travel in wagons, it took nine long nights to walk to the Otherworld, shod in special Hel shoes. The *Saga of Gisli the Outlaw* says, "Tis the custom . . . to bind the hellshoe on men, so that they may walk on them to Valhalla."[16]

The Hagalaz, with an H shape, was an early shape of the ninth rune, but it eventually became Hail written with a star shape. The star of Hail is a healing star, the hale and hearty symbol adapted by EMTs: ✳. Ice, brimstone (sulfur), and salt brine from Hel's womb all contain healing qualities.

OGHAM

The ritual center of Troy was remembered, like the coil of Teth, as a labyrinth. Mycenaean Greeks attacked and conquered Troy to reclaim Helen who had been stolen away to that city. After the fall of Troy,

Fig. 65. Maiden in a Troy town maze, Sibbo, Finland, c. 1400 CE. These represented Virgin Dances where the suitor needed to find his way through the labyrinth to find the maiden.

Image from the Labyrinthos website

Fig. 66. From an Etruscan vase or wine-server, c. 630 BCE, from Tragliatella
near Caere, with detail showing a soldier riding away from a Troy town
maze. Next to the maze lies a mating couple seeding new life.
(Early magic was very earthy.)

G. Q. Giglioli, "L'Oinochoe di Tragliatella," *Study Etrusci,* vol. III, Firenze, 1929

"The Walls of Troy were rebuilt by . . . architects of Crete after the
model of the Cretan Labyrinth which was an exact representation of
the stellar universe."[17] After Troy's defeat, fleeing Trojans carried their
"Troy town" mazes throughout Europe.

Bird Ogham's ninth character, Starling (Truith), hints at another
captive princess. The Welsh *Mabinogion* tells the tale of the sister of
Bran the Blessed, who is unhappily married to an Irish king. Imprisoned,
she sends a starling to tell her brother about her mistreatment. Bran, the
Alder king we met at the fourth and sixth charms, comes to rescue her.
After being killed in the battle, Bran's head is cut off. Still able to speak,
the head was carried about the land by seven survivors of the battle for
numerous years. Bran's head was eventually brought to Britain and buried under the Tower of London. As long as it remains there, it is said,
London, once known as Troy town, will be safe from capture. Bran is
associated with ravens; his ravens also protect the Tower.*

Fort Ogham's ninth character is Tara, the seat of Ireland's High
Kings. Tara is named after the hot, lustful, wanton goddess Tea.
Remembering Celtic kings could not rule without marriage to the land,

---

*Among Bran's names is the Blessed Crow. Fearn, the purple alder tree, is associated with
a giant named Bran whose name can mean alder, grain, or raven. The word *alder* ultimately derives from Proto Indo-European *el,* El being one of the names associated with
giant Orion.

the Milesian king, Eremon, wed Tea. The land of Tara was once the ancient seat of the High Kings in the center of Ireland. Among Tara's treasures is a large megalithic passage grave from around 2500 BCE. Like the seven labyrinthine walls attributed to Troy and Jericho, Tara had seven ramparts from which Irish kings watched each morning lest the armies from Fairy take them unaware.

Assistant Ogham's ninth character is Talamon (or Teilmon). He sailed with Jason's Argonauts in search of the Golden Fleece.* On the way home, in the company of Hercules, whose own journey took him through the sky, Talamon stormed the walls of Troy. First over the wall, he took home a daughter of Troy as prize.

Holly (Tinne, but later Teine, meaning fire) is Tree Ogham for this position. Fitting to this charm of mazes and labyrinthine coils is Ireland's Holly-wood Stone, found near Wicklow. It is engraved with a maze. Winter-green Holly is sacred to the Hag variously known as Hel, Holle, and Hulda. In keeping with older memories of sacred cow goddesses, the fey children of Hulda, the hulder maidens, have cow tails.

Describing a rune list whose Hag (ninth) rune is glossed with A, philologist René Derolez noted that of all the glossed runes, only the ninth rune is capitalized, writing: "I admit there is no reason to have a capital H here."[18] Perhaps the scribe was paying tribute to Mother Earth. The letter A, remember, is the shape of a woman's womb as well as of a cow goddess's head. Within her coiled womb, hidden treasures are kept safe for another generation.

Adapting early stories to later ones, Holly became the thorn crowning a sacrificed Jesus. "And at the ninth hour . . . Jesus cried with a loud voice, and gave up the ghost" (Gospel of Mark, 15:34–37). And in the ninth month the sun finally loses its battle with the dark. After the autumn equinox, days become shorter; the sun continues his fall.

---

*Io, the ancestor of Cadmus, was a goddess of Argos. Danaus, first a ruler of Libya, became a king of Argos. Also descended from Io, Danaus had fifty daughters. Fifty is a number associated with both Ogham history as the number of foster children of the Hag of Beare and with the fifty Sanskrit letters Kali the black goddess of India wears around her neck.

ᴎ
Tenth Letter
Judgments of Fate

Phoenician/Old Hebrew	Yod (hand)
Greek	Iota
Ogham	Col (Hazel)
Runes	Naudiz, Nyd (need)
Hieroglyph	Mouth
Tarot	Wheel of Fortune

Decimate: Choosing one in ten by lottery for a sacrificial offering.

JUDGMENTS OF FATE

With the tenth charm, we encounter both the pointing finger of Fate and the measurements of time as the moving finger writes in the Book of Life.* Ten is a spinning charm of fate, fire, and judgment. In the Western calendar, we arrive at the tenth month, containing such festivals of the dead as Halloween.

The Day of Atonement (Yom Kippur), celebrated ten days after the

---

*In astrology, the pointing finger of a Y-shaped formation, known as a *yod,* represents the compulsion of Fate.

New Year of fall, is also here. Standing in the hand of Fate, facing the compulsion of Time, we await judgment, measured by the actions of our life. The end of Yom Kippur represents "the transformation from the stern judge of Yom Kippur to the sheltering mother of Sukkot."[1]

> *I know, O Lord, that your judgments are right.*
> PSALM 119, TENTH STANZA,
> BEGINNING WITH THE LETTER YOD

This is the month for the final judgments to be written in the Book. Here will be inscribed "Who shall live and who shall die, Who shall reach the end of his days and who shall not, Who shall perish by water and who by fire."[2] Ten's symbolism includes the judgments of life's deeds. On October 31 (Halloween), the feast day of Saint Erc is celebrated in Cornwall. A verse dedicated to his memory comments: "Whatever he judged was rightly judged. Whosoever gives a just judgment shall receive the blessing of bishop Erc."[3]

Among the ten halls described in the *Grímnismál*, Glistener, tenth hall of the Norse gods, is where we find Forseti, god of justice and reconciliation. "Here Forseti lives every day, settling all causes. Without exception, all who come to him in legal disputes go away reconciled. That is the best court known to gods and men."[4]

Time is a taskmaster, *task* being synonymous with *tax*. Tithing is the one in ten due the gods and must be collected by the eleventh hour. Earth magic has always demanded her gifts be shared. The judgment

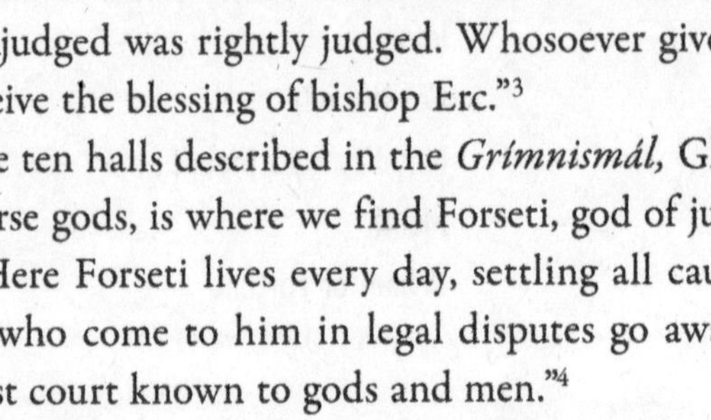

Fig. 67. Modern advertisement for tithing,
based on decimation's one in ten

souls receive as they enter the Dark Land is determined by what they share on Earth. With spells ending at midnight and life's deeds soon to be judged, by the last day of the tenth month, "one should give alms to the poor."[5]

The Lyke-Wake Dirge, a traditional English folk song sung while keeping company with the dead body, reminds the living to be generous:

> *If ever thou gave either hosen or shoon,*
> *Every night and awle,*
> *Sit thee down and putt them on,*
> *And Christ receive thy sawle.*
> *But if hosen nor shoon thou never gave naen,*
> *Every night and awle,*
> *The whinnes shall prick thee to the bare beane.*
> *And Christ receive thy sawle.*[6]

THREE FATES

With the help of the ninth letter (teth as clew, a ball of yarn), we entered the Underworld family of Hel. Among the Greeks and Romans, the first of the three goddesses of Fate spun that yarn. Romans called their Fates Nona (nine), Decima (ten), and Morta (death). We are now traveling with Decima, who measures and records the thread of life. It will be cut and collected at the next charm. Although she embodies the fate coming for all who travel the world of time, Decima also promises a continuation. As ten, she allows the circle to go on after each decimation: $1 + 0 = 10$, $10 + 1 = 11$, $10 + 2 = 12$, and so on.

These three Wyrd Sisters act together, their stories overlapping. Irish names for the Fates are Holly (ninth ogham), Spindle, and Bag. With Bag gathering the debts along with Morta (eleventh charm), what is due must be settled before midnight. In the north, the debt is collected by Skold, third of the three Norse Fates. Her name translates as "should" or "debt."

Depictions of the Fates from Roman times show Nona with her spindle, Decima with her scroll in which the deeds of life are recorded,

Fig. 68. The Wheel
of Fortune
Rider-Waite Tarot

and Morta with her distaff. Debts must always be paid in full before the journey can be continued.*

The Fates are daughters of Necessity (married to Need, the tenth rune). In her Greek form, Necessity is married to Chronos, Time himself. Together, they keep the seasons circling the year. Tarot places a spinning Wheel of Fortune as its tenth card. The figures around the turning Wheel represent the spinning seasons.

Mother Goose's counting rhyme carries on: "Eight for Heaven, Nine for Hell, and Ten for the Devil's ain self." The tenth month being the season for witches to dance, Mother Goose sometimes sings, "Ten will be a Dance." Like spiders, witches heading for their revels travel out from their bodies attached to a long silver thread. If the thread breaks, they lose the way home. Knowing this need, the Norse god Odin employs a charm to disrupt their journey:

---

*There is some variation in the depiction of the Fates. Some traditions place the spinner at the ninth position, some at the tenth position. Nonetheless, ten is a place of final judgment before meeting Morta at the eleventh hour.

> *A tenth I am able when witches do ride*
> *high aloft in the air:*
> *I can lead them astray out of their forms,*
> *Out of their minds.*[7]

This association remains today: a circling finger pointed at the head means crazy, someone led astray, someone who has lost their mind.

The Hag of coming winter now dances, shaking apart the dying world. As an aspect of Time, she is the strongest of the goddesses, for Time consumes everything in her fires. As Nemesis, she is divine retribution; the hour of her wolf is approaching.

Like Halloween and the Day of the Dead, the festivals of Kali, India's black goddess of fate and time, are celebrated in late October or early November, announcing the coming end of a year: "At the end of each cycle, during which one creation lasts, [Kali] gathers up . . . the seeds of the universe that is extinct, out of which a fresh creation is started." Black sister of Lakshmi, India's golden goddess of luck, is Alakshmi. She too arrives the tenth month, dressed in witches' black to sweep up dying souls with her broom.*[8]

JUDGMENTS OF FATE

> *What Halloween inaugurates is winter, and much of the*
> *uncanniness of the night, when man seems powerless in the*
> *hands of fate, will prevail until the dawn of another summer.*
> —ALWYN REES AND BRINLEY REES,
> *CELTIC HERITAGE*

Scandinavians knew the triple Fates as Norns: "*Weird* [Urd] they called the first of them, the second *Becoming* [Verandi] . . . they carved on a tablet—*Should* [Skold/Debt be] the third."[9] The North had no fatal judgments, only gold and pleasure, until three Giant Women arrived along with their laws. "In their dwellings at peace they played at tables.

---

*In northern fairytales, if the witch carries a rake, some souls escape between its teeth; if it is a broom, she sweeps everyone before her.

Of gold no lack did the gods then know, till thither came up giant-maids three . . . out of Jotunheim [giant land]."*[10] Verse 20 says, "Laws they made there, and life allotted to the sons of men, and set their fates."[11]

Henceforth, although the warriors might sail off to enjoy their battles, and their dead heroes might still be rewarded by a Heaven filled with games, drink, and war, they must now bear a lingering worry that their actions will be judged.

The Tree Ogham for the tenth position is Hazel (Col). A tree of concentrated wisdom, hazelwood was favored for divining rods, for making magic wands, and for passing judgments. Robert Graves notes, "In England a forked hazel-stick was used until the seventeenth century for divining . . . guilty persons in cases of murder and theft."[12] In Iceland, described in *Egil's Saga* (c. 1230 CE), "court was held on a level stretch of ground on which hazel poles had been arranged in a circle. . . . Inside the circle sat the judges."[13]

The Assistant Ogham for this charm is Cae of the Fair Judgments. Irish philologist Eugene O'Curry noted, "It was stated in very old copies of the 'Book of Invasions' [*Lebor Gabála Érenn*] . . . that it was the Mosaic law that the Milesians brought into Erinn at their coming; that it had been learned and received from Moses, in Egypt, by Cae . . . who was himself an Israelite."†[14]

MILLS OF FATE

The spinning Mill of Fate grinds slowly but exceedingly fine as the gold of summer blood-reddens with winter's arrival. In Earth magic, one must share Earth's blessings to avoid retribution. What goes around the Wheel of Fortune comes around. Describing the tenth rune, the Old Icelandic Rune Poem states: Need is "the grief of the bondmaid and state of oppression and toilsome work."[15]

---

*Scoring on wood is how runes were carved.

†Note that the mythic ancestors of the Celts denote cultural as well as physical heredity. After traveling from the lands of Asia, a large army of Celts served in Egypt under the pharaoh, Ptolemy II (Ellis, *The Druids*, 27). Continuing on to Spain, myth remembers the black daughter of a pharaoh, Scotia, traveled with the sons of Mil. In time, she becomes known as the Hag of Beare.

The Norse poem *Grottasöngr* tells of a once generous King Frode (whose name means "prosperity"). He acquired two giant women as bondmaids and set them to turning a great millstone. They ground out gold, peace, and good harvests. When they grew tired and pleaded for rest, he refused. Daughters of ancient mountain gods, they then ground out an army to slaughter Frode. Carried off by the victor, they were forced to continue grinding. This time they ground out salt, sinking the boat they were traveling in. The sunken mill still spins off the coast of Norway, creating a whirlpool, a maelstrom, that is one of the strongest in the world (the Moskstraumen).

The name of the handle by which the mill was turned is Mundilfoeri. *Mund* means "hand" (as does yod, the tenth Phoenician letter). Mund also means "a point in time." That is, it can represent a point, a jot, an iota, a period. Yod, the pointing finger of fate of old Hebrew, became such a jot in the modern Hebrew script: י. Smallest of the letters in the Hebrew alphabet, it is one of the most powerful. Standing in the center of the circle, it becomes the seed out of which new letters emerge after Time's decimations. Every modern Hebrew letter contains a small yod.

ALCHEMICAL FIRES

After entering the Underworld, after having been measured and judged, the soul must continue its journey toward the light. In Egypt, after being swallowed by the mouth (tenth hieroglyph) of a sky cow, the soul might travel through the belly of the goddess in a grand boat. Others might be eaten by black vulture goddesses and flown through the dark. The Color Ogham for this position is dark Cron. An early Irish goddess, Cron was "identified as swallower and personification of the pitch-black abyss."[16]

Less fortunate people needed to trudge the long weary way. Finally, some eventually learned to set fires with the twirling of two Need sticks (tenth rune), the fire sticks used to set funeral fires. Burning off the dross of the dead allowed both souls and prayers to rise with the smoke from these fires. Bird Ogham's character is Crane (or Cron). As Gerald of Wales wrote in the twelfth century, "The liver of this bird is . . .

of such a fiery heat, that, when by chance it swallows iron, its stomach digests it."[17] Crane is actually missing from the known ogham lists. Robert Graves claims "the omission of corr, the crane . . . is intentional; the contents of the [magical] crane bag were a close secret and all reference to it were discouraged."[18*]

Crane's relative, the stork, will eventually return the soul to Earth, tenderly placing small babies under cabbages. Cabbages, one should notice, are crucifers, with their four petals forming a cross, the + symbol promising a proper return of soul or profit. And the fourth letter of the alphabet is the delta, the door of birth.

Regarding the Crane Bag, the king of the sea was the owner. It was said to appear at low tide before disappearing.

ᚴ
Eleventh Letter
Visionaries and Payment of Debts

Phoenician/Old Hebrew	Kaph (palm of the hand)
Greek	Kappa
Ogham	Quert (Apple)
Runes	Isaz (Ice)
Hieroglyph	Reed shelter (house)
Tarot	Strength

VISIONARIES AND PAYMENT OF DEBTS

I have become like a bottle in the smoke . . . how much longer must I wait?

PSALM 119, ELEVENTH STANZA,
BEGINNING WITH KAPH

The third Roman Fate, Morta, following her sisters Nona (nine) and Decima (ten), rules death and divination. As number eleven, she mandates a pause before continuing the journey through the Underworld. The Mora fish, a "dreadful fish that hath deserved the name of death [morta]," compelled ships to stay motionless (the word *mora* means "a delay," as in the word *moratorium*).[1]

The eleventh is a charm of icy stasis, death, and visionary deep dreaming. It also mandates a final collection of debts before the soul continues its journey. In the Western calendar, the season includes November and early December. In the frozen months of late fall, we pause to balance ourselves after the spinning magic of the preceding Fates. Standing exactly halfway through the twenty-two letters of the Hebrew alphabet, kaph, usually translated as "palm" (of a hand), has the additional meaning of a pan of merit (see below). Measurements of the pan of a balance scale should be equal on each side.

In England on Martinmas (Saint Martin's Day), "no beame doth swinge, nor wheel go round, upon Gurguntum's walled town."[2] Gurguntum (modern-day Norwich) had eleven gates into the city. Martinmas, celebrated on November 11 (11/11), signals the final slaughter of animals before winter freezes the land. On Armistice Day, also November 11, we remember the sleeping dead with blood-red poppies that the dreaming priestess from Crete (fig. 69) wears on her head. Out of her dream state come visions to determine future actions.

Fig. 69. Poppy goddess figurine from the sanctuary at Gazi, Crete, c. 1350 BCE
Image by Jebulon, CC0

Eleven, a tricky number mirroring one (1-1), also represents two (1 + 1). We met the undivided twin at the first charm and the divided twin at the house of the second. Eleven is a moment where the bright twin and his shadow stand in perfect balance. Writing in 1839, Victor Hugo observed, "K is the angle of reflection equal to the angle of incidence."[3] That is, a twin and his shadow are identical. In Hebrew, the eleventh letter kaph, when added to words, instills this twin meaning, signifying "like."*

In Egypt, the shadow twin of man is literally the ka. Surviving the body at death, the ka (⊔) is depicted, like the dreaming priestess (fig. 69), with raised palms. An African tradition provides another link between eleven and visionary dreamers; here, "number Eleven is one of the most dangerous . . . the number of wizards and demons. It is also the number associated with . . . speaking with the dead."[4]

Morta, as icy Death, perhaps gets its name "from '*morsu*,' that bite of the first man, when, munching fruit from the forbidden tree, he merited death."†[5] Apple is Tree Ogham's choice of symbols for the eleventh position. According to legend, the Celtic king of the sea owned an apple branch. Ringing the three golden apples on its bough caused the listener to fall into a deep, healing sleep. "So delightful was the music of the branch that the sick, the wounded, and women in childbed would fall asleep when they heard it."†[6]

Color Ogham chose Quiar, Mouse. It implies the same stillness of deep sleep implicit in these other symbols of death and visionary travel through the Underworld: "In some areas, the mouse . . . is the visible separable soul of a sleeper."[7] And "their flesh if put in one's food begets oblivion."[8]

---

*Variant of Greek letter kappa: $\mathcal{K}$. Note the shape of the Magician and Aleph (א, one).

†According to E. C. Krupp (*Beyond the Blue Horizon*, 150), the three apples, present in numerous myths, adjusted the cycles of solar and lunar calendars. Every eight years, three additional months must be added: 8 + 3 = 11.

FAR-SIGHT AND DIVINATION

*Ice is very cold and immeasurably slippery; it glistens, clear
as glass.*

OLD ENGLISH RUNE POEM FOR THE ELEVENTH RUNE,

BELLOWS TRANS.

Eleven's magic continuing the journey through the Underworld, many
symbols refer to vision and visionary far-sight of dreamers. Pliny the Elder
(23–79 CE) claimed that hardened crystals of ice produce the crystal ball
of fortune tellers.[9] Quartz crystal was used as a talisman to correct eyesight. Many of the saints of early winter evoke this theme: Saint Lucy, eye-
balls in her hand, wanders the world in early December. Saint Matthew
(celebrated on November 16), a tax collector associated with the sign of
visionary Aquarius, wears spectacles when he comes to collect his debts.
In Rome, Aquarius as eleventh house of Western astrology is represented
by Juno's peacock, bearing multiple eyes on its watchful tail.[10]

> *I know an eleventh spell;*
> *if I lead old friends into a battle,*
> *I enchant their shields*
> *so that they will have the victory;*
> *they will go to battle unharmed,*
> *and return from battle unharmed.*
> *They will come home without harm.*[11]

Quartz crystals as unripe diamonds were, according to Pliny,
formed from ice. Like cracking ice, crystals sing like bells. Held to the
light, they produce rainbow bridges leading to the Otherworld. Each
time the soul travels through the Otherworld, it gains strength (the
eleventh Tarot card), as well as vision.[12] The Japanese hiragana shape for
ka derives from two symbols meaning "add strength to an argument."
Eventually the shape became simply "addition"

The Old Icelandic Rune Poem, describing the eleventh rune says,
"Ice is the rind of the river and the roof of the waves and a danger

Fig. 70. Watermark boar with apple in its mouth, bearing K upon its back

From Bayley, *Lost Language of Symbolism*, 89

for fey men." The poem is glossed with *jofurr,* a wild boar, wild boar helmet, or, in Thorsson's translation, "one who wears the boar-helm."[13]

A fey man is both a traveler through the Underworld and one facing death, that final fee collected from every mortal passing through the world of time. The Norse Earth god, Frey, originally from Anatolia, owned a magic boar helm. His twin Freya, who rode a golden boar into the Otherworld, taught the art of far-seeing to the northern gods. Their kings, having learned to far-travel like witches, communed with spirits while sitting on the graves of their ancestors. When wearing the boar helm into battle, the helmet, like the eleventh spell of the High One cited above, "they will go to battle unharmed, and return from battle unharmed," protected warriors.[14]

FAR-TRAVEL AND SAILING MAGIC

Ice we call the broad bridge; The blind man must be led.
OLD NORWEGIAN RUNE POEM, DICKINS, TRANS.

The Milky Way, the River of Stars, the path of souls, flows between the constellations of Orion/Gemini and Scorpio/Sagittarius. After pouring over star maps, I realized the Milky Way branches into two paths: a broad one and a narrow one near the womb of our Universe, the galactic center. This necessitates a choice: "The road which they travel . . . divides and they must choose which to take. Forked ways in the Land of the Death are to be found in the Mystery Religions and were known to

the Pythagoreans."[15] In images of the Milky Way, the broad road leading to hell is the one that heads toward Scorpio.

The celestial river may have reinforced Tree Ogham's choice of
Apple (Quert) for this position. Forty days before the winter solstice
(December 21), Adam picked his ripe apple and was expelled from the
Garden of Eden, his mythic Fall occurring in late fall. Weeping, he
stood forty days in the River Jordan until the sun's rebirth gave him
hope to live and ultimately to die. Among their many incarnations,
Gemini/Orion at one end of the river and Scorpio/Sagittarius on
the other represent Adam and Eve, the apple forever stuck in Adam's
throat.

There are many ways to travel the Underworld. For those who
can't ride, walk, or fly, a ship will sail the River of Stars. It is docked
at the eleventh letter, K (quay). The *Grímnismál* notes, "Noaton [Ship's
Rest] is eleventh. There, Njord has built him a hall." Skade, Bride of
Scandinavia, was once married to Njord. She wanted to live in her
mountains; Njord preferred the sea and the unhappy marriage did
not last. As Bride, Skade later married the kings of her northern land.
Originally from Anatolia, Njord has been identified as an aspect of
Saturn. His son Frey is one owner of the boar helm discussed above.

Sagittarius now rules the late November–early December skies.
Given that the River of Stars intersects the zodiac near that constellation, the saints of early winter include sailors as well as eyeglass-
wearing visionaries and tax collectors. One of Saint Nick's emblems is
an anchor. He protects sailors, as do Saint Jude and bespectacled Saint
Matthew. Another sailor saint of early winter is Andrew (celebrated on
November 30).

That same Saint Nick who ascended chimneys to fly through the
sky is associated with eleven's icy stasis: "A curious practice . . . refers
to this patron saint. When a boy is hard pressed in any game . . .
he cries out Nic'las, upon which he is entitled to a suspension of the
play for a moment."[16] Nicholas's saint's day is in the early December
of Sagittarius.

COLLECTION OF DEBTS

Fierce Nemesis, who lives behind the right ear whispering morality along with mortality, carried an apple bough. Her name translates as "what is due." By the eleventh hour, preceding the hour of the wolf, debts must be paid in full. "Debt" is an alternate translation for the name of Skold, third goddess of the Germanic Fates. Other debt collectors are also associated with the eleventh charm. Saint Matthew's saint's day is celebrated during November, our eleventh month. Associated with Aquarius, the eleventh house of astrology, "Matthew was a publican"—that is, he was a tax collector.[17]

On December 6, Saint Nicholas travels Europe on his white horse. Like wolfish Nemesis, he rewards the good and punishes the bad. Saint Jude (celebrated on October 28) arrived earlier to help hopeless causes. In Tibet, the Buddha of Compassion wears eleven heads. His single head broke apart as he mourned the suffering of the world. From his tears sprang the beneficent Tara (Star). Like Saint Lucy, White Tara carries eyes in the palms of her hands.

One final comment on our eleventh letter, kaph ("palm of the hand"): this is a moment along our path where we pause on our journey. What is due is now collected. As the cup of the hand, only an empty palm is useful. Describing a foolish man who brought no container to market and thus lost both his food and his money, the twelfth-century text *Bahir* called kaph "the pan of merit."[18] That is, it is an empty palm that possesses merit. Note: Square Hebrew, emphasizing its developing spiritual needs, changed the twin shape of the reflective Phoenician kaph (א) to כ, the empty space of the useful palm.

We make a vessel from a lump of clay. It is the empty space within the vessel that makes it useful.

LAO-TZU, *TAO TE CHING*, ELEVENTH VERSE,

TRANS. JOHN WU

ㄥ

Twelfth Letter

Upside-Down Teacher and
L's Name of God

Phoenician/Old Hebrew	Lamed (ox goad or rod of a teacher)
Greek	Lambda
Ogham	Muin (Vine or neck)
Runes	Jera, Ger, or Ar (harvest or year)
Hieroglyph	Plaited wick (upside down)
Tarot	The Hanged Man

THE UPSIDE-DOWN TEACHER
AND THE NAME OF GOD

In the twelfth charm, El, the potent sower of the seed of the third charm, now harvested, hangs upside down: ㄱ (Phoenician gimel) becomes ㄥ (lamed). To some, Roman numeral 50, also written L, is the proper number of years to retire from work. But Earth magic implies a return after traveling the dark. The journeying soul cast off its mortal coil earlier in our story. Here we find our traveler sacrificed again on Twelfth Night. El's Saturnalia is celebrated in the twelfth month, when the world turns upside down and kings serve their slaves.

Fig. 71. The Hanged Man
Rider-Waite Tarot

Explanations for the twelfth Tarot card emphasize that this is not a card of death; rather, the hanging is voluntary, and the rope is not tied. The Twelfth hieroglyph, ⅄, also upside down, is a wick for lighting torches. Frayed edges burning, they are extinguished by plunging upside down into water or wine. Bird Ogham's Titmouse (Mintan) continues this theme: Tom Tit, the tufted titmouse with his kingly crown of feathers is "extremely active, hanging upside down . . . in the busy search for insects."[1]

> *I see that all things come to an end, but your commandment*
> *has no bounds.*
>
> PSALM 119, TWELFTH STANZA,
> BEGINNING WITH THE LETTER LAMED

HARVESTED RULER'S WISDOM OF INSPIRATION

The Christian saint inheriting Orion's L-shaped mason's square was Doubting Thomas. His stories, "Gnostic or Manichean in origin," tell of the mason-saint traveling to India. After building a golden temple, he died, like the sun and El, in the twelfth month, at the winter solstice.[2]

Square Hebrew (c. 250 BCE) is properly scribed with the letters dropping down from an invisible line. Among its letters, only the ruler El (lamed) rises above this line: ל. The literal meaning of the letter lamed (root "LMD") denotes the acquiring of knowledge. As twelfth letter, it represents a (twelve-inch) ruler's wisdom shared with his people. As a preposition, L means "to," a moving toward, as is proper for a divinity.*

Although a broken and long hidden tradition, the alphabet's Mysteries resurface in surprising places. In Arabic, another Semitic language that derived its script from a descendent of the Phoenician alphabet, Allah derives from El: "According to the reconstructed Proto-Semic (P-Sem) lexicon the name of God in Proto-Semitic religious tradition consisted of two letters, 'l. . . . These letters are in Western scholarship conventionally (and somewhat arbitrarily) vocalized as El or Il. More recent data allows us to be more precise. It is the second letter which is actually the 'nucleus' of the divine name."[3] That is, L represents the High God.

As L (El), a high king bequeaths inspiration and good harvests for his peoples. Fort Ogham's twelfth character, Meath, hints at the kingly owner of this position. Around 130–160 CE, King Tuathal the Legitimate became high king of Ireland. He took Meath as the personal estate of the high kings.[4]

Fig. 72. Albania, c. 4500 BCE
Gimbutas, *Language of the Goddess*, 295

---

*Persians likened the belt of Orion's stars to "the letter of the Persian alphabet that was similar in form to the Greek lambda λ." (Allen, *Star Names*, 319).

Marija Gimbutas notes, "Whirls and four-corner designs are symbols of becoming and the turnings of cyclical time."[5] The whirling symbols in figure 72 echo the shape used thousands of years later as the twelfth rune Ger (harvest): ᛃ. A variant of the twelfth rune is Ar (year). Our year, of course, has twelve months. The term Ar was "early used for the dead patriarchs who are supposed to give good seasons."[6]

Advice of these ruler-kings was often sought from beyond the grave. The *Hávamál* recites:

> *That twelfth I know if on a tree I see*
> *a hanged one hoisted on high:*
> *thus I write and the runes I stain*
> *that down he drops*
> *and tells me his tale."*[7]

Witches and magicians traveled the Underworld at will. Eventually, royalty learned the secrets of Otherworld flight. Kings as well as poets sat on burial mounds to commune with the dead. "There are . . . scattered references . . . to kings and seers sitting on burial mounds, not only in order to make a claim to the title of a former king after his death, but also when they desired to seek inspiration."[8]

Referring to the secrets of Otherworld travel, the twelfth character in Color Ogham is Mbracht (variegated), while Assistant Ogham's is Murrath. These suggest the speckled colors worn by Celtic magicians. After the slaughter of the Battle of Moyrath (Murrath), it's said, the poet-king Sweeney (Suibhne) went mad, growing feathers and flying among the trees. There is also the story of a Druid named Mog Ruith (Irish names come in multiples, many multiples, of spellings). According to the ninth-century *Glossary of Cormac*, "Mog Ruith's skin of the hornless, dun-coloured bull was brought to him then and his speckled bird-dress . . . with its winged flying. . . . And he rose up, in company with the fire, into the air and the heavens."[9]

JOHN BARLEYCORN, VINE KINGS, ELIXIRS, AND SPIRITS

The twelfth charm continues the soul's travel through the Underworld, which was entered through the gate of the eighth (heth/gate). The journey is taken yearly (twelve months) by Vine Kings (Tree Ogham) and daily (twelve hours) by the sun. They travel in numerous ways. In Mesopotamia, Gilgamesh, in search of the elixir of immortality, sails along the cosmic river to the end of the world: he travels along the road of the sun" and eventually meets Siduri, the divine barmaid, who "has the ritual intoxicating beverages which comfort the dreary souls who are denied the drink of immortality."[10] The Norse god of the sea, Aegir, and his wife, Rán, who live at the bottom of the sea, are also known for their hospitality; they serve alcohol to drowned sailors and visiting gods.

The twelfth house of astrology belongs to watery Pisces, a sign representing deep dreaming, alcohol, and endings. Its ruler is traditionally Jupiter, high king of the gods, whose planet takes twelve years to circle the zodiac. Neptune came to rule Pisces after winning her in a lottery game. Neptune's spirit-blue planet is identified by psi (ψ), the same symbol that represents barley. Adapting symbols from older cultures, Greeks used the letter psi to represent the butterfly souls (psyche) of psychic far-travelers. In time, psi became the twenty-third Greek letter. The twenty-third rune, Dagaz, was written with a butterfly shape: ᛞ

Like all of twelve's symbols, barley will be sacrificed and hung for his people. In the *Allvísmál,* we find the speaker questioning the dwarf Alvíss (All-Wise): "Tell me, then Allwise, How is the Seed, which the sons of men sow, called in each of the worlds? [Answer]: 'Bigg' among Men, 'Bear' (barley) among Gods . . . ; in Hell they call it Hnipinn [hanging]."*[11] In time, barley's symbol turned upside down will symbolize peace.

> *Then sayde the trees unto the vyne. Come thou and be oure kinge.*
>
> Coverdale Bible, Judges IX, 12

The modest vine refused the kingship, preferring her task of sharing her spirits. Vine is Tree Ogham for this position, and wine is associated with Poseidon (a.k.a. Neptune). Ancient Greece's wine

---

*I use the term *hanging* in place of the usual translation as "drooping."

festival was celebrated in the month of Poseidon (December) in honor of Dionysus. His mother was the grain goddess Semele, herself the daughter of Phoenician Cadmus and Harmonia. His father was Zeus. When Semele was burned to a cinder (in some stories by Zeus's lightning powers), Zeus snatched Dionysus from her dying womb to save him.

Dionysus "possessed himself of the festivals of Demeter, took over her threshing-floor and compelled the anomaly of a winter threshing festival."*[12] (The Temple of Solomon was built upon such a threshing floor.) He became a wanderer, traveling from India to Britain and transmitting his Mysteries of the vine.

Al-kohl (alcohol), like al-khema (black earth, as alchemy), was an important Mystery tradition. The spirits aided the flights of such high kings as Old King Cole (Coal) along their journeys through the Underworld. Christmas revels included cards, gamboling, gambling, and drink. The merriment associated with the twelfth month was so strong that even during the puritanical years of late Christianity, the Church never banned the celebrations.

The Mystery of the vine was literally lifesaving. Wine has the god-like power to purify water by killing disease-causing microorganisms. Mixed with water (in a 1:1 ratio), it can destroy any *E. coli* in the water in three minutes, cholera within fifteen, and typhoid germs within twenty-four hours. As Dr. Guido Manjo explains, "The effect of wine is . . . truly bactericidal, not bacteriostatic."[13] That is, it kills off the bacteria. The property is specific to wine rather than to alcohol, wine vinegar also being beneficial.

> *The weapon-blessed Odin lives on wine alone.*
> GRÍMNISMÁL, TWELFTH HALL OF THE GODS.

> *Apres moi, le Deluge*
> SPOKEN BY A SUN KING

---

*Described earlier, like other teachers of Mystery traditions, he entered the Underworld, returning with his mother.

ᛗ

Thirteenth Letter

Breaking Waters and the Deluge

<hr/>

Phoenician/Old Hebrew	Mem (water)
Greek	Mu (associated with a Deluge)
Ogham	Gort (Ivy) or Gart (Garden)
Runes	Ihwaz (yew tree)
Hieroglyph	Placenta
Tarot	Death

<hr/>

BREAKING WATERS AND THE DELUGE

"The Sumerian term for year, usually twelve lunar cycles, sometimes thirteen, was MU."[1] Myths of Mu, like those of Atlantis, include an Island of the Wise disappearing under water.

The thirteenth charm, like the second, is associated with the moon. With this moon number, we will recross myths of water and blue spirits: Underworld openings leading to wisdom, endings, and rebirth. Stories of the thirteenth moon are darker than those of the Virgin Spring awaiting her purification and plowing at the second charm. Although the thirteenth letter includes many of the same themes as the second, death dwells among its stories.

Unlike the faithful sun, which shifts slowly north toward the sum-

Fig. 73. Moon god, Abris de las Vinas,
Paleolithic Spain, c. 9000 BCE

From Gerald Hawkins, *Mindsteps to the Cosmos*, 13

mer solstice and then back to a southeast rising at midwinter, the inconstant moon appears at different sites along the horizon with each rising. Tracing out the shape of our English M, it takes thirteen lunar months to match the sun cycle of twelve. The thirteenth moon, occurring twice in one month of a solar year, is a blue moon.

Knowledge of lunar magic appeared thousands of years before a Spanish moon at Abris de las Vinas (c. 9000 BCE) described his sinuous passage against the horizon. The stones of France hold the Venus of Laussel (c. 20,000–18,000 BCE). Full breasted and saggy, she caresses her full belly with one hand; the other cheerfully raises a drinking horn. The horn carries thirteen marks, which "may symbolize the

Fig. 74. The Venus of Laussel,
France, c. 20,000–18,000 BCE

Photo of the original kept by the Museum of
Aquitaine, France, CC BY-SA 3.0

Fig. 75. Death

Rider-Waite Tarot

nearly 13 cycles the moon experiences in a year or the number of days of visible waxing moon."[2]

The thirteenth Tarot card shows Death come riding on his white horse. Most interpretations describe this card as being not a physical death, but the end of a cycle prior to regeneration. It can mean that "you need to let go . . . of what is stagnant. . . . New possibilities, perhaps a rebirth will result."[3] The sage ordering Egypt's twenty-four hieroglyphs placed a delivering woman's placenta in the thirteenth position.

Like the placenta of the thirteenth hieroglyph and the full-bellied Venus with her horn of thirteen notches, esoteric tradition relates the thirteenth Hebrew letter, mem (water), with the womb: "What is a Mem? Do not read Mem, but Mayim (water). Just like water is wet, so is the belly always wet. Why does the open Mem include both male and female, while the closed Mem is male? . . . The opening was . . . added to it for the sake of the female. . . . Just like the female has an opening with which to give birth, so can the open Mem give birth."[4] Square Hebrew has some dual-shaped letters. A closed mem appears only at the end of words; the open mem can precede (birth) other letters.

The motherly waters of life offered salvation from death long before Christians adopted its blessings. Water, whether salty, bloody, or clear from a well, was protective. Practical knowledge was once contained in riddles and poems before degenerating into mere verbiage. Boiling wool in water results in a thick felt fabric. Vinegar, brewed by adding a mother to wine (another aqua vita), was used by the Gauls to felt wool: "the Wool is compressed also for making a felt, which, if soaked in vinegar, is capable of resisting even iron; and, what is still more, after having gone through the last process, wool will even resist fire."[5]

> Thirteenth I know, if they wish me to sluice
> with water a citizen's son,
> He shall not fall, though outnumbered he be,
> He shall not fall by a sword.[6]

Yew, the symbol for the thirteenth rune, is an intensely toxic tree traditionally planted by graveyards and known as "the keeper of the Fire" in the Old English Rune Poem. As people adapted the alphabet symbols to their own needs, yew wood became the last rune, meaning "grave," of the Younger Futhark (c. 800 CE) and the final Tree Ogham. The early Irish used Yew staves, the "coffin of the vine" to store wine,[7] but the yew vats fell out of use from the poisonous nature of the wood, by which some had lost their lives.

Celtic and Norse warriors emphasize the death aspects of this letter, though not totally ignoring the promise of protection and rebirth. Yew's strong flexible wood is prized for making lethal longbows. The verse for the Yew rune of the Old Icelandic Rune Poem reads: "Yew is a strung bow and brittle iron and Firbauti of the arrow."*[8] Yew bows and brittle iron weapons, which break easily, lead to a warrior's death. Firbauti is the father of Loki, the trickster god whose demon children were responsible for the death of the northern gods at Ragnarok.

Glosses added to this verse of the poem are "rainbow" and

---

*In this poem, Yew is the last of sixteen runes.

"descendant of Yngvi." "Rainbow" refers to either the glittering ice bridge over which trolls and giants traveled to kill the northern gods at Ragnarok or the promise of Noah's rainbow that life would continue after the destruction, that the wisdom of the arcana would return over the waters. Yngvi, the second gloss, is another name for Frey, the Norse god responsible for Earth's fertility. His descendants died in various crop-significant ways: his son drowned in a cauldron of ale; his grandson, after marrying a daughter of Snow, was crushed by a nightmare; other descendants were sacrificed after bad harvests, hung until dead by the daughter of Froste, or killed by peasants wielding hay forks.

The Fort Ogham character for this thirteenth position is Gabur. In the Battle of Gabhra (Gabur), hero Fionn Maccumhail's army was slaughtered. This was "the last great battle in which the Fianna took part and in which they were exterminated."[9] Fionn, son of the sun, was already dead, drowned while jumping over a river. His son was away in Fairyland, so Fionn's grandson led the troops into their final battle. After the destruction, Fionn returned over the waters of death to mourn their passing.

TRANSMISSION OF WISDOM AFTER DEATH

As in the myths of the moon and the water stories of the second charm, we find blue spirits aiding far-travel in the thirteenth. Mirrorlike wisdom reappears here, with hints of knowledge transmitted after each Flood. By this later time, however, respect for the wisdom of the old ways is fading.

> *I have more understanding than my teachers. I am wiser than my elders.*
>
> PSALM 119, STANZA BEGINNING
> WITH THE LETTER MEM

The Tree Ogham's choice is either Gart (Garden) or Gort (Ivy). The Roman playwright Plautus, according to Pliny, assigned custody of all gardens to Venus.[10] Venus, like the moon, has thirteen cycles through the sky. During the eight years it takes Venus to travel the zodiac, she circles Earth thirteen times. The Ogham as Garden recalls the story of death entering the world after the fruit of the Tree of Knowledge was eaten. Another story remembers Seth, third son of Adam and Eve, who was given a branch of the Tree of Life growing in that garden. His descendants included Enoch, who did "not see death" (Hebrews 11:5), and Noah, who sailed out of a flood carrying secrets of astronomy and alchemy. Noah's arcana included the knowledge of winemaking.

Ivy (Gort), as a symbol of learning, names our universities the "halls of ivy." Supplying a hallucinogenic drink used in the Dionysian revels, the ivy bush associated with Dionysus came to symbolize taverns.[11] The wine used for the revels may have been mixed with opium, henbane, or cannabis, which was known to the Scythians, but ivy infusions themselves could cause delirium.[12] Blue Gorm is Color Ogham's choice, and drinking too much Blue Ruin* was said to make one gormless (witless).

Blue is the color of the spirit world, the color of coats worn by Underworld travelers, the color flames burn when spirits draw near, the color of the thirteenth moon. Blue is also the color associated with Kobolds, little goblins who appeared to metalworking miners.[13] The poisonous blue cobalt took its name from the kobolds who were associated with the ore. Gaibneacht (Smithwork) is the Arts and Crafts Ogham's character for this position.

The thirteenth letter's attributes of ivy, wisdom, metallurgy, astronomy, brewing, and death come sliding together in this ninth-century Irish poem, about an Ivy spray (which does not mention Ivy). Attributed to Saint Govan, it describes: "My little hut . . . a mansion would not be more ingenious, with its stars to my wish, with its sun, with its moon. It was Gobán that made it. . . ; my darling, God of Heaven, was the thatcher that roofed it. A House in which rain does not fall . . . as open as if in a garden without a wall."[14]

Brigit, Bride of Ireland, was the midwife-smith who brewed ale.

---

*An eighteenth century epithet for gin.

Gobán (Goighiniu, Gobhan) was an Indo-European smith arriving in Ireland with his brothers. Keeping with the protective magic of thirteen's waters of life, Gobán "presided over the Otherworld feast . . . at which he served a special ale that rendered all who drank it exempt from disease and death." He killed Brigit's son, occasioning the first lament to be heard in Ireland.[15]

By the Western calendar, we have completed a year of twelve months. After the Capricorns of letter twelve's December, we have arrived at thirteen's waters of Aquarius. The fish of Pisces follows.

After the Deluge of ancient Mesopotamia, the Goddess cries out

Fig. 76. Detail from a vase showing a Hag figure with a fish-child in her belly, Boeotia, Greece, c. 700 BCE. Note the peacocks of Aquarius above the lions of Leo. The city founded by alphabet-bearing Cadmus following his cow is in Boeotia.
American School of Classical Studies at Athens, Alison Frantz Photograph Collection

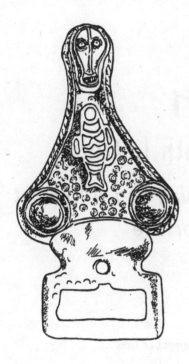

Fig. 77. Hag with a fish,
France, c. 600 CE

From Johnson, *Lady of the Beasts*, 237

"like a woman in travail. How could I bespeak evil . . . ordering battle
for the destruction of my people, when it is I myself who gave birth to
my people!"[16] A new generation now arrives out of the breaking waters
of death. Following the path of our alphabet calendar, Nun (serpent-
fish) arrives as the messiah of the fourteenth letter. After the Deluge
comes an allotment of fortunes.

ᛍ
Fourteenth Letter

Return of a Messiah and Allotment of Fortune

Phoenician/Old Hebrew	Nun (serpent or fish)
Greek	Nu
Ogham	Ng* (Reed) or Pethboc (Guelder Rose)
Runes	Perth, Peorth (lot or dice box for casting lots)
Hieroglyph	Belly of animal with teats (i.e., a nursing mother)
Tarot	Temperance

*Ngetal is thought to be the oldest form.

RETURN OF A MESSIAH AND ALLOTMENT OF FORTUNES

Thus, there were fourteen generations in all from Abraham to David, fourteen from David to the exile to Babylon, and fourteen from the exile to the Messiah.

MATTHEW 1:17*

The serpent-fish-son-Messiah now arrives in his ark. The fourteenth Phoenician letter, nun (serpent-fish), is written with a shape similar to the drawing of Draco (fig. 78a). Draco was once the ruler of the pole stars before they began slipping away. Figure 78c, the South Iberian script for letter nun, even shows Draco's horns. In Arabic, *nun* still means Leviathan.†

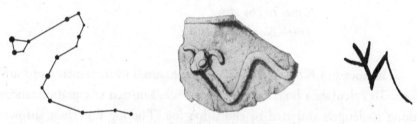

Fig. 78a. Draco. Fig. 78b. Yugoslavia, c. 4000 BCE. Fig. 78c. So. Iberian "N."

Fig. 78a. Dirk Hünniger, CC 3.0

Fig. 78b. From Gimbutas, *Civilization of the Goddess*, 237

Fig. 78c. From Diringer, *The Alphabet*, vol. 2, 174

After each Great Flood, a hero must carry the accumulated wisdom of the previous world over the waters of death to bequeath them to a new generation. Noah in his ark was one such hero: "This Art

---

*Matthew apparently had to fudge the generations to reach the proper fourteen for this Messiah to arrive in the Age of Pisces. (Due to the Precession, we are now moving toward the Age of Aquarius.)

†In the biblical story of Moses, that greatest of prophets never entered the Promised Land. It was Joshua, the "son of Nun," who made the crossing over the River Jordan.

was first imparted to Adam by the Holy Spirit, and He prophesied
. . . that the world must be renewed, or, rather, purged with water.
Therefore his successors erected two stone tables, on which they
engraved a summary . . . , in order that this arcanum might become
known to posterity. After the Flood, Noah found one of these tables
at the foot of Mount Ararat."[1]

Like Noah, the poet Taliesin was set sailing over the waters to safety.
Like other Gnostics, he knew the names of all the stars "from the north
to the south." Taliesin hints at arcane alphabet secrets of reincarnation:

> *Johannes the Diviner*
> *I was called by Merddin [Merlin],*
> *At length every King*
> *Will call me Taliesin.*
> . . .
> *I was in the Ark*
> *With Noah and Alpha.*[2]

The speed of Noah's ark was once measured in increments of fourteen. To calculate a boat's speed, a rope was knotted at equal distances
along its length and tied to the ship's log. The log was then thrown
overboard, and the speed at which the knots played out behind the
moving vessel was measured against a sand glass marked by fourteen
notches (or twenty-eight for a slow-moving boat).[3]

In India, Sanskrit's sound of aum (om) is said to hold the power to
create each new universe. As written in Devanagari, it contains the seed

Fig. 79. The aum (om) sound
written in Devanagari

in its arc floating above the potential of alpha. (The seed represents the sound of M.)

While floating on the Cosmic Waters, the god Vishnu, in the form of a fish (like fourteenth Hebrew letter, nun), warned Manu about the coming Deluge. Like Noah, Manu carried the wisdom of his ancestors (Vedas) in his boat and sailed to safety, creating a new people from his seed. After each of fourteen Deluges destroys the world, another form of Manu arrives to people each new period of Creation.

"To escape from the fear of the Underworld," Vishnu has a ceremony, called Ananta Caturddaçi, lasting fourteen years. On the fourteenth day of each month, the devotee offers fourteen gifts. At completion, one dons an armband of fourteen threads tied with fourteen knots.[4]

THE RETURN OF THE LEVIATHAN'S SON

Having carried his arcana safely over the waters in the ark, Noah gifted Western alchemists with their hermetic knowledge of Mysteries: "For this same Hermes flourished both before and after the Flood, and is identified with Noah. Then this Art found its way into Persia, Egypt, and Chaldaea. The Hebrews called it the Cabbala, the Persians Magia, and the Egyptians Sophia."[5] The arts included such skills as the calendars of astronomy and temple building. They also included the magical art of the vine.

Noah's ark is sometimes said to be literally a "mother ship." Welsh writer Edward Davies posits that "Rhea, or the mother of the gods . . . was the same as Ceres, Venus, Isis or Deceto. She was, in short, the Ark of Noah, from which issued all the hero gods of paganism."*[6] Noah, according to Davies, is another incarnation of Saturn, god of the common man.

Noah's ark landed with his arcana on Mount Ararat in Armenia. Serpent-fish being part of our tale, the Armenian Saint Blaise, whose feast day is in February, died choking on a fishbone. In Ireland and China, dragons and serpents still appear in the month of February.

---

*Edward Davies, quoting from the Mysteries of the Cabiri, notes that Orion, also known as Saturn, rides the dragon-fish-tree of the Milky Way.

Having circled the zodiac with December's twelfth charm, the sign following the breaking waters of Aquarius is the messianic fish of Pisces (February/March).

Safely over the waters, the sailor emerges from the watery womb of the Mother Ship, though our young hero will not fully surge into the light of day until the opening eye of the sixteenth charm (ain/eye). Echoing this theme, the fourteenth Egyptian hieroglyph is a nursing mother ("animal with teats").

Tree Ogham's fourteenth character Ng (or Ngetal, thought to be its oldest form) is usually translated as Reed. It was a reed who delivered a god in Armenia, discussed below. Ng is not an Irish sound, so Pethboc (Guelder Rose) eventually replaced Ng. The Guelder Rose (*Viburnum opulus*), otherwise known as cramp bark, "was part of their repertory of drugs to ease the pain of childbirth."[7] This would help a mother deliver her young fish.

ALLOTMENT OF FORTUNE

The twin fish of Pisces appear in the Egyptian zodiac of Dendera (c. first century BCE), a bas-relief ceiling from a temple dedicated to Hathor, with a game board of chance and divination between their tails. Festivals of lots and deliverance from death is part of the February story. The fourteenth charm also includes the allotment of inheritances. When the new world begins after each Deluge, fortunes must be redistributed.

> *Your decrees are my inheritance forever.*
> PSALM 119, STANZA BEGINNING WITH
> THE FOURTEENTH LETTER NUN

The gods of ancient Greece, having overthrown an older rule of giants, divided the world by gambling: Neptune (Poseidon), ruler of Pisces, won the sea; Jupiter, the former ruler of Pisces, inherited the sky.

Celestial gamblers used the game board of Pisces. Renowned Egyptologist E. A. Wallis Budge wrote, "The draught-board, which

Fig. 80. Pisces and a game board on the zodiac of Dendera,
Egypt, c. first century BCE

Photographer unknown, CC 3.0

seems to have been introduced into Egypt from Babylonia, was used in connexion [sic] with astrology, and later the dead made use of it when playing against . . . the serpent-god."*[8] When a Christian zodiac was created to replace the pagan, Saint Mattias was given ownership of Pisces. Chosen to replace the banished Judas, he was selected by lottery.

As society changed, the promise of the afterlife and a hope of a better future became more prominent. "With the growth of class inequalities, the use of the lot for the distribution of wealth became more and more restricted, with the result that the Moirai [Fates], who had asserted the birthright of all men to the fruits of their labour, were transformed into inexorable Fates whose authority was used to reconcile men with their lot, however meagre, in the new social order. . . . And

---

*And from Matthew 27:35, about soldiers gambling for the clothes of the crucified Jesus: "They parted my garments among them, and upon my vesture did they cast lots."

Fig. 81. Temperance, mixing
waters from cups

Rider-Waite Tarot

consequently, robbed of their birthright in the real world, . . . they were
driven to console themselves . . . with the mystical hope of recovering
their lost heritage in an illusory world beyond the grave. The birthright
became a death right."[9]

Temperance as the fourteenth Tarot card has the meaning of: to
mix, blend, combine, or measure. "The Angel Temperance blends two
opposite aspects or essences, producing life giving energy."[10] The fourteenth Futhark rune is the dice box (Peorth) used in gambling. Like
Temperance's actions, the box is shaken and mixed before casting the lots.
Lots, once cast to divine the will of the gods or to bestow an inheritance,
devolved into a pleasurable game of chance. The Old English Rune Poem
describes, "Peorth is a source of recreation and amusement to the great,
where warriors sit blithely together in the banqueting-hall."[11]

Given that the alphabet mystery hides mathematical secrets as well
as those of an alchemical soul journey, fourteen's gamble has the power
to turn a circle of 360 degrees into a workable calendar of 365 days.
An Egyptian goddess married to the sun took a lover in his absence.
When she became pregnant, the enraged sun refused to let the child be

born on any of the 360 days he owned. The distraught mother asked Thoth the Measurer to help. In turn, Thoth gambled with the moon for some light. Winning 1/72 of the moon's light, he had enough to create five extra days, each containing 1/14 of the light he won (360 / 72 = 5). The Hebrew Festival of Lots, Purim, when the Persian Jews rejoiced after vanquishing their would-be executors, is celebrated on the fourteenth day of Adar, which is in February or early March. Similarly, the five Egyptian "extra" holidays, each giving birth to one of the five gods described earlier, are celebrated in early spring.

For the sage creating the Tree Ogham series, Reed (Ng) had multiple associations with the fourteen's attributes. Like the I Ching yarrow sticks or Germanic rune staves, reeds were once cast as divining rods. Reed in this position may also have been chosen because baskets of reeds carried both Moses and the shining magician Taliesin safely over the water. Like the Leviathan, Moses has been depicted with horns. Like Noah, Moses brought the secrets of the alphabet, law, and Golden Rule to his people. In the modern calendar of twelve months, we have now circled back to the second month of February. Reed is the second hieroglyph in the Egyptian alphabet. Celts, the creators of Ogham, cited Jews, Egyptians, Milesians, and Trojans among their hermetic sources.

Reed contains additional stories that qualify it as a symbol for this charm. For example, it is both the container and the contained. Vahagn, fire god of ancient Armenia, where Noah's ark landed, was "born of a purple sea . . . delivered through the neck of a slender reed." His mother, Anahit (Anna Heth; see the eighth charm, heth) like other great goddesses, had the power to purify the seed of all men.[12] And Noah's ark, delivering the seed of a new world, was also made with reeds: "Make yourself an ark of Gofer wood. With Reeds make the ark" (Genesis 6:14).

Assistant Ogham for this position is Gomers. The inventor of this Ogham may have thought Gomers suitable for a charm whose theme is the hero emerging from a flood. Gomer, Noah's grandson by Japeth, was a mythic ancestor of the Celts. He began his travels in the Black Sea area of Armenia.

Fourteen's Bird Ogham is Ngeigh (Goose). It is proper that wise

Fig. 82. Rosicrucian watermark
of a goose

Bailey, *Lost Language of Symbolism*, 93

Mother Goose's son be reborn as a gander. We consider the goose a "silly" bird, a witless bird, a stupid gomer, a gormless bird, but the word goose originally meant "blessed" or "holy." In the past, the goose was seen as courageous and wise. When it was eaten, the power and knowledge of this bird was said to pass into the bodies of those fortunate enough to share in the feast.

Discussing the watermarks of a hissing goose, English scholar Harold Bayley wrote, "The meaning of the geese emblems herewith puzzled me for a long while until the idea struck me that the flame emerging from the mouths was intended to represent the goose's hiss . . . that the goose was assumed to be full of the Holy Spirit, and that its sibilant hiss was understood to be the emission of Spirit. The word *goose* is evidently allied to *goost*, the ancient form of ghost, i.e. 'spirit.'"[13] Ancient Celtic Christians depicted the Holy Spirit as a wild goose called Ah Geadh-Glas. Like the Holy Spirit, it could not be tamed.

Fifteenth Letter
Devas, Devils, and Protection

*Deities took on different planetary and stellar appellations.
. . . They could also take on more than one appearance at
the same time.*

NORMAN DAVIDSON,
ASTRONOMY AND THE IMAGINATION

DEVAS, DEVILS, AND PROTECTION

There are associations between the third, fifth, and fifteenth objects in
a series. The third position in our story belongs to the lusty sower of the
seed fertilizing his land to dry her red sea. His male aspects include a

youthful Saturn, Orion, Mars, stormy red Set, or the seductive Devil as the horned humpbacked camel-serpent Samael. Whatever their name, in third position, they impose the bolts and bonds of material Time. At the fifth charm, he became the teacher, a virtuous priest-king bestowing the great wisdom and harvests produced by his potency. At the fifteenth, he represents either a sign of protection and wealth for his land or a materialistic devil.

I believe that when the alphabet first developed, the deity represented by the fifteenth letter was revered. As the fertile god of an ancient people, he was eventually demonized into the Horned God as Tarot's Devil. The fifteenth Egyptian hieroglyph, Bolt, was a symbol of Egypt's red storm god as a devil: Set identified with the Baals of Phoenicia.

Several alphabets, including the South Iberian from Spain, drop the fifteenth letter. Ogham, as explained earlier, dropped Deus as the deuce. Ogham also dropped Samekh, perhaps because he had become associated with evil. Hebrew kept the letter, but the devilish serpent-camel Samael, seducer of Eve into eating the apple, became identified as "Samekh-Mem." By Jewish tradition, he remained as God's helper, though never quite trusted.

Away from me, you wicked!
PSALM 119, STANZA BEGINNING WITH
THE FIFTEENTH LETTER, SAMEKH.

In his commentary on the Tao Te Ching, Man-jen Cheng offers this thought describing the fifteenth verse: "In ancient times, well educated people were mysterious and in communication with heaven."[1] In his translation of the ancient text, John Wu offers this translation from the fifteenth verse: "He who keeps the Tao does not want to be full. But precisely because he is never full, he can always remain like a hidden sprout, and does not rush to early ripening."[2]

In the fifteenth position, the young traveler has grown up and become more powerful. For those in communication with the Mysteries of the Heavens, the male deity of the fifteenth charm may appear as a potent Bull of the full moon. The moon takes thirty days to travel the sky-round, becoming fully bright on the fifteenth day. Saturn and Mars are other names associated with the number fifteen because of their planetary travels around the sky. Mars circling the zodiac takes fifteen years and once every fifteen years the planet is particularly bright. The planet Saturn, king of a lost Golden Age, is also most brilliant every fifteen years, during his thirty-year journey around the sky.[3]

Apollo is yet another name for the Horned God. As the morning aspect of Mercury, growing horns as he emerged from his Earth's shadow, he was Apollo. As the horned planet Venus in her morning aspect, he was Lucifer, the devilish archangel thrown from Heaven for his presumptive brightness. Apollo, originally a wild god of dark northern woods, ultimately became a sky god: "They had a king over them which is the angel of the bottomless pit whose name in the Hebrew tongue is Abaddon; but in the Greek tongue is Apollyon" (Revelation 9:11). This fallen star once held the keys to Earth's bottomless storehouse.

Before they became devils, many ancient gods wore horns. One name for the fifteenth rune is Algiz, "elk" or "elk sedge." *Elk* has additional meanings: yew, yew bow, swan, or the Horned God himself.

Fig. 83. Detail from the Gundestrup Cauldron, Denmark, c. 150 BCE, showing a horned god surrounded by animals

Photo by Malene Thyssen, CC BY-SA 3.0

The word *elk* derives from the name algiz (Alces), a proto-Germanic word. The Alcis, twins like wild Apollo and Artemis, once traveled as horned stags.* According to northern myths, when the Ghost Riders of the Wild Hunt thunder through the sky they may chase the elk god. Alternatively, the Horned One leads the Hunt.

PROTECTION

The Eolh-sedge is mostly to be found in a marsh; it grows in the water and makes a ghastly wound, covering with blood every warrior who touches it.

OLD ENGLISH RUNE POEM, DICKINS TRANS.

Recalling the connection between the numbers three and fifteen, we note that fifteen, like martial three, is a triangular number (see the profile of letter twenty-one for a definition). Sedges, including the horned elk sedge,† have triangular stems with sharp edges, which has earned them the name "sawgrass"—and a reputation as plants to avoid touching, as I once learned to my dismay. As one scholar has observed, "The primary meaning of (this) rune is protection."[4] Reeds, on the other hand, have smooth round stems, good for building boats or delivering fire gods.

Fig. 84. Drawing of sedge with its horns

UC Integrated Pest Management Program

---

*Priests of the Alcis, remnants of a mother goddess tradition, wore women's clothing. In our modern world, Alces represents the genus of mammals (order Artiodactyla) comprising the moose and the European elk.

†To see photos of elk sedge, go to the University of Florida's Gardening Solutions website.

The Horned God, in various manifestations, has offered protection and fertility to the land since the most ancient Paleolithic times. Eventually agriculture developed. The symbol depicting the fifteenth rune as an elk, Y, eventually became the symbol for the horned barley. Like Horned God, Barley dies for his people. As a shield for protection, he offers a way of making peace with the use of the word *barley*. In their book about the language of children, the Opies told "when you feel like a rest in a game you cross your fingers and shout Barley upp!" Barley is "a term used in the games of children, when a truce is demanded."[5] Derived from an older, wilder magic, beneath the civilized journey of John Barleycorn lies the path followed by an older shaman toward the light. The grave symbol that gave peace and food, sacrificed and hung upside down, became the modern peace symbol: ☮.*

Sustain me, according to your word that I may live. . . .
Sustain me so that I may be safe.

PSALM 119, FIFTEENTH STANZA BEGINNING
WITH THE LETTER SAMEKH

NUMBER OF THE BEAST

Tarot places the Devil in the fifteenth position. As Lucifer, his pentacle is upside down, befitting a fallen angel or barley hanging as a sacrifice. Lucifer's tradition ties him to the Hierophant, the papal Bull of the fifth charm, whose name "belonged to the high priest of the Greek Eleusinian mysteries. . . . Here the [Hierophant] signifies initiation into a secret doctrine."[6]

The Hierophant card carries as his patriarch's cross the Phoenician symbol for samekh: ☨. That symbol is still carried by popes in ritual processions. Because Masonic masters also carry it, the papal cross is seldom seen in public. Also known as the Cross of Salem, "it is the insignia of the Grand Master and Past Grand Masters of the Grand Encampment of Knights Templar of the United States."[7]

---

*Designed by Gerald Holtom, 1958, it was a symbol of death within a circle.

Fig. 85. The Devil

Rider-Waite Tarot

THE DEVIL .

Poor Horned God—once the savior of his land, the singer at the gates of dawn has become a beast. Along with fifteen, the Beast is connected to the number 666. This number really irritated me since number magic is, in its own way, extremely logical. I wasn't satisfied with the explanation that the number of the Beast slouching toward Jerusalem was the numeric name of an unpopular emperor. Emperor Nero supposedly learned black magic from an Armenian magician, but apparently he was an inept student of the art.[8] An ancient manuscript has been found using the number 616 (6 + 1 + 6 = the unlucky 13). Later transcribers may have changed the number to 666 to reflect other mythic needs.

Armed with a calculator, I went looking: by tradition, 7 is the age of a child; 14 a youth; 21 the age of a man (and reason). Fifteen beyond the age of reason is 36, a number belonging to Orion's yardstick and to the thirty-six Righteous Ones who sustain the world. One of the measuring ruler's multiple names is "yard arm" (a yard having 36 inches). Adding all the sums of each progressive number: 1 + 2 + 3 . . . + 36 equals 666.

The Egyptian twenty-four-hieroglyph alphabet employs Bolt as its fifteenth symbol. Described above, it is associated with the red storm god Set. "It is probably more than chance that . . . Satan shares so many of Set's characteristics," writer John Anthony West observed. It is Set, who is sometimes identified as a phallus, "that imprisons spirit in matter." (See the third charm for discussion of terrification of the spirit by "pricks.") His bolt must be drawn back to let the spirit escape its material cage; The Pyramid Texts of Unas (c. 2600 BCE) intone, "Draw it [the bolt] back! . . . The phallus . . . is drawn back . . . they make a road for the king that [Horus] may pass."[9] The Papyrus of Ani also states, "The bonds of Seth which restricted my mouth have been loosened."[10]

INITIATION INTO MYSTERIES

Fifteen steps into the Mystery; fifteen small mysteries of the rosary celebrate the greater Mystery of Redemption.

> *Mystery: an incident in the life of our Lord . . . regarded as having a mystical significance. Hence, each of the fifteen divisions of the rosary corresponding to the "mysteries of redemption."*
>
> OXFORD UNIVERSAL DICTIONARY

Seven steps after entering the Underworld through eight's gate (heth), we arrive at the heart of an ancient Mystery. A bell rings, the veil pulls back. The treasure hidden deep in the labyrinth is as mutable as Earth and sky. It may appear materialistic and gross like the Tarot's Devil or shine like an alchemist's gold. In the Grecian city of Eleusis, the Mystery may even have appeared as a simple sheaf of glowing grain.

Odin, singing these charms of the alphabet, is one of the leaders of the devilish Wild Hunt. The fifteenth charm is the stage just before the Underworld traveler arises into the light of a new sun. He will emerge through the opening eye of the next letter. At this fifteenth stage, he is still deep in the Mystery, getting ready to greet the coming dawn.

> *I know a fifteenth, which the dwarf Thiodrerir*
> *chanted before Delling's [Dawn's] doors:*
> *power he sang for the Aesir and before the elves,*
> *thoughtfulness to Hroptatyr [Odin].*[11]

Norfi or Narfi had a daughter called Night. Her last husband was called Delling [Dawn] and together they had a son called Day. Odin took "Night and her son Day and gave them two horses and two chariots and set them up in the sky so that they have to ride around the earth every twenty-four hours."[12]

O

Sixteenth Letter

Opening Eye of the Sun

Phoenician/Old Hebrew	Ain (eye)
Greek	Omicron*
Ogham	Straif (Blackthorn)
Runes	Sig or Sigel (Sun or Victory)
Hieroglyph	Folded cloth
Tarot	Lightning-Struck Tower

*Greek expanded the Phoenician alphabet, placing "Big O" (omega) as the last of its twenty-four letters. Omicron is "Little O."

Which is the way to Somewhere Town? O, up in the morning early. The round red Sun is the door to go through. That is the way quite clearly.

KATE GREENAWAY, 1846–1901

OPENING EYE OF THE SUN

There are several possible endings for the alphabet journey. The earliest Spell may have ended with the stories of the first seven letters, rising up through the gate (heth/eighth letter) of the first octave. A watery Deluge

235

Fig. 86. Serpent emerging from the Egyptian eye of the sun.
Note the sixteen dots.

Illustrator unknown, from a book by E. A. Wallis Budge (1857–1934)

(mem/thirteenth letter) ending the lunar calendar of thirteen months is another possible ending. The sixteenth letter, the opening eye of the sun, is yet another ending. According to Diodorus, "'thirteen letters' . . . formed the 'Pelasgian alphabet' before Cadmus increased them to sixteen."[1]

These letters may or may not have ended with the encircling sun's embrace, or even the X-shaped gift of tav promising a multiplication of lives. Once a symbol is placed at a numbered slot, however, it assumes the attributes of that position, modifying those of its original placement.

The serpent-fish of letters fourteen and fifteen emerges through the eye of Egypt's sun, spitting out sixteen dots. Ain (eye) is the sixteenth Phoenician letter: O. This is the eye through which the devilish lover we met at the third charm as a camel now slips through, but only after sharing his golden wealth.

> *More than gold and precious stones . . . . I love thy commandments above gold, yea, above fine gold.*
> PSALM 119, STANZA SIXTEEN,
> BEGINNING WITH AYIN/AIN

> *It is easier for a camel to go through the eye of a needle, than for a rich man to enter into the kingdom of God.*
> MARK 10:25

Following our calendar of twelve months, the thirteenth month returned us to Aquarian January and the waters of the letter mem. Fourteenth is the Piscian February, when serpents and festivals of lots reappear. In March, we reentered the material world of time engendered by the phallus of fifteen's devil. Now in April, the sun once again grows strong; ice melts; seasons continue their circle.

The Old Icelandic Rune Poem tells us: "Sun [the sixteenth rune] is the Shield of the clouds/And a shining glory/And the life-long sorrow of ice." The two glosses, added by later sages answering the riddles posed in the poem, are *rota* ("wheel") and *Siklingr* ("descendent of the victorious one").[2] They may refer to the story of the valkyrie Sigrun. Her name translates as "victory rune" or "sun rune," and her story tells of her rebirth into the wheel of time. As told in the second lay of Helgi Hundingsbane, Sigrun marries Helgi, son of Sigmund the Volsung, but the lovers tragically die. Eventually they reincarnate to wed once again. "Sigrun was short-lived for the sorrow and woe [that she had]. It was the belief in the old days . . . that men were born again, but that is now called an old wife's tale. Helgi and Sigrun are said to have been born again; he was then called Helgi Harding's Scathe, and she Cara Halfdan's daughter—as it is said in the Lay of Cara—and she was a Walcyrie."[3]

Smolach, the song-loving Thrush welcoming the day, is the Bird Ogham character for this position. The twelfth-century writer Gerald of Wales claimed that mistletoe was formed from the dung of thrushes. The seeds passing through the sticky dung attach to trees and grow. Mistletoe, the golden bough, is a plant associated with a return from the land of death. In Vergil's *Aeneid,* the Trojan prince, on his way to a new home in Rome, is guided into the world of death where souls are waiting to be reborn. He is told to carry the golden bough with him to give to the queen of the Underworld. After his visit, he returns safely home through the gate of sleep. Pliny, in his Natural History (16:95), stated that mistletoe gathered by the druids "taken in drink, will impart fecundity to all animals that are barren." The ultimate gateway back into the world of Time.

The Celtic sun goddess is Aine, her name being akin to ain (eye), the Phoenician letter for the sixteenth position. Golden "Aine as mother-to-be appears in the word *ain* 'meaning in my womb.'" Laboring to produce her golden harvest, in Ireland Aine sits on her birth chair "when the earth is 'in travail' to turn the green corn to gold."[4] The sheaf of corn is Aine's child. In a number of traditions, sixteen years is the proper age for the young mother to deliver her rising son.

The full womb, after winter's quiet, is now again warming and contracting to deliver Earth's sun back into the spring. The golden child is leaving his hiding place in the delta, surging greenly into the light of his mother's opening eye. This is the season when Earth should be kissing the stubby green toes of her fur-feathered sun, washing him with dew. Then, after her labor, she should briefly rest until her child dances her awake. Islamic scholar Annemarie Schimmel notes, "In many languages there is a break after 16."[5]

Earth as Ireland's black Hag of Beare remembers the passing of her fertile powers. In her poem, written as a now cloistered nun, placed there by Christians entering her land, old ways passing, she will never take young lovers to return the yellow of old age to green: "I have had my day with kings, drinking mead and wine; now I drink whey-and-water among shrivelled old hags."[6]

As a Great Goddess, she carried the alphabet Mysteries from Asia Minor, where Noah found tablets inscribed with the Mysteries, to Egypt. As Scotia, black daughter of Egypt's pharaoh traveling with the Milesians, she brought the magic to Britain. Having multiple names, she also traveled as Bera, a queen from Spain, the land where the Sons of Mil settled before sailing to Ireland. Robert Graves notes: "Bera [Beare] and Scotia seem to be the same person." Bera is otherwise known as the Hag of Beara.*[7]

Tree Ogham's choice of symbols for this position is Straif, or Blackthorn. Blackthorn is a thorny wizard's tree ringing the sleeping fairy forts of Ireland. Poets were warned against burning the tree for it provided mothering shelter for birds. The French, another Celtic

---

*Beare is associated with the Ogham script, the majority of samples being found in Munster, the Irish province considered to be the chief stronghold of the Hag (Dames, *Mythic Ireland*, 56).

people, recall blackthorn as *mer du bois,* "mother of the woods."

Color Ogham is Sorcha, meaning purple-black, the color of the blackthorn's sloes, which are used to make a sun-warm brandy; the color of the thrush now singing at dawn's gates to greet the sun. A common name for thrush is mavis, which can also mean "purple."

Although most rune verses cite a warrior's use of the letter's power, some derive from an older, earthier magic. This spell to warm a maiden's heart from the *Hávamál* recalls the Hag's happier days:

> *That sixteenth I know, if I seek me some maid,*
> *to work my will with her:*
> *the white-armed woman's heart I bewitch,*
> *and toward me I turn her thoughts.*[8]

Mistletoe, like this rune charm, bestows a kiss for lovers lucky enough to stand under it.

CIRCLING SUN GODS

The ouroboros holding its tail represents the bright and dark cycles of the circle of time. The sixteenth charm, like the eighth, is a place where one can step off the wheel of life or, like Sigrun, return to the world. Among the Norse, the Midgard serpent biting his tail circles the earth. At the destruction of the world of northern gods, Ragnarok, this

Fig. 87. Line drawing from Cleopatra the Alchemist, c. third century, of an ouroboros

Image reproduced from the *Codex Marcianus Graecus,* c. tenth century serpent lets go of his tail to bite Thor, slaying one of the great gods. The serpent holding its tail implies the continual cycle back into the world; when it lets go, karma's wheel is no longer a rolling circle and the world will end.

Both the Old Norse and the Old Icelandic Rune Poems moved the yew rune from the thirteenth rune of the Elder Futhark to the sixteenth (and last) position of the Younger Futhark. We looked at the Icelandic poem in our discussion of yew at the thirteenth position, another number of endings and beginnings. As the sixteenth rune, the yew may reflect memories of the Tree of Life symbolism bestowed on the light returning to the world. As with all myths, there are multiple origins. The placental tree of life grows between the navel of each newborn child and the watery well of its mother's womb.

There is another World Tree belonging to the newly delivered child. The spinal column contains twenty-four vertebrae, the same as the number of hours of the turning dark and bright fortnights of each year, the number of hours in day and night. Inside is the spinal cord. Two nerves branch from each side of a vertebra. At the top is the head

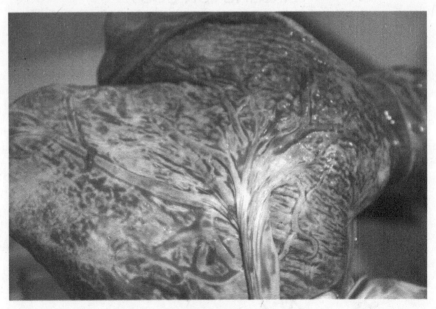

Fig. 88. Placental tree

with its small opening in the skull for illumination to enter and the enlightened soul to exit. At the spine's base, the nerves form a tangle of roots traveling down to well-planted feet.

> *[Yew] is a tree with rough bark, hard and fast in the earth supported by its roots, a guardian of fire and a joy upon an estate.*
>
> OLD ENGLISH RUNE POEM, TRANS. DICKINS

An old name for Ogham's Blackthorn is Straif. Another name, according to Edward Davies writing in 1809, is Draighean, recalling words like *draoi* (wizard) and *draig,* defined as "a generative principle or procreator, a fiery serpent, a dragon. . . . In the mythology of the primitive world the serpent is universally the symbol of the sun." Referring back to the above description of the Blackthorn, it is a thorny wizard's tree ringing the sleeping fairy forts of Ireland.[9]

UNRAVELING OF THE WEB

Egypt's twenty-four-hieroglyph alphabet ends with the returning serpent. The sixteenth hieroglyph, folded cloth, may illustrate another symbol of death and the hope of rebirth. "Beginning as early as the 4th Dynasty, men (and, less commonly, women) were frequently depicted holding a folded bolt of white cloth, typically in . . . non-royal funerary monuments. While Egyptologists have traditionally interpreted the folded cloth as a symbol of rank or office, I hypothesize that it signified the deceased status of its holder. . . . White linen was [used] in the ritual care of the divine images of the Egyptian gods. In both cases, the act of shrouding the figure in cloth was intended to provide protection and facilitate rebirth."[10]

But after number sixteen, the hieroglyphic alphabet's story has begun to unravel. I am losing the threads. The last seven hieroglyphs may hide mathematical or astronomical secrets, just as do the runes, Tarot, and the Phoenician alphabet, but I haven't found a key. The key may be found among the twenty-four letters of the Greek alphabet if it is true, as according to Isidor of Spain, that Isis, coming from Greece, brought the alphabet to Egypt.

Fig. 89. The Tower

Rider-Waite Tarot

The Lightning-Struck Tower, as the sixteenth Tarot card, hints at the precession of the equinoxes responsible for the fall of the Tower of Babel. The sun, aligned against a tower or fixed landmark, faithfully continues to rise in its correct season. But the background stars, once matching the sun's calendar, are not fixed. Slowly, over thousands of years, they retreat backward through the sky. A tower (or pyramid) aligned to no-longer-ruling stars becomes obsolete as the world's ages change. We will meet the tower again in the next letter, but this tower marking the calendar has fallen: it no longer reflects the correct stars of the seasons.

By this late time, the world of ancient Earth mothers is ending. War and warriors entering the older farming communities have affected the myths and the "sun rune" (Sigrun) now offers battle victory rather than rebirth: "The charms of Sigrdrifa, which she spake to Sigfred—Runes of Victory [sigrun] thou must know, if thou wilt have victory; and thou shalt grave them on thy sword-hilt; some on the rims, some on the carnage-brands, and twice name Ty."*[11]

---

*Tyr is a form of the war god, Mars. Sigrdrifa is another name for the battle goddess, Brunhilda.

Third Family:
Letters of the Heavens

Introduction to the Third Family

As discussed throughout this book, the order of the twenty-two letters of the early alphabet hints at an early knowledge of astronomical cycles. This third family describes the Heavens as the sun, moon, and stars circle the sky. We begin with the seventeenth letter (pe/command), as the north star that once ruled the sky. The travels of the moon (eighteenth letter) and sun (nineteenth letter) bring us to the head (ros/twentieth letter) of each new cycle. We end with the plus sign of a good return, the multiplication implied by tav's original shape of X or +. Like the Phoenix after whom the early alphabet was named, the mark (tav) promised an escape from death: "Tav [you] will be put as a sign on the foreheads of the righteous so that when the destroying angel comes . . . he will see the letter . . . and spare them."[1]

ך

Seventeenth Letter
Pi's Control of the Circle

Phoenician/Old Hebrew   Pe (mouth or commandment)

Greek   Pi

Ogham   Ruis (Elder)

Runes   Tir or Tiuwaz (god of the North Star)

Hieroglyph   Lake or sea

Tarot   The Star

Controlling the area over the North Pole is a pole star, around which all the stars of Heaven are seen to circle. The Greeks use letter pi (π), Hebrew employs pe, "commandment," while the Tarot simply uses Star as the seventeenth card. In China, pi (or bi) is a jade circle representing the emperor's mandate from Heaven. This symbol is a circle of Heaven, sometimes pierced by an arrow.

PI'S CONTROL OF THE CIRCLE

Shining over the entrance to the north is a way star, pathfinder guardian of an ancient world. With the wobbling of Earth, the original star slipped slowly away from the north, leaving an empty space in Heaven: a ravenous mouth threatening to consume the world.

I opened my mouth and panted. For I longed for thy commandments.

PSALM 119 STANZA, BEGINNING WITH PE,
MEANING "MOUTH" OR "COMMANDMENT"

Zodiac stars also slipped eastward. They no longer rose in their proper season, raising fear of chaos and apocalyptic endings. In *Hamlet's Mill,* De Santillana and von Dechend discuss the grinding mill threatening to destroy the world (see the spinning mill of letter ten). These fears are evoked by the "astronomical process, the secular shifting of the sun through the signs of the zodiac. . . . Great structures collapse; pillars topple which supported the great fabric [of the world]; floods and cataclysms herald the shaping of a new world."[1]

Symbolizing the new world arising after the destruction of the old may explain the seventeenth hieroglyph, "lake or sea." In Egypt, the primordial chaos was a vast sea named Nun. Out of this rose a hill beginning Creation. In time "the earth which had emerged from Nun might one day again be swallowed up into the primordial waste of waters."[2] In time, the mound will re-emerge and the Phoenix will announce a new world.

By the time our seventeenth symbol was developed, war was marching into once peaceful farming villages of Old Europe. New peoples, possibly driven by famines due to changing climates, were on the move with their herds and warriors. Annemarie Schimmel observes, "In classical antiquity, [the number] 17 appears in connection with warfare and heroism."[3]

Finally, a new star captured the empty space, imposing order on the stars. By this time, the old ways were dying. New heroes became rulers rather than lovers of Earth's once Bottomless Pit. The Black Mother disappeared underground to sleep with fallen kings and dragons until the coming of another Golden Age.

The seventeenth through the twenty-first letters seem to hide a variety of astronomical and magical secrets but not a true story. Several scripts associate the seventeenth symbol with the command of the pole star, the eighteenth with the moon, and the nineteenth with the sun because of their astronomical cycles.

Fig. 90. The Star

Rider-Waite Tarot

Although Egypt had an early hermetical working concept of pi and its mathematics commanding the circle (22 / 7 = π),* the final hieroglyphs (seventeen/lake, eighteen/hill, nineteen/basket) don't seem to refer to the circling pole stars nor to sun and moon cycles. If they do, I haven't found the proper key, though I may guess at possibilities. Several, however, seem to refer to the story we have been following in the alphabet.

THE PILLAR BETWEEN
HEAVEN AND EARTH

Tir is one of the guiding marks (tacn); It keeps its faith well toward princes. Above nights' clouds it is always on its path and never fails.

OLD ENGLISH RUNE POEM, R. I. PAGE TRANS.

---

*The Rhind Mathematical Papyrus, c. 1550 BCE, demonstrates mathematics for calculating the area of a circle, including an approximation of the value of pi.

The arrow of Tir illustrates the seventeenth Germanic rune. Tir, a northern god identified with Mars, Orion, and the revolving pole stars, is a god of law who never broke a pledge.

Tir's arrow (↑) still points north on maps and compasses. As the north star it is one of the way stars that help travelers navigate the way over land and sea. An alternate name for Tarot's Star is the Navigator. Orion spinning the wheel of the year through the seasons has also been depicted as an arrow, as has Mars.

Although ancient wisdom is couched in story and myth, I find it contains astute observations and hidden technologies. As Hermes/Mercury, the god of order's planetary cycle of eighty-eight days he quarters the Earth in each lunar cycle (4 × 88 = 352). Returning to his original zodiac sign in the same month as the sun takes seven years, during which time Mercury has twenty-two cycles (22 / 7 = π).

According to archaeoastronomer E. C. Krupp, Widukind, a tenth-century leader of the Saxons against the Frankish forces of Charlemagne, wrote in his chronicles that "Hermin, or Irmin, was the Saxon name for the god Mars, and he described a huge column they dedicated to Mars. This idea is strengthened by the name of the city in which the Irminsul [the pillar] was located; it is . . . Marsberg. . . The Norse counterpart of Mars was said to be Tyr."[4] Charlemagne destroyed the Irminsul in 772 CE and then seized control of the pole stars. Once known as Irmin's Wagons, they were renamed Charley's Wains.

The guiding star, centered over the North Pole, is said to mark one of the entrances to the Underworld. In England, under the name of Ermine Street, Herman's Way heads north toward Harrowsgate, where, in the 1800s, the oldest yew, a tree associated with death, grew by a healing well. Here, "the "sulphurous waters are of considerable strength and efficacy. . . . [Near here,] Robin Hood had his famous encounter with the 'curtall fryer.'"[5] Robin Hood, like Tir, was known for his archery. Harrowsgate and its sulfur suggest another entrance to the Underworld through which heroes enter to "harrow hell" and release the dead.

STAR AS WAY-FINDER

Polaris, the North Star since 1000 CE, is a faint star whose importance lies not in its size but in its powers of regulation. Each night as the world turns, the other stars whirl around this director. Polaris never sets; on a clear night one could travel straight east or west by keeping it at a constant height above the horizon. By knowing the height of the star for each destination, a sailor could be reasonably safe setting off beyond sight of shore and arrive at the expected port by keeping the star at the proper measurement above the horizon. Travelers over desert or sea corrected direction by sighting other stars as they rose in the east during the night.

"Then the traveller in the dark thanks you for your tiny spark. How could he see where to go, if you did not twinkle so?"[6] Even with the stars above, finding one's way in unfamiliar territory was a risky endeavor for ancient travelers. Roman historian Priscus of Panium (c. fifth century) told the story of a Roman convoy that once began a night march facing the setting sun but were greeted at dawn by the rising sun in their faces—a complete turn-around.[7] Eventually, the mystery of pathfinding was solved with a simple tool: the lodestone.

LODESTONES

A lodestone is a magnetized piece of iron that traditionally belongs to Mars/Tir. When suspended, it points steadily toward the magnetic north. Magnetic north and true north, as indicated by the pole star, are not quite identical. In Scandinavia and the Classical world, the longitudes of both closely correspond, but as one moves east or west of this line, the stone points back to the magnetic north. The Greek explorer Pytheas, visiting Britain around 300 BCE, noted that the pole star was not over the true north.[8] The Greek Thales of Miletus having discovered the property of magnets by 600 BCE, Pytheas possibly had a lodestone to help him make that determination.

Although the Chinese were using the magnetic stone for navigation as early as 2700 BCE, it was not openly used in Europe for another 3000 years. "Sailors in Europe may have been using crude magnetic compasses of Arab origin as early as 1000 A.D. A thirteenth-century writer wrote "when in cloudy weather [no longer profiting] by the light of the sun, or when the world is wrapped up in darkness . . . of night and they are ignorant to what point of the compass their ship's course is directed, they touch the magnet with a needle [which was either floated in a cork or suspended by a thread], which is whirled round in a circle until, when its motion ceases, its point looks direct to north."[9]

Norsemen were not above using a lodestone's magnetic powers to warm their beds through the cold dark northern nights. The lodestar of love and lodestone of all hearts is evoked by Odin singing this charm to a dying dragon, Loddfáfnir, in the *Hávamál*:

> *That seventeenth I know, (if the slender maid's love*
> *I have, and hold her to me:*
> *thus I sing to her) that she hardly will*
> *leave me for other man's love.*"[10]

Made of the same iron running through a red-blooded lover's veins, the lodestone, love stone, was carried by prostitutes in ancient Europe, fed water and iron on Fridays by Mexicans, and formed by Greeks into statues of lovers. In that country, a lodestone goddess was set free once a year to rush toward her lover made of iron.[11] The lodestone's magnetic powers of attraction could not help but redirect a traveler's wandering footsteps or recall a woman to man by stirring her blood.

Alas, its powers were not enough to keep Earth's northern gaze from wandering from Draco toward the Wagons (Dipper). Having replaced Tir as leader of the northern gods, Odin continues his song: "For a long, long time shall you, Loddfafnir, be lacking in these lays."[12] The dragon Loddfafnir is the dragon slain for his treasure in our fifth charm. A new ruler now controlled the pole stars, and it will be thousands of years before the precession of the equinoxes returns control of the star to the dragon.

In time, Odin himself will be killed. He tore a branch from the World Tree supporting the worlds to make his spear. The tree began to die, the well at its foot dried up, and in time its wood supplied the fires at the Twilight of the Gods.* Eventually, out of the chaos, a man and woman, Life (Lif) and Lover of Life (Lifthrasir), emerge from their hidden place in the forest around the World Tree to birth a new world.

BROKEN PROMISES

Some of the stories attached to the seventeenth position recall the broken pledges of the guiding star that was once trusted implicitly. Describing the seventeenth rune, the Old Icelandic Rune Poem describes Tyr as a "god with one hand, and leavings of the wolf and the prince of temples." The glosses below this line are "Mars" and *tiggi,* "a poetic word for king."[†13]

Long ago, the order of the northern world was about to be consumed by a ravenous wolf. The gods, or Aesir, held council, considering how to bind him. Fetters were made from "the tread of the cat, from a woman's beard, from fishes' breath, and birds' milk, from a hill's roots, and a bear's tail: out of all these things Gleipni [the Shackle] was fashioned." The gods then approached the proud wolf, challenging him to a test of strength. They promised to release him if he failed to break the bonds. Tir, the god who never broke an oath, served as guarantee. He held his hand in the wolf's mouth as promised. "Then, when the Aesir would not loose him, he [the wolf] bit off the hand at the place now known as the 'wolf-joint.' [So Týr] is one-handed and he is not called a peace-maker."[‡14]

The Tree Ogham's choice is Ruis (Elder). Fitting with the theme of broken oaths, Judas, sealing his broken vows with a kiss, hung himself on an elder tree. Older tales remember fairies riding switches of elder to fly to the Otherworld opening under the pole star. "Elder . . . that furnishes horses to the armies from the *sidh* [fairy], burn so that he be charred."[15]

The Color Ogham is Ruadh (red). A fragment of an Irish tale tells of King Aed Ruadh (Fire Red). He engaged a soldier and then refused

---

*This is Richard Wagner's version. In the Icelandic *Poetic Edda,* although the world ends when Ragnarok occurs, the World Tree survives.

†Thorsson translates *tiggi* as "director."

‡In Rome, the statue of the Mouth of Truth still bites off the hand of liars.

to pay his wages. The soldier "set the sea" against the king, who "broke upon the soldier the stars, visible and invisible." The meaning of the phrase is unknown but certainly involves magic. Aed Ruadh dies. Like Tir and Judas, he "flouted the rules of fair exchange."*[16]

Odin, who includes the name Tyr among his many namings, was another oath breaker.[†] He will be killed by the Fenris wolf who breaks loose at Ragnarok, ending the northern world. "A ring-oath Woden swore to Gundfled and broke."[17] He stole into a giant's home to steal the mead of poetry. Spending three nights romancing the giant's daughter, he betrayed her, stole the mead she was guarding, and fled without her.

---

*The Assistant Ogham seventeenth character is Reuben, the eldest son of Jacob, who did not receive his father's blessing to lead the twelve tribes after dishonoring his father. He was associated with a tower called the Stone of Bohan (Joshua 15:6; 18:17).

†Examples of Odin as Tyr include the names Hangatyr, Valtyr, and Fimbultyr.

ⲣ

Eighteenth Letter

Tsadiks, Moons, and Midwives

Phoenician/Old Hebrew	Tsade (hunt or fish hook)
Greek	Sigma
Ogham	Ailm (Elm, Palm, or Fir)
Runes	Berkana (Birch)
Hieroglyph	Hill
Tarot	The Moon

MOONS AND MIDWIVES

Many traditions associate the eighteenth symbol with the wandering moon because of her eighteen-year cycle. One is the saros cycle, in which, every eighteen years and eleven days, the sun and moon's nodes (where the moon crosses the ecliptic) line up and either a solar or lunar eclipse can occur. Every three cycles (fifty-four years), the eclipse occurs in the same zodiac sign. There is another lunar cycle of 18.6 years when the very erratic moon is close to Earth, the super moon appearing very large in the sky. An eclipse of this brilliant moon would have been especially impressive. Being able to predict eclipses was an important power of ancient scholar priests.

Fig. 91. The Moon
Rider-Waite Tarot

Early star-watching peoples were aware of the moon/sun cycles. Tarot uses the Moon as its eighteenth card. The growing and waning moon is associated with childbirth in many traditions. Sin, the moon god of Mesopotamia, assisted his beautiful cow, Geme-Sin, to deliver her child; an incantation from an Old Babylonian "magical-medical text" offers help. The incantation ends with a supplication: "'may this woman give birth as easily as Geme-Sin' suggesting this text's role in human child-birth."[1]

Cadmus carried his alphabet and its Mysteries to Greece, with whom, as detailed earlier, the Egyptians, Phoenicians, and Mesopotamians had a long history of interaction. The Greek moon was the midwife and huntress Diana/Artemis, and the Phoenician letter tsade, in its meaning as "hunt," may refer to this aspect of a moon goddess. Like the Babylonian moon's aid in giving birth, Artemis midwifed her brother.

Given the memory that every word, every letter, every number in the wheel of the Torah has a hidden meaning, the following is undoubtedly significant. Eighteen, as explained above, is a number associated with the moon. In chapter eighteen of Genesis, angels announce to long-barren Sarah that she will become a mother.* In Hebrew, eighteen represents the number of life (chai).

Square Hebrew (Ketav Ashuri), replacing letter-shapes of the earlier Old Hebrew/Phoenician, has a tradition known as gematria that assigns number values to letters. After the tenth letter (yod), the values increase by tens. Letter eighteen (tsade), therefore, has the value of ninety, Sarah's age when she receives her annunciation in chapter eighteen of Genesis. Out of her womb emerge the People of the Book.

In Psalm 119, the stanza beginning with tsade declares: "Righteous art Thou, O LORD, and upright are Thy judgements." The eighteenth Phoenician/Old Hebrew letter, tsade (also written tzade), is usually translated as "hunt" or "fish hook" but has been associated with the story of thirty-six (2 × 18) hidden tzadikim (righteous people) who sustain the world. The twelfth-century Kabbalah text, the Bahir, reiterates the tzadikim's role in sustaining the world: "What is the letter Tzadi? . . . It is thus written (Proverbs 10:25), 'The righteous (Tzadik) is the foundation of the world.'"[2] Hebrew has two forms of tsade, thus 2 × 18.

Tree Ogham has had several characters representing the eighteenth position, including Elm, Fir, and Pine. Another is Palm (Ailm).† Palms do not grow in Ireland but do grow in Spain, from which the Celts sailed to conquer Ireland. It was under a palm tree that Nemesis birthed her sun, Apollo, and the moon as Diana. Diana, born first, helped deliver her brother. As a midwife "palm," her dates are fingers (dactyls). Although couched as myth, the moon as twin of the sun is truly a reflection of his light.

> The old palm-tree [of Delos] played midwife for Leto . . .
> under its branches she bore Apollon and Artemis.
> NONNUS OF PANOPOLIS (C. FIFTH CENTURY),
> DIONYSIACA, TRANS. ROUSE

---

*According to gematria scholar Bethsheba Ashe, the chapter divisions of the Bible were created by Stephen Langton in 1227, a scholar certainly aware of the numbered Mysteries.
†According to Robert Graves (White Goddess, 190), in Old Irish the name ailm can mean the palm tree.

The mothering palm gave birth to another set of twins: Zerach and Peretz of Hebrew tradition. "Why was Tamar [palm tree] worthy of being the mother of Peretz and Zerach? It was because her name was Tamar. . . . Why were they called Peretz and Zerach? Peretz was named after the moon. The moon breaks out (*paratz*) at times. . . . Zerach was named after the sun, which always shines (*zarach*) in the same manner."[3] The line of Judah comes from the offspring of the moon, Peretz.

The eighteenth rune is Berkana, birch. As one of the first trees to bud out after winter, the birch is a symbol of fertility and regeneration. Associated with a number of mother goddesses including Freya, the lady birch, like all mothers, produces a nourishing sap each spring to feed her children. Cradles made from birch were believed to protect newborn babies from malicious spirits, and in the folklore of the Highlands, it was said that a pregnant cow herded with a birch stick would bear a healthy calf: "and if the animal was barren, she would become fertile."[4]

The *Sigrdrífumál* uses a rune (Biargrunar) as a midwife: "if help thou wilt a woman to bring forth her babe: on thy palms wear them, and grasps her wrists, and ask the disir's [fates] aid."[5] Like the incantation to Gema Sin above, it offers help in delivering a child. And like the old palm tree of Delos who acted as midwife to help Leto deliver her sun and moon, the midwife's palms play the role in this Birthrune.

Biargrunar are runes helping a woman in labor. As the birch tree contains both male and female aspects, the Old Norwegian Rune poem ties birch to the trickster Loki. He fathered some of his children; and as a mother, gave birth to others.

The Bird Ogham character is Aidhircleog (Lapwing). Associated with the Underworld, lapwings are connected to moon symbolism, feeding mostly during the day except for the few days around the time when the moon is full, when it feeds at night.

The history of Greek's eighteenth letter, sigma (Σ or, sometimes, a crescent-shaped "lunate sigma") is obscure, but it possibly derives from the twenty-first Phoenician letter, Shin or Sin (W). The shape echoes the sinuous moon's path measured out against the horizon behind the moon god from Paleolithic Spain (fig. 73, p. 211). Sin was the midwife moon god of ancient Babylon.

Φ

Nineteenth Letter

The Number of the Sun

Phoenician/Old Hebrew	Qopf (monkey)
Greek	Phi (represents the golden ratio)*
Ogham	Ohn (Furze)
Runes	Ehwaz (horse)
Hieroglyph	Basket with handle (represents a lord)
Tarot	The Sun

*The Greeks eventually changed the order of their letters, moving their nineteenth symbol, phi, to become the twenty-first letter instead.

THE NUMBER OF THE SUN

The number nineteen has a connection to a golden sun cycle. Every nineteen years, without further adjustment, the calendars of the sun, moon, and Mercury realign. They reappear in the sky together on the day they joined nineteen years earlier.*[1] Phoenicians' choice of "monkey" for the nineteenth letter seems odd, but in Egypt, a country influencing the Phoenicians for thousands of years, monkeys were associated with the lordly sun.

*The exact calculations work out to between nineteen and twenty years.

Fig. 92. A monkey stands
next to the midwife palm,
symbolizing the sun god's daily
rising; Egyptian amulet bead, c.
1300 BCE

Image from the Walters Art Museum

Babylonians by at least 500 BCE knew this nineteen-year sun-moon-Mercury cycle. The image in figure 93, from the Bronze Age, suggests an earlier knowledge of the cycle. The dragon boat carrying the sun has nineteen prongs. The solar cross on the boat may have been used for navigation before the sextant was invented.[2]

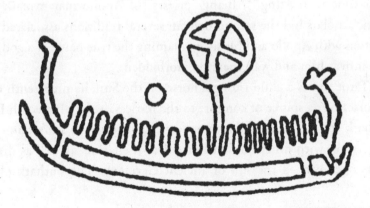

Fig. 93. Sun boat, Bronze Age Scandinavia, c. 3000 BCE

Gimbutas, *Language of the Goddess*, 249

APOLLO AND THE HYPERBOREANS

Apollo began his journey as a god of the north before eventually becoming a Greek sun god: "Until the Christian era this name [Apollo] for the god of day was the title of the planet Mercury when [he appeared as a] morning star."[3] We first met Apollo at the second charm. His mother, traveling as a wolf, was Leto/Nemesis. One tradition has her born in Anatolia.

Diodorus (c. 60–30 BCE) states: "Leto (mother of Apollo and Artemis—Zeus was their father) was born on this island [of the Hyperboreans, said by some to be Britain] . . . and the inhabitants are looked upon as priests of Apollo. . . . The god visits the island every nineteen years, the period in which the return of the stars to the same place in the heavens is accomplished. . . . At the time of this appearance of the god he both plays on the cithara and dances continuously the night through from the vernal equinox until the rising of the Pleiades."[4] I haven't discussed the Pleiades in detail, but these faint stars rising just before Taurus were important calendar markers. Maia, mother of hermetic Mercury, is one of the Pleiades.

Hyperboreans were said to be people from beyond the North Wind. They are often assumed to be related to, if not actually, Celts. Last survivors of the Golden Age, Pindar (c. 518–438 BCE) claimed they "knew neither sickness nor old age and instead of toiling or fighting wars, pass their time in feasting."*[5] Being "priests" of Apollo may explain why Celtic scholars hid the second ogham; several traditions associated that position with Apollo and his sister. Naming the true name of a god gave power over him and was, therefore, forbidden.

Tarot shows a child riding a horse on the Sun, its nineteenth card. A horse, ever a source of comfort to the restless, is the nineteenth Elder Futhark rune. The rune does not seem to suggest the sun's numerical association with nineteen, but horse-drawn chariots as well as dragon boats once carried the sun of ancient Germany. The Futhark placed

---

*Per *The Bacchae*, the ancient Greek tragedy (405 BCE) by Euripides, Cadmus and his wife, after becoming dragons, headed north to retire in the land of the Hyperboreans.

Fig. 94. The Sun

Rider-Waite Tarot

Fig. 95. Trundholm sun chariot drawn by horse, Denmark, c. 1400 BCE. On this sun disk, ornaments on the golden side number 366; on the dark side, there are 354, the days of the lunar calendar.

Photo by Malene Thyssen, CC BY-SA 3.0

Sig (sun) as the sixteenth rune, The Valkyrie Sigrun (discussed above, whose name translates as "sun rune" or "victory rune") rode through the air on her flying horse. The Norse sun goddess and the moon god traveled the sky in a chariot pulled by horses. A later rune depicting a horse, ᛚ, is a variant for the Sig rune, ᛋ.

Mundilfaeri (a period of time) had two beautiful children. "He called the one Moon and his daughter Sol [sun]." Jealous gods set them up in the sky. "They made Sol drive the horses that drew the chariot of the sun. . . . Moon guides the course of the moon and controls its waxing and waning."[6]

POTENCY OF THE SUN

The generative power of our warm, lordly sun is a reality. Therefore, myths of potency should and do appear among those of the nineteenth symbols. The nineteenth hieroglyph is a basket, but when added to Egyptian words, it represents a lord, perhaps because his potency produced both golden wealth and grain.

The nineteenth Hebrew letter qoph (monkey), 𐤒, would seem to relate to the English word *copulate,* the sexual act of a potent generation. The dictionary derives *copulate* from a Latin root, but the suggestive shape of Phoenician qoph hints at an older lineage.

Although I have emphasized that the qualities of each symbol derive from its number placement, symbols copied from older shapes transposed to new positions in the order contain the qualities inherent in the original. In ancient Greek, qoph's shape has become the letter phi (ϕ), representing the golden ratio of mathematics and art. Gold being the color of the warm sun, phi in philosophy is shorthand for a "generic act," which produces a family of copies. Copulate meaning "join together," the same ϕ symbol in Brahmi represents the "cha" sound, signifying "and," which is, of course, a joining. "Cha" joined to other words is known as a dvandva construction, with "cha" having a copulative linguistic function.

ᛝ
Twentieth Letter

New Year after Sun/Moon/Mercury Nineteen-Year Cycles

Phoenician/Old Hebrew	Ros (head)
Greek	Upsilon
Ogham	Uhr (Heather)
Runes	Mannaz (man)
Hieroglyph	Stand for jugs
Tarot	Judgment

START OF A NEW CYCLE

Uiseoc, the Bird Ogham, is the lark singing at the dawn of day. The twentieth Tarot card shows the dead emerging from their graves on Judgment Day. After the finality of the nineteen-year sun cycle, a new beginning returns with each twentieth year. I believe this is the reason the twentieth Phoenician letter is ros, meaning "head"—the head, or start, of each new cycle.

Fort Ogham is Usney. Also spelled Uishigh or Uisneach, it is a hill in the center of the five Irish provinces. Here a great assembly would

Fig. 96. Judgment
Rider-Waite Tarot

JUDGEMENT.

gather for the lighting of Beltane fire (May 1) in Spring. Like other of the twentieth symbols announcing a new beginning, the fire marked the arrival of Summer in Ireland.[1]

In ancient Israel, two kingdoms competed for the crown after the death of Solomon: the northern kingdom of Israel and that of Judah. Israel began its new year with the vernal equinox (March); Judah, surviving after the ten lost tribes of Israel were scattered by the Assyrians, continues to celebrate its new year, Rosh Hashanah, each fall.

There is another twenty-year cycle: the great rulers Jupiter and Saturn conjunct every twenty years, an importance marked by the brightness of their joining. There are five such conjunctions every hundred years. The grand conjunction of 6 BCE may have announced the arrival of the Age of Pisces and its messiah.

Starting each new cycle, one must choose a path. Phoenician-born Pythagoras of Samos used a dowser's Y-shaped upsilon (the twentieth Greek letter) to represent the forked path mandating one's decision. Known as the Samian letter, it represented the path of virtue or vice.

When Reason doubtful, like the Samian letter,
Points him two ways, the narrower is the better.
ALEXANDER POPE, *THE DUNCIAD*

The path of the Milky Way splits into two paths around the womb of our galaxy (the Galactic center) near the constellation Scorpio, associated with the Black Goddess. It is the broad road that leads to hell. The straight and narrow path moves away from her womb.

Note that although runes derive most of their shapes from the Germanic tribes' own hoard of images, the twentieth Phoenician letter is ◁, the same shape used for the thorn or "prick" of the third rune. Three is the position when the world of time begins with the seeding of Earth and the drying of her waters with impregnation. As the third month of Mars, the vernal equinox marks the new year of the ancient world. The head of each zodiac cycle, the zero point of time, occurs when Aries (Mars) passes over the Green Witch of England (Greenwitch Mean Time). And once man enters the world of time, he enters the world of death, augmenting the dust from which he came. The Younger Futhark rune for man, Ψ, when turned upside down indicated the date of death in some early documents. The Younger Futhark's upside-down shape became their sixteenth and final rune, Yew, the toxic tree associated with graveyards.

Maðr [Man] is an augmentation of the dust;
Great is the claw of the hawk.
OLD NORWEGIAN RUNE POEM, DICKINS TRANS.

W

Twenty-First Letter

A Triangular Number of a Sinuous Moon God

Phoenician/Old Hebrew	Shin (tooth)
Greek	Phi
Ogham	Eodha (Poplar)
Runes	Laguz or Logr (lake, ocean, or leek)
Hieroglyph	Bread (rising bread, not a flat wafer)
Tarot	The World

Sin (or Shin) was the moon god of Mesopotamia, and bore the name of the twenty-first Phoenician letter. This moon-Bull was said to mate with the mountains to fertilize his land. Many of the twenty-first symbols seem to hint at fertility.

The twenty-first rune, Laguz/Logr, is shaped like the third Phoenician letter: 𐤂. And the qualities of the twenty-first symbol seem to relate to those of the third: 2 + 1 = 3. I found this very confusing until I discovered triangular numbers, which are obtained by adding the natural numbers. Twenty-one, for example, is the sum of the first six natural numbers (1 + 2 + 3 + 4 + 5 + 6 = 21).

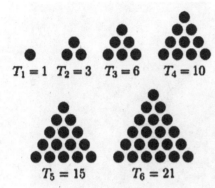

$T_1 = 1$ $T_2 = 3$ $T_3 = 6$ $T_4 = 10$

Fig. 97. Grids of
triangular numbers

$T_5 = 15$ $T_6 = 21$

These numbers are called "triangular" because they can form a triangular grid of points, where the first row contains one point, and each subsequent row contains one more point than the preceding one $(1 + 2 + 3 + 4 \ldots)$, forming a triangle.

The Younger Futhark reduced the number of runes from the twenty-four found in the Elder Futhark to sixteen. The Younger Futhark's movement of the watery lake rune from the twenty-first to the fifteenth symbol may have been determined by fifteen's association with triangles; fifteen, like three and twenty-one (lake's Elder Futhark position), is a triangular number.

Both the third and fifteenth symbols, like the twenty-first, carry the attributes of fertility. This would seem another explanation for the twenty-first symbol's early association with the third symbol. The third rune is a thorn, with all of a prick's phallic connotations leading to birth; the fifteenth is that old black devil who induced Adam and Eve to enter the world of time and bear the children of Man.

Laguz/Logr is traditionally translated as "lake" but sometimes as "leek." The "leek" interpretation is based not on the rune poems, but rather on early inscriptions where the rune is thought to abbreviate *laukaz,* a symbol of fertility. One example are the inscriptions on the Bülach fibula (pin), found at a grave site in Switzerland and dating to the late sixth century. The rather phallic leek is a member of the onion family. The Elder Futhark runes inscribed on the fibula form a message, begging: [Lover- penis, you- vulva: receive me: leek! penis! leek! penis!"[1]

Fig. 98. A bulbous leek emerging from its hairy nest
Photo by Björn König, CCO

In India, another civilization sharing myths with the West, devout Hindus do not eat onions or their relatives due to the family's sexually stimulating nature.

The Greeks eventually placed the phallic phi as the twenty-first of their twenty-four letters rather than leaving it in its original nineteenth position (which became their Q). The last four Greek letters became phi (Φ), chi (X), psi (Ψ), and omega (Ω).

X or +

Twenty-Second Letter

Escape from Death and the Promise of a Good Return

Phoenician/Old Hebrew	Tav (mark) or + (the plus of a good return)
Greek	Chi
Ogham	Ioho (Yew)
Runes	Ingwaz
Hieroglyph	Hobble for cattle
Tarot	The Fool, who continues the circle

The twenty-second rune representing Ingwaz is an alchemist's symbol for lead: ᛉ. Like Saturn, the sower of the seed before he aged into blackened lead, Ingwaz (sometimes known as Ingvi-Frey) was responsible for his Earth's fertility. Like precessed Orion (himself known as both Saturnus and the Fool), he went "east over the waves." Frey is a son of Earth (Njord) who is associated with Saturn. (Remember that very often in myth, the father is reborn as the son.) Like the Hebrew patriarch Jacob later named Israel, Ingvi fathered people named after him.

The Greek alphabet placed the crossroads of chi, X, as the twenty-second letter. In Plato's *Timaeus* (c. 360 BCE), he describes a cosmic geometric structure in which two circles are cut "into two parts length-wise; and then . . . laid the twain one against the other, the middle of one to the middle of the other, like a great cross"—that is, the letter X. This great cosmic X formed the underpinning for the formation of the soul of the world, which then "began a divine beginning of unceasing and intelligent life lasting throughout all time."[1]

The path of the ecliptic, along which the planets, sun, and moon travel, crosses the path of the Milky Way near Orion/Taurus/Gemini and again near Scorpio/Sagittarius. At Time Zero, the two equinoctial "hinges of the world" were in Gemini and Sagittarius, connected by the Milky Way.*[2] The zodiac light of their passage appears as an X, offer-ing a stairway to the stars by the river. Angels and souls once descended and ascended along this ladder, but travel between Heaven and Earth is only possible when the Milky Way touches Earth on the quarter points of the year, either on the solstices or equinoxes.

Each age named after the stars rising on the spring equinox lasts about 2,000 years. The Age of Gemini began about 6450 BCE, followed by Taurus/Scorpio, which still touched the hinges of Earth. For more than two thousand years after Aries rose in spring (c. 2150–1 BCE), the crossroads in the Milky Way hovered in the sky. When Pisces came to rule the spring equinox and Virgo the autumn, the gates now open-ing at the solstices once more touched Earth in Gemini and Sagittarius. Pisces opposite Virgo and Gemini opposite Sagittarius form a square, their stars now rising during the equinoxes and solstices.

Death and rebirth themes continue in Ogham's spell. The last char-acter of Bird Ogham is Eagle. Sea eagles of ancient Britain, like the vul-tures of Anatolia, consumed the flesh of exposed bodies. The mortal flesh was flown toward Heaven; the bones might join their ancestors in the dark sanctuary of communal tombs. Some of these passage graves were oriented to receive the midwinter sun into their womb. At mid-winter, the sun dies and is reborn into another year.

Thousands of years after a pattern was laid into our alphabet to sing the world into existence, we still follow its hopeful trail through our cal-

---

*The four zodiac signs form a square.

Fig. 99a. The twenty-first Tarot card is the World, representing an ending to a cycle of life, a pause before the next big cycle, which begins with the Fool (Fig. 99b), the cipher, the zero, who exists both at the beginning and end of time.

Rider-Waite Tarot

endar. We still expect life to return after each cold winter; we still expect that after each dark night, a sun will rise above a nurturing Earth.

> *While earth remains, seedtime and harvest, cold and heat,*
> *summer and winter, day and night shall not cease.*
>
> GENESIS 8:22

We have now come to the end of the Phoenician alphabet, but in Mystery traditions, the end is always embedded in the beginning and the beginning in their end. While the X of the final Phoenician letter now appears on dying trees slated for destruction or warns of death on poison bottles, it once promised a return into the Circle of Life. Phoenician ends with tav, the X "mark" of multiplication promising an increase, or the plus (+) promising a good return. The Greek alphabet continues on until its twenty-fourth letter, the womb of omega: Ω. That alphabet is now bookended by the alpha and the omega. The runes, too, carry on for twenty-four symbols, ending with the womb-shaped Othala (inheritance or homeland): ᛟ.

The very first "sign" in the Torah was placed by God himself, who inscribed a single letter on Cain's forehead. Some maintain the sign was made in the form of a tav (mark).

> And the LORD said unto him, Therefore whosoever slayeth Cain, vengeance shall be taken on him sevenfold. And the LORD set a mark upon Cain, lest any finding him should kill him.
>
> GENESIS 4:15 (KJV)

Described earlier, Cain's people, the Canaanites, became city dwellers along the coast of the Levant and ultimately became known as the Phoenicians whose alphabet contains the secrets of an enlightened return to life.

A Review

There was a crow sat on a clod.
That's an end to my story that's very odd.

We now leave our story. Regardless of where the story ends, the first and last symbols of these ancient scripts hint at a ceaseless circling of time. Each end is embedded in each beginning. Each beginning is embedded in each end.

As I hope to have made clear, the ordered symbols of the alphabet and its descendants contain too consistent a story to have been carelessly chosen. Our alphabet emerged out of an ancient Spell, a spell reminding the winter-dead to remember the promise of spring. Each letter was once a mnemonic for a verse sung to enchant an evolving creation. The attributes of the letters were determined by their placement in the series. At its root, our alphabet is based on number magic.

Fig. 100. Crow, Crete, c. 1500 BCE
From Marija Gimbutas, *Civilization of the Goddess,* 240

A CAVEAT

I have followed the alphabet trails of ancient goddesses from a long-past Golden Age. To properly understand their magic, the wary reader should continually remember to read between the lines. Even those straight lines were the gift of a shape-changing enchanter. Linus (Flax) was one of the children of wild Apollo. Along with Hemp (Cannabis), Vine Kings, John Barleycorn, and other winter Capri-corns (Wild Grains), Flax is beaten and flayed to provide linen to shroud his people. The older magic dancing rebirth, his music devolved into dirges lamenting the dying year.[1] Readers clinging to the littoral shore of fact will be dismayed by the fey riddles of mythmakers following wandering cows and trader crows along ancient paths as they distributed the wealth and secrets of an older civilization.

The bread and cheese are on the shelf.
If you want any more, cut it yourself.

APPENDIX 1

Astronomical Calendar Cycles

The cycles of the sun, moon, and five wandering planets able to be seen by the naked eye have been carefully observed and recorded since Paleolithic times. As deities, their travels became the basis of calendars and the timing of festivals. As an Earth-centered tradition, they do not include Earth.

SUN—It takes Earth 365.25 days to orbit around the sun (a circle of 360 degrees + 5 days to regulate the calendar). Many methods have been devised to adjust the calendar to keep it accurate. We employ a leap day every 4 years to keep our calendar consistent with the seasons. Unadjusted, the sun and moon (and Mercury) cycles realign every 19 years (in what's known as the Metonic cycle). Number 18 is given to the moon, and 19 to the sun (recall fig. 93, p. 257).

MOON—The moon needs 27.3 days to travel from fixed star to fixed star, 29.5 days from phase to phase, and 352 days to revolve the 360 degrees of the zodiac. The full moon occurs every fifteenth day (360 / 15 = 24, the number of letters in some alphabets). By tradition, the moon cycle is usually given as 30 days. In a lunar year, there are 13 full moons, with the blue moon being the second moon in a solar month (recall fig. 73, p. 211).

Eighteen is a moon number. Every 18.6 years, the full moon is at its closest to Earth, appearing much brighter and larger than in other years. This cycle may not have been known when the alphabet was first ordered, but it was definitely known by the time of Tarot, runes, and

Ogham. Tarot places the Moon as its eighteenth card, followed by the Sun as the nineteenth.

In what is known as the saros cycle, every 18 years and 11 days the sun and moon's nodes (where the moon crosses the ecliptic) line up and an eclipse occurs. Every 3 cycles (54 years), the eclipse occurs in the same zodiac sign.

MERCURY—Mercury is the innermost planet circling the sun. Like the moon and Venus, Mercury occasionally passes behind the sun on his travels. As he emerges from its shadow, he wears a crescent shape and is depicted with horns as his symbol: ☿.

It takes 88 days for Mercury to circle Earth. Mercury thus quarters the Earth 4 times in a lunar year ($4 \times 88 = 352$). The number 4 is therefore associated with Mercury. In our 7-day week, the fourth day is Mercredi or Wednesday (Woden's day).

Mercury is also linked to the number seven; in planetary form, he spends 7.3 days in each of the 12 zodiac signs. Returning to the original zodiac sign in the same month as the sun takes 7 years, during which he has 22 cycles. Pi ($22 / 7$), the mathematical commander of each circle, is the seventeenth Greek letter. In Hebrew, the seventeenth letter, pe, translates as "command" or "mouth."

Mercury's calendar aligns with the sun and moon every 19 years, with all three meeting in the same zodiac sign. As the evening star, Mercury was known as Hermes. Rising with the sun, his name was Apollo, the deity sacred to the Celts.

VENUS—This planet orbits Earth in 224.7 days, spends 236 as a morning star, then disappears for 90 days; she appears for 250 days (close to the 9 months of pregnancy) as the evening star, then disappears for 8 days. It takes her 1.6 years between morning risings. Five such heliacal risings, each occurring in a different zodiac sign, mark out a pentacle in 8 years. The numbers 5 and 8 are therefore both associated with Venus. She orbits Earth 13 times during the 8 years. The horned moon, another of the Great Goddess's aspects, has 13 months per solar year.

As an inner planet, Venus circles between the sun and Earth. Like Mercury and the moon, she appears as a crescent as she emerges from the sun's shadow. Ancient statues often depicted her with horns. As the evening star, she was known as Venus in her peaceful female aspect. As the morning star, she is either male or a fiery woman warrior. The fierce morning star is also known as Lucifer, a great light thrown from Heaven (see the profile of the fifth letter).

MARS—The third planet seen from Earth, Mars orbits the sun in 687 Earth days. Every 15 years, Mars reaches its closest point to Earth and shines its brightest. For this reason, it is associated with the number 15. Being a hot red planet, Mars is sometimes identified with a devil.

JUPITER—Jupiter takes 11.9 years (that is, about 12 years) to orbit the sun. As a great ruler (12 inches, 12 months) of the sky, Jupiter, king of the gods, appears in one zodiac sign a year on his 12-year journey. As a measuring ruler, he became the supreme god of the Romans. In the form of letter L (El), he appears with the rod of a teacher (lamed) as our twelfth letter.

SATURN—It takes Saturn 29.5 years (30 years) to orbit the sun. The number 30 is therefore associated with Saturn (whose name means "seven"), as are 7 and 50. Fifty is the biblical Jubilee number, when, after 7 × 7 years, on the fiftieth, the land rests and slaves are set free. Saturn, traditionally associated with the common man, allows workers the leisure to celebrate the Sabbath (the seventh day). On the year's last month in winter, the Saturnalia is celebrated. Having reached his southernmost position, the sun reverses his path on the winter solstice to head back north toward summer. On the Saturnalia, the world is turned upside down and masters serve their slaves.

Jupiter and Saturn conjunct every 20 years. As an important and bright conjunction, this possibly appeared as the Christmas Star that was followed by magi looking for the Christ Child.

Note: Orion, also known as Saturn, became Tarot's zero, the Fool.

As Fool, an early form of the wealth-bringing cipher as 0, zeros were written with the number 30. When the Babylonians began using the zero (c. 500 BCE), they wrote it with the symbol for 30.

In alchemy, Saturn is a blackened aspect of Mercury. As the last of the planets seen by the naked eye, he again symbolizes an end that refers back to the beginning.

THE POLE STARS—Phoenician's seventeenth letter pe ("mouth" or "commandment") is associated with the pole star, around which the stars circle. (Greek's seventeenth letter, pi, is associated with command of circles.) The current pole stars are traditionally seven, replacing the older Draco, who lost control of the pole star position around 3000 BCE. Tarot depicts the Star as its seventeenth card; the Elder Futhark runes place Tir, god of the North Star, in this position, his arrow (↑) pointing toward the North Star.

SIRIUS—The Dog Star following Orion in the sky was also an important calendar marker, rising just before the sun (heliacal rising) near the summer solstice around 4500 BCE. This preceded July's yearly flood of the Nile.[1] Decan stars, those travelling the same circle as Orion and Sirius, rise in the east every ten days. After setting in the West, they take 72 days to reappear, to be reborn, in the night sky. Zodiac stars like Taurus, rising 30 days apart, take 40 days to reappear. Hoping for a return to the light after passing through the darkness of death, some ancient people wheeled the dead in wagons for 40 days before placing them in the tomb. Jesus appeared for 40 days after his resurrection before ascending to Heaven.

Table of Alphabet Patterns Compared

Position	Tarot	Phoenician	Egyptian	Futhark	Tree Ogham
1	The Magician	Aleph (ox)	Vulture	Fehu, Feoh, or Fe (cattle or money)	Beth (Birch)
2	The High Priestess	Beth (house)	Reed	Urus or Ur (aurochs, ore, dross, shower or rain)	Unspoken
3	The Empress	Gimel (camel or rope)	Forearm	Thurisaz or Thurs (thorn or giant)	Luis (Rowan)
4	The Emperor	Dalet (door)	Quail	Ansus or Os (high god or mouth)	Nion (Ash) or Fearn (Alder)
5	The Pope	Hey (window or "sound of rough breathing")	Leg	Raido or Rad (ride or wheel)	Saille (Willow)
6	The Lovers	Vav (nail)	Seat	Kenaz, Ken, or Kaun (torch or canker/sore)	Fearn (Alder) or Nion (Ash)
7	The Chariot	Zain (weapon)	Snake with horns	Gyfu or Gebo (gift)	Huath (Hawthorn)
8	Justice	Heth (gate or fence)	Owl	Wynn (joy or white)	Duir (Oak)
9	The Hermit	Teth (wheel or coil)	Water	Hagalaz (Hag god, hail, or heal)	Tinne (Holly)

Position	Tarot	Phoenician	Egyptian	Futhark	Tree Oghan
10	Wheel of Fortune	Yod (hand)	Mouth	Naudiz, Nyd (need)	Col (Hazel)
11	Strength	Kaph (palm of the hand)	Reed shelter	Isaz (ice)	Quert (Apple)
12	The Hanged Man	Lamed (ox goad or rod of the teacher)	Plaited wick (upside down)	Jera, Ger, or Ar (harvest or year)	Muin (Vine)
13	Death	Mem (water)	Placenta	Ihwaz (yew tree)	Gort (Ivy) or Gart (Garden)
14	Temperance	Nun (serpent or fish)	Belly of animal with teats	Perth or Peorth (lot or dice box for casting lots)	Ng (Reed) or Pethboc (Guelder Rose)
15	The Devil	Samekh (prop or fish)	Bolt	Algiz (elk/horned deity or elk sedge/protection)	Unspoken
16	Lightning-Struck Tower	Ain (eye)	Folded cloth	Sig or Sigel (sun or victory)	Straif (Blackthorn)
17	The Star	Pe (mouth or command)	Lake or sea	Tir or Tiuwaz (god of the North Star)	Ruis (Elder)
18	The Moon	Tsade (hunt or fishhook)	Hill	Berkana (birch)	Ailim (Elm, Palm, or Fir)
19	The Sun	Qopf (monkey)	Basket with handle	Ehwaz (horse)	Ohn (Furze)
20	Judgment	Ros (head)	Stand for jugs	Mannaz (man)	Uhr (Heather)
21		Shin (tooth or bow)	Bread	Laguz or Logr (lake or leek)	Eodha (Poplar)
22	The World	Tav (mark)	Hobble for cattle	Ingwaz (Earth god)	Ioho (Yew)
23			Hand	Dagaz (day)	
24	The Fool (zero)		Snake	Othala (homeland or inheritance)	

Notes

INTRODUCTION
TO THE ALPHABET AS
A SPELL OF RESURRECTION

1. Bouisson, *Magic,* 99.
2. As quoted in Jean, *Writing,* 195.

CHAPTER 1.
ALPHABETS AS ROSARIES
OF LETTERS

1. Bayley, *Lost Language of Symbolism,* 72.

CHAPTER 2.
ASTRONOMY AND CALENDARS

1. Allen, *Star Names,* 303ff.
2. To further explore the myths concerning this traumatic loss of stability between Earth and sky, see *Hamlet's Mill* (1977), by Giorgio De Santillana and Hertha von Dechend.
3. See the image in Gadon, *Once & Future Goddess,* 11.
4. Jacobsen, *Treasures of Darkness,* 95. In particular, Jacobsen describes this in relation to An, the Sumerian supreme deity, as the fecund breed-bull whose name means "sky."

CHAPTER 3. ANATOLIAN, MESOPOTAMIAN, EGYPTIAN, AND EARLY SEMITIC SCRIPTS INCLUDING PHOENICIAN

1. Holst, *Phoenician Secrets*, 14.
2. Sanders, *The Invention of Hebrew*, 50.
3. Hymn to Demeter, verse 470 & 480 (c. seventh–sixth century BCE), from H. G. Evelyn-White, *Hesiod, Homeric Hymns, Epic Cycle, Homerica*, H. G. Loeb Classical Library, vol. 57 (Cambridge, Mass.: Harvard University Press; London: William Heinemann Ltd., 1914), as quoted on the website of the Theoi Texts Library.

CHAPTER 4. THE EGYPTIAN TWENTY-FOUR-HIEROGLYPH ALPHABET

1. Betro, *Hieroglyphics*, 11.
2. As quoted in Graves, *White Goddess*, 232.
3. I use the order of 24 hieroglyphics given by Betro, *Hieroglyphics*, 22, and Diringer, *Alphabet*, 63.
4. David Diringer (*The Alphabet*, 63) equates the vulture with aleph. I can't determine whether this is his own gloss or from an earlier source. Most sources simply use A.
5. Personal correspondence from Jim Loy.
6. Jacq, *Fascinating Hieroglyphics*, 106.
7. Rami Arav, "Excarnation: Food for Vultures," *Biblical Archaeology Review* 37, no. 6 (November/December 2011).
8. Poe, *Black Spark, White Fire*, 158.
9. Gimbutas, *Language of the Goddess*, 242.

CHAPTER 5. SPREAD OF THE PHOENICIAN SCRIPT

1. Holst, *Secrets of the Phoenicians*, 22.
2. Calasso, *Marriage of Cadmus and Harmonia*, 386.
3. Grimal, *Dictionary of Classical Mythology*, 156–57, and Bell, *Women of Classical Mythology*, 196.
4. Holst, *Phoenician Secrets*, 94ff.

5. King, "Differential Y-Chromosome Anatolian Influences on the Greek and Cretan Neolithic."

CHAPTER 6. TRADITIONS FROM HEBREW AND THE KABBALAH

1. Naveh, *Early History of the Alphabet*, 112.
2. Kaplan, *Sefer Yetzirah*, xiv.
3. Bischoff, *The Kabbala*, 65.
4. Scholem, *On the Kabbalah and Its Symbolism*, 96.

CHAPTER 7. VARIOUS WESTERN TRADITIONS

1. Gadon, *The Once & Future Goddess*, 216.
2. Baigent, Leigh, and Lincoln, *Holy Blood, Holy Grail*, 54.

CHAPTER 8. CELTIC OGHAM

1. *Mabinogion: The Red Book of Hergest*, trans. Lady Charlotte Guest (1877), 427.
2. As quoted in Graves, *White Goddess*, 116.
3. Diringer, *The Alphabet*, 174, shows the Iberian letters.
4. Barry, *Greek Qabalah*, 21.
5. O'Curry, *On The Manners and Customs of the Ancient Irish*, 20.
6. Namely, *Lebor Gabála Érenn* (eleventh century) and *Auraicept na n-Éces* (fourteenth century). Also, Graves, *White Goddess*, 1948, 236–38.
7. York Manuscript No. 1.
8. Rolle, *World of the Scythians*, 8.
9. John Michell, *At the Center of the World* (Thames & Hudson, 1994), as quoted by Bob Trubshaw, "Loch Finlaggan, Islay: Archaeologists Confirm John Michell's Research," At the Edge website, updated November 2008 (originally published in *Mercian Mysteries*, no. 23, May 1995).

CHAPTER 9. GERMANIC RUNES

1. Vigfusson and Powell, *Corpus Poeticum Boreale*, vol. 1, 29.
2. Vigfusson and Powell, *Corpus Poeticum Boreale*, *Grimnismal*, 69ff; *Havamal*, 23ff.

3. As quoted in Titchenell, *Masks of Odin,* chapter 8.

4. Page, *An Introduction to English Runes.*

CHAPTER 10. INDIA'S BRAHMI, SANSKRIT, AND CHAKRAS

1. Examples of Brahmi, see Diringer, *The Alphabet,* vol. 2, 254.

2. Khanna, *Yantra,* 43.

3. For further discussion, see White, *Tantra in Practice.* See also Avalon, *Serpent Power,* 177.

4. Avalon, *Serpent Power,* 165.

5. Benfey, *Sanskrit-English Dictionary,* 168.

CHAPTER 11. CHINA'S I CHING AND TAO TE CHING

1. Goodrich, *Peking Temple of the Eastern Peak,* 80.

2. DeSantillana and Von Dechen, *Hamlet's Mill,* 273.

3. Harris, "The Word Made Flesh," 20.

4. Legge, *I Ching,* xiv.

5. Walters, *Alternate I-Ching,* 20.

6. This list comes from Whitlock and Ehrmann, *Story of Jade,* 56–59.

7. Lemoine, *Yao Ceremonial Paintings,* 54, 60.

FIRST LETTER

1. Vigfusson and Powell, *Corpus Poeticum Boreale,* vol. 1, 92ff.

2. Bray, *The Elder or Poetic Edda,* 105.

3. *Oxford Classical Dictionary,* 2nd ed. (1972), 502.

4. Grahn, *Another Mother Tongue,* 14.

5. Benham, *Book of Palmistry,* 624.

6. *Uncle Thor's Magazine* 2, no. 3 (Trollwise Press, May 1993). No longer available.

7. Hua-Ching Ni, *Book of Changes,* 33.

8. Bayley, *Lost Language of Symbolism,* 350.

9. Jaschke, *Tibetan English Dictionary,* 603.

10. Kaplan, *Bahir,* 8.

11. See Diringer, *Writing*, 146.

12. Jaschke, *Tibetan English Dictionary*, 603.

13. Atwood, *Hermetic Philosophy and Alchemy*, 500ff. All quotes of the Keys come from this text.

14. As quoted in Motoyama, *Theories of the Chakras*, 167.

15. From "Song of the Forest Trees," by Standish Hayes O'Grady, as translated by Eleanor Hull in *Poem-book of the Gael*, 99.

16. Green, *Symbol & Image in Celtic Religious Art*, 55.

17. From "Online Index to the *Lebor Gabála Érenn (Book of Invasions)* based on R.A.S. Macalister's translations and notes," compiled by Michael Murphy, 2008, on the website of CELT (Corpus of Electronic Texts).

SECOND LETTER

1. "The Lament of the Old Woman of Beare," in Murphy, *Early Irish Lyrics*, 75.

2. Rees and Rees, *Celtic Heritage*, 134–35.

3. Quoted in Wong, *Cultivating Stillness*, 11.

4. Caras, *North American Animals*, 75.

5. Jacobson, *Treasures of Darkness*, 37.

6. Herder, *Dictionary of Symbols*, 14.

7. Napier, *Masks, Transformation, and Paradox*, 160.

8. Caesar, *Conquest of Gaul*, 146.

9. Wolkstein and Kramer, *Inanna*, 37.

10. Jacobsen, *Treasures of Darkness*, 36.

11. Goodrich, *Peking Temple of the Eastern Peak*, 82.

12. Bray, *The Elder or Poetic Edda*, 105.

13. Golowin, *World of the Tarot*, 206.

14. Farmer, *Oxford Dictionary of Saints*, 66.

15. White, *Book of Beasts*, 219.

16. Beer, *Unicorn*, 11.

17. Harrison, *Prolegomena*, 42–55.

18. Atwood, *Hermetic Philosophy and Alchemy*, 289.

19. Dickins, *Runic and Heroic Poems of the Old Teutonic Peoples*.

20. Kalweit, *Shamans, Healers, and Medicine Men*, 237–39.

21. As quoted in Motoyama, *Theories of the Chakras*, 169.

22. Thorsson, *Runelore*.

23. Legge, *I-Ching*, 193.

24. Walters, *Chinese Geomancy*, 46.

25. Kaplan, *Bahir*, 80.

26. *Haustlong* poem, in Sturlson, *Edda*, trans. Faulkes, 87.

27. From the Lay of Atli in Vigfusson and Powell, *Corpus Poeticum Boreale*, 422.

28. Rohde, *The Old English Herballs*, 18.

29. Berg, *The Essential Zohar*, 58. Commentary transcribed by Moses de Leon, 1279 CE.

THIRD LETTER

1. White, *Book of Beasts*, 219.

2. Graves, *White Goddess*, 198.

3. Leland, *Gypsy Sorcery and Fortune Telling*, 104.

4. Lawrence Carter, "The Rowan Tree," on an Angelfire website.

5. Kaplan, *Bahir*, 8.

6. Thorsson, *Runelore*, 189.

7. Johnson, *Lady of the Beasts*, 190.

8. Cooper, *God Is a Verb*, 47. For a deeper story of Samael, gimel, and Eden, see 42ff.

9. From the *Svipdagsmál*, as translated in Vigfusson and Powell, *Corpus Poeticum Boreale*, 94.

10. Davidson, *Scandinavian Mythology*, 64.

11. Gundarsson, *Teutonic Religion*, 366.

12. Titchenell, *Masks of Odin*, verse 146, 163.

13. As quoted on the inside cover of *Parabola*, vol. 20, no. 3 (August 1995).

14. Legge, *I-Ching*, li.

15. Nichols, *Jung and Tarot*, 30.

16. As quoted in Motoyama, *Theories of the Chakras*, 170–71.

17. Bayley, *Hidden Symbols of the Rosicrucians*, 16.

18. Ni, *The Book of Changes*, 85.

19. Walters, *Chinese Geomancy*, 155.

20. Cooper, *Symbolic & Mythological Animals*, 226–27.

21. Walters, *The Alternative I Ching*, 68.

22. Neugebauer, *Exact Sciences in Antiquity*, 27.

23. Lao-tzu, *Tao Te Ching*, trans. John Wu, verse 42.

24. Dennis, *Encyclopedia of Jewish Myth, Magic and Mysticism*, 228.

FOURTH LETTER

1. Lao-tzu, *Tao Te Ching*, trans. D. C. Lau, verse 4.
2. Grimal, *Concise Dictionary of Classical Mythology*, 231.
3. Tichnell, *Masks of Odin*, 163.
4. Dickins, *Runic and Heroic Poems of the Old Teutonic Peoples*.
5. Graves, *White Goddess*, 390.
6. Cooper, *Symbolic & Mythological Animals*, 186–87.
7. Gaster, *Festivals of the Jewish Year*, 31.
8. Swadesh, *Origin and Diversification of Language*, 186.
9. Nichols, *Jung and Tarot*, 103.
10. Modern spelling, mine. Line of the Old Icelandic Rune Poem from Thorsson, *Runelore*.
11. Aswynn, *Leaves of Yggdrasil*, 25.
12. As quoted in Motoyama, *Theories of the Chakras*, 173.
13. Harrison, *Prolegomena*, 338.
14. Allen, *Star Names*, 107.
15. "The Lament of the Old Woman of Beare," in Murphy, *Early Irish Lyrics*, 77.
16. Bell, *Magic of Numbers*, 163.
17. Bell, *Magic of Numbers*, 85.

FIFTH LETTER

1. Kaplan, *Bahir*, 94.
2. Rabbi Shmuel Bornsztain, *Shem Mishmuel* (1927), as translated by Rabbi Zvi Belovski in "The Nature of the Shalosh Regalim," on the Aish website, accessed May 21, 2023.
3. White, *Book of Beasts*.
4. Graves, *White Goddess*, 274.
5. Magnus, *Book of Minerals*, 119.
6. Tichnell, *Masks of Odin*, 163.
7. Graves, *White Goddess*, 278.
8. Betro, *Hieroglyphics*, 154.
9. Kaplan, *Bahir*, 53.
10. Potter, *Compendia of Materia Medica*, 50.
11. Swiggers, "The Iberian Scripts," in *The World's Writing Systems*, 109.
12. White, *Book of Beasts*, 218.

13. Grahn, *Another Mother Tongue*, 80.

14. *Tibetan Book of the Dead*, trans. Fremantle and Trungpa.

15. 5th rune, "Rat end os uuritan," *Abcedarium Nordmanicum*, c. 800 CE.

16. *Tao Te Ching*, trans. Hamill, 7.

17. Dames, *Mythic Ireland*, 191.

18. Gregory, *Gods and Fighting Men*, 2.

19. Dillon, *Early Irish Literature*, 35.

20. Thorsson, *Runelore*.

21. Whitlock and Ehrmann, *Story of Jade*, 56–59.

SIXTH LETTER

1. Holst, *Phoenician Secrets*, 50.

2. Lurker, *Gods and Symbols of Ancient Egypt*, 71.

3. Gimbutas, *Language of the Goddess*, 318.

4. Rutherford, *Celtic Lore*, 106.

5. Thorsson, *Runelore*, 102.

6. De Breffny, *The Land of Ireland*, 135.

7. Dibner, *Agricola on Metals*, 32.

8. Dickins, *Runic and Heroic Poems of the Old Teutonic Peoples*.

9. Lao-tzu, *Tao Te Ching*, trans. John Wu, verse 6.

SEVENTH LETTER

1. "The Lay of Grimnir," in Taylor and Auden, *Elder Edda*, 63.

2. Gikatilla, *Gates of Light*, 271, 273.

3. Dillon, *Cycles of the Kings*, 38–40.

4. "The Lament of the Old Woman of Beare," in Murphy, *Early Irish Lyrics*, 77–83.

5. Anne Pasko, personal communication. Anne studied Irish wells with Earth Watch.

6. "The Lament of the Old Woman of Beare," in Murphy, *Early Irish Lyrics*, 77–83.

7. Bray, *The Elder or Poetic Edda*.

8. Strassfeld, *Jewish Holidays*, 85.

9. E. A. Wallis Budge, *From Fetish to God in Ancient Egypt*, 94.

10. Johnson, *Lady of the Beasts*, 144.

11. Burkhardt, *Chinese Creeds and Customs*, 56–57.

12. As quoted in Allen, *Star Names*, 203.

13. Lissner, *Man, God, and Magic*, 182.

14. Leland, *Gypsy Sorcery and Fortune Telling*, 81.

15. Gikatilla, *Gates of Light*, 374.

16. McKenna, *Food of the Gods*, 224.

17. Thorsson, *Runelore*, 95.

18. Gikatilla, *Gates of Light*, 69.

EIGHTH LETTER

1. Titchenell, *Masks of Odin*, 159–73.

2. As quoted in Jean, *Writing*, 195.

3. Davidson, *Astronomy and the Imagination*, 68.

4. Davidson, *Myths and Symbols in Pagan Europe*, 16.

5. Vigfusson, *Poetry of the Old Northern Tongue* (1883), vol. 1, 430.

6. Tichnell, *Masks of Odin*, 163.

7. Graves, *White Goddess*, 176.

8. Novello, *The Armenians*, 84.

9. Grimal, *Concise Dictionary of Classical Mythology*, 401.

10. Brand, *Observations on the Popular Antiquities*, vol. 2, 292.

11. Dennis, *Jewish Myth, Magic and Mysticism*, 153–54.

12. Joyce, *Social History of Ancient Ireland*, vol. 1, 232.

13. Rutherford, *Celtic Lore*, 109.

14. Poole, *From Domesday Book to Magna Carta*, 114.

INTRODUCTION TO THE SECOND FAMILY

1. Diringer, *Alphabet*, vol. 1, 168–69.

NINTH LETTER

1. Barry, *Greek Qabalah*, 73.

2. Barry, *Greek Qabalah*, 73.

3. As quoted in Jean, *Writing*, 195.

4. Imperial Record Department, *An Alphabetical List of the Feasts and Holidays of the Hindus and Muhammadan*, 20–26.

5. *Li Chi,* trans. Legge, 292–94.

6. Neumann, *Great Mother,* 162.

7. Kaplan, *The Bahir,* 47.

8. Vigfusson and Powell, *Corpus Poeticum Boreale,* vol. 1, 41.

9. Groa's spell, *Poetic Edda,* trans. Hollander, 142.

10. *The Poetic Edda,* trans. Hollander, 46.

11. *The Poetic Edda,* trans. Hollander, 39.

12. *Pliny's Natural History,* 23, 28.

13. Fisher, *Labyrinth,* 144.

14. Rhie and Thurman, *Wisdom and Compassion.* See also Getty, *Gods of Northern Buddhism,* 149–50.

15. Imperial Record Department, *An Alphabetical List of the Feasts and Holidays of the Hindus and Muhammadan,* 20–26.

16. *Gísla saga Súrssonar,* trans. G. W. DaSent, 1866.

17. R. W. Morgan, *The Trojan Era* (1857), as quoted in Matthews, *Celtic Reader,* 104.

18. Cotton Ms, Domitian A9, saec XI, cited in Derolez, *Runica Manuscripta,* 10.

TENTH LETTER

1. Strassfeld, *Jewish Holidays,* 145.

2. *Unetanah Tokef* prayer for the Day of Atonement

3. Farmer, *Oxford Dictionary of Saints,* 133–34.

4. Sturluson, *Prose Edda,* trans. Jean Young.

5. Budapest, *Grandmother of Time,* 208.

6. Brand, *Observations on the Popular Antiquities,* vol. 2, 275.

7. Tichnell, *Masks of Odin, Hávamál* verse 154.

8. Imperial Record Department, *An Alphabetical List of the Feasts and Holidays of the Hindus and Muhammadan,* 2, 45.

9. Vigfusson and Powell, *Corpus Poeticum Boreale,* vol. 1, *Voluspa,* 791.

10. *Voluspa,* trans. Bellows, verses 8.

11. *Voluspa,* trans. Bellows, verse 20.

12. Graves, *White Goddess,* 182.

13. Palsson and Edwards, *Egil's Saga,* 119.

14. O'Curry, *Manners and Customs of the Ancient Irish,* vol. 2, 20.

15. Dickins, *Runic and Heroic Poems of the Old Teutonic Peoples.*

16. Michael Dames, *Mythic Ireland*, 35.

17. Cambrensis, *The Historical Works of Giraldus Cambrensis*, 35.

18. Graves, *White Goddess*, 299.

ELEVENTH LETTER

1. White, *Book of Beasts*, 208–9.

2. Brand, *Observations on the Popular Antiquities*, vol. 1, 404.

3. As quoted in Jean, *Writing*, 195.

4. Ulufudu, *Zulu Bone Oracle*, 68.

5. T. H. White, *Book of Beasts*, 225.

6. Rees and Rees, *Celtic Heritage*, 310.

7. Jones, *Larousse Dictionary of World Folklore*, 311.

8. White, *Book of Beasts*, 91.

9. Magnus, *Book of Minerals*, 83.

10. See the entry "Saint's Days" in Farmer, *Oxford Dictionary of Saints*; see also Allen, *Star Names*, 46.

11. Crawford, *The Poetic Edda*.

12. Henshall, *Guide to Remembering Japanese Characters*, 131.

13. Thorsson, *Runelore*, 102.

14. Davidson, *Myths and Symbols in Pagan Europe*, 49–50.

15. Rutherford, *Celtic Mythology*, 117.

16. Brand, *Observations on the Popular Antiquities*, vol. 1, 417.

17. Farmer, *Oxford Dictionary of Saints*, 294.

18. Kaplan, *Bahir*, 74.

TWELFTH LETTER

1. Roger Tory Peterson, *Field Guide to the Birds* (Houghton Mifflin, 1947), 119.

2. Farmer, *Oxford Dictionary of Saints*, 406–7.

3. Wesley Muhammad, "Origin and Meaning of Allah," 7. Available on the Academia website.

4. Ellis, *Dictionary of Irish Mythology*, 168.

5. Gimbutas, *Language of the Goddess*, 295.

6. Vigfusson and Powell, *Corpus Poeticum Borele*, vol. l, 418.

7. *Poetic Edda, Hávamál*, trans. Hollander, stanza 157.

8. Davidson, *Scandinavian Mythology*, 81.

9. As quoted in Tolstoy, *Quest for Merlin,* 145.

10. De Santillana and Von Dechen, *Hamlet's Mill,* 294.

11. Vigfusson and Powell, *Corpus Poeticum Boreale,* vol. 1, 86.

12. Harrison, *Prolegomena,* 147.

13. Manjo, *Healing Hand,* 186–89.

THIRTEENTH LETTER

1. Cohen, *Cultic Calendars of the Ancient Near East,* 4.

2. Krupp, *Beyond the Blue Horizon,* 71.

3. Golowin, *World of the Tarot,* 180.

4. Kaplan, *Bahir,* 31.

5. Pliny, 8.73, from *Pliny the Elder, The Natural History,* trans. John Bostock and H. T. Riley. London: Henry Bohn, 1855.

6. Tichnell, *Masks of Odin,* 164.

7. Woodland Trust website s.v. "Yew," accessed June 22, 2023.

8. Thorsson, *Runelore,* 103.

9. Ellis, *Dictionary of Irish Mythology,* 131.

10. Wethered, *Mind of the Ancient World,* 119.

11. Graves, *White Goddess,* 183.

12. Rätsch, *The Encyclopedia of Psychoactive Plants.*

13. Rose, *Spirits, Fairies, Leprechauns, and Goblins.*

14. Jackson, *Celtic Miscellany,* 72.

15. Ellis, *Dictionary of Celtic Mythology,* 115.

16. Pritchard, *Ancient Near East,* 69–70.

FOURTEENTH LETTER

1. Edward Kelly, *Theatre of Terrestrial Astronomy,* 9.

2. From the poem "Hanes Taliesin" (History of Taliesin), originally recorded in the Welsh *Mabinogion,* as quoted in Graves, *White Goddess,* 91.

3. As described in an early 1800s book on sailing. I no longer have the source.

4. Imperial Record Department, *An Alphabetical List of the Feasts and Holidays of the Hindus and Muhammadan,* 31.

5. Kelly, *Theatre of Terrestrial Astronomy,* 10.

6. Edward Davies, *The Mythology and Rites of the British Druids* (1809), as quoted in Matthews, *Celtic Reader,* 63.

7. Reader's Digest, *Magic and Medicine of Plants,* 215.

8. Budge, *From Fetish to God in Ancient Egypt,* 42.

9. Thomson, *Studies in Ancient Greek Society,* 347.

10. Nichols, *Jung and Tarot,* 249

11. Dickins, *Runic and Heroic Poems of the Old Teutonic Peoples.*

12. Novello, *The Armenians,* 84.

13. Bayley, *Lost Language of Symbolism,* 93.

FIFTEENTH LETTER

1. Lao-Tzu, *Tao Te Ching,* trans. Man-jen Cheng.

2. Lao-tzu, *Tao Te Ching,* trans. John Wu, verse 15.

3. Davidson, *Astronomy and the Imagination,* 130, 134.

4. Aswynn, *Leaves of Yggdrassil,* 70.

5. John Jamieson, *An Etymological Dictionary of the Scottish Language* (1818), as quoted in Opie, *Lore and Language of Schoolchildren,* 148.

6. Pollack, *Seventy-Eight Degrees of Wisdom,* 49.

7. As defined by Mackey in his *Encyclopaedia of Freemasonry and Its Kindred Sciences,* 187.

8. Wethered, *Mind of the Ancient World,* 158–60.

9. West, *Serpent in the Sky,* 140–41.

10. Quoted inside the cover of *Parabola* vol. XX, no. 3 (August 1995).

11. Larrington, *Poetic Edda.*

12. *Gylfaginning,* in Sturluson, *Edda,* trans. Faulkes.

SIXTEENTH LETTER

1. Graves, *White Goddess,* 225.

2. Thorsson, *Runelore.*

3. Vigfusson and Powell, *Corpus Poeticum Boreale,* vol. 1.

4. Dames, *Mythic Ireland,* 99–100.

5. Schimmel, *Mystery of Numbers,* 216.

6. "Caillech Bérri" (Old Woman of Beare), trans. Gerald Murphy.

7. Borlase, *Dolmens of Ireland* (1897) quoted in Graves, *White Goddess,* 213.

8. Hollander, *Poetic Edda,* 40.

9. Edward Davies, *The Mythology and Rites of the British Druids* (1809), as

quoted in Matthews, *Celtic Reader,* 94, 96–97. Davies tells that Blackthorn translates as Ogham: *Straif;* Scots Gaelic: *Draighionn;* Irish Gaelic: *Draighean;* Welsh: *Draenen ddu.*

10. Lorenz, "The Significance of the Folded Cloth in Egyptian Iconography."
11. Vigfusson and Powell, *Corpus Poeticum Boreale,* vol. 1, 40.

INTRODUCTION TO THE THIRD FAMILY

1. Schwartz, *Tree of Souls,* 250. A mark on the forehead saving one from death appears in Ezekiel 9: 4–6.

SEVENTEENTH LETTER

1. De Santillana and von Dechend, *Hamlet's Mill,* 1–2.
2. Ions, *Egyptian Mythology,* 22–23.
3. Schimmel, *Mystery of Numbers,* 219.
4. Krupp, *Beyond the Blue Horizon,* 288.
5. Hoppin, *Old England,* 229–32.
6. Jane Taylor, "Twinkle, Twinkle, Little Star," *Golden Book of Poetry* (1947).
7. Cary and Warmington, *Ancient Explorers,* 17.
8. White, *Medieval Technology,* 132–33. There is controversy over the dating of the use of a lodestone. See also Hyde, *Ancient Greek Mariners,* 319, as well as the section on Pytheas, 124–34. Pytheas's book *On the Ocean* no longer exists, but he was quoted by early Greeks, including Polybius.
9. Dill, "Lodestone and Needle."
10. Hollander, *Poetic Edda,* 40.
11. Walker, *Woman's Dictionary of Symbols and Sacred Objects,* 516.
12. *Havamal,* trans. Tichnell, verse 161.
13. Dickins, *Runic and Heroic Poems of the Old Teutonic Peoples.*
14. Vigfusson, *Corpus poeticum boreale,* stanzas 47–50, 16.
15. Hull, "Song of the Forest Trees," from *Song Book of the Gaels,* 100.
16. Dames, *Mythic Ireland,* 172.
17. Vigfusson, *Corpus poeticum boreale,* 422.

EIGHTEENTH LETTER

1. Stone, "Nanna/Suen/Sin (god)."
2. Kaplan, *Bahir,* 22 (verse 61).

3. Kaplan, *Bahir,* 79.
4. Woolf, "Tree Folklore."
5. *Poetic Edda,* trans. Hollander, 233.

NINETEENTH LETTER

1. Moore, *Stargazing,* 152.
2. Miller, "Celtic Cross Ancient Science."
3. Allen, *Star Names,* 230.
4. As quoted in Hawkins, *Stonehenge Decoded,* 129–30.
5. Rutherford, *Celtic Mythology,* 124–28.
6. *Gylfaginning,* in Sturlson, *Edda,* trans. Faulkes, 14.

TWENTIETH LETTER

1. Ellis, *Druids,* 72; also see Logan, *The Scottish Gael,* vol 2, 326.

TWENTY-FIRST LETTER

1. H. Klingenberg, "Die Runeninschrift aus Bülach," *Helvetia Archaeologica* 7 (1976): 116–21, as translated on the Wikipedia page for the Bülach fibula.

TWENTY-SECOND LETTER

1. Plato, *Plato in Twelve Volumes,* vol. 9, trans. W. R. M. Lamb, sections 36b–e.
2. De Santillana and Von Dechend, *Hamlet's Mill,* 62–63.

A REVIEW

1. Graves, *Greek Myths,* vol. 2, 214 (section 147).

APPENDIX I.
ASTRONOMICAL CALENDAR CYCLES

1. See Joanne Conman, "The Egyptian Origins of Planetary Hypsomata," *Discussions in Egyptology,* vol. 64, available on the Academia website.

Bibliography

Allen, Richard. *Star Names*. 1899. Dover, 1963. Available online.

Apollonius. *Voyage of the Argo*. 250 BCE. Trans. E. V. Rieu, 1959. Penguin, 1987.

Aswynn, Freya. *Leaves of Yggdrasil*. Llewellyn, 1990.

Atwood, M. A. *Hermetic Philosophy and Alchemy*. 1850. Julian Press, 1960. Available online.

Avalon, Arthur (Sir John Woodroffe). *Serpent Power*. 1919. Dover, 1974. Available online.

Baigent, Michael, Richard Leigh, and Henry Lincoln. *Holy Blood, Holy Grail*. Delacorte Press, 1982.

Barry, Kieren. *The Greek Qabalah*. Weiser, 1999.

Bayley, Harold. *Hidden Symbols of the Rosicrucians*. 1903. Surefire Press, 1988. Available online.

———. *Lost Language of Symbolism*. 1912. Rowman & Littlefield, 1968.

Beauval, Robert, and Adrian Gilbert. *Orion Mystery*. Crown, 1994.

Beer, Rudiger Robert. *Unicorn*. Mason & Carter, 1977.

Beinfield, Harriet, and Efrem Korngold. *Between Heaven and Earth*. Ballantine, 1992.

Bell, Eric. *Magic of Numbers*. 1946. Dover, 1991.

Bell, Robert. *Women of Classical Mythology*. ABC-CLIO, 1991.

Bellows, Henry Adams, trans. *Voluspa*, 1936.

Benfey, Theodore. *Sanskrit-English Dictionary*. 1866. Asian Educational Services, 1991.

Benham, William. *Book of Palmistry*. 1900. Newcastle, 1988.

Berg, Rav P. S. *The Essential Zohar*. Bell Tower, 2002.

Betro, Maria Carmela. *Hieroglyphics: The Writings of Ancient Egypt.* Abbeville Press, 1996.

Bischoff, Erich. *The Kabbala.* 1910. Weiser, 1998.

Bouisson, Maurice. *Magic: Its History and Principal Rites.* E. P. Dutton, 1961.

Brand, John. *Observations on the Popular Antiquities.* 3 vols. Bohns, 1849.

Brier, Bob. *Ancient Egyptian Magic.* Quill, 1980.

Briggs, Katharine. *British Folk Tales.* Pantheon, 1977.

Bryant, Jacob. *A New System, or, An Analysis of Ancient Mythology.* T. Payne, P. Elmsly, B. White, and J. Walter, 1774. Available online.

Budapest, Zsuzsanna. *The Grandmother of Time.* Harper Row, 1989.

Budge, E. A. Wallis. *Egyptian Language.* 1889. Dover, 1983.

———. *Egyptian Magic.* 1901. Dover, 1971.

———. *From Fetish to God in Ancient Egypt.* 1934. Dover, 1988.

Burkhardt, V. R. *Chinese Creeds and Customs.* South China Morning Post, 1966.

Caesar. *Conquest of Gaul.* Circa 50 BCE. Trans. S. A. Handford. Penguin, 1960.

Calasso, Roberto. *Marriage of Cadmus and Harmonia.* Knopf, 1993.

Cambrensis, Giraldus. *The Historical Works of Giraldus Cambrensis.* G. Bell & Sons, 1913.

Campbell, Joseph, and Richard Roberts. *Tarot Revelations.* Vernal Equinox, 1982.

Caras, Roger. *North American Animals.* Meredith Press, 1967.

Carmichaell, Alexander. *Carmina Gadelica.* 1899. Lindesfarne, 1992. Available online.

Cary, M., and E. H. Warmington. *The Ancient Explorers.* Penguin, 1963.

Cheng, Man-Jen. *Lao-Tzu: "My Words Are Very Easy to Understand."* Trans. Tam Gibbs. North Atlantic Books, 1981.

Cleary, Thomas, trans. *The Essential Tao.* Castle Books, 1998.

Cohen, Mark. *Cultic Calendars of the Ancient Near East.* CDL Press, 1993.

Cooper, Rabbi David. *God Is a Verb: Kaballah and the Practice of Mystical Judaism.* Riverhead, 1997.

Cooper, J. C. *Symbolic & Mythological Animals.* Aquarian, 1992.

Crawford, Jackson. *The Poetic Edda: Stones of the Norse Gods and Heroes.* Hackett, 2015.

Dames, Michael. *Mythic Ireland.* Thames and Hudson, 1991.

Daniels, Peter T., ed. and William Bright, ed. *The World's Writing Systems.* Oxford: Oxford University Press, 1996.

DaSent, G. W., trans. *Gísla saga Súrssonar,* 1866. Available at Icelandic Saga Database website.

Davidson, H. R. Ellis. *Gods & Myths of Northern Europe*. Penguin, 1971.

———. *Myths and Symbols in Pagan Europe*. Syracuse, 1988.

———. *Scandinavian Mythology*. Peter Bedrick, 1988.

Davidson, Norman. *Astronomy and the Imagination*. Routledge, 1985.

De Breffny, Brian. *The Land of Ireland*. Harry N. Abrams, 1985.

Deane, Seamus, ed. *Field Day Anthology of Irish Writing*. Vol. 1. Norton, 1992.

Dennis, Rabbi Geoffrey. *Encyclopedia of Jewish Myth, Magic and Mysticism*. Llewellyn, 2008.

Derolez, R. *Runica Manuscripta*. University of Ghent, 1954.

De Santillana, Giorgio, and Hertha von Dechend. *Hamlet's Mill*. 1977. Godine, 1992.

Dibner, Bern. *Agricola on Metals*. 1556. Burndy Library, 1958.

Dickins, Bruce. *Runic and Heroic Poems of the Old Teutonic Peoples*. 1915. Available online.

Dill, J. Gregory. "Lodestone and Needle: The Rise of the Magnetic Compass." Ocean Navigator website (January 1, 2003).

Dillon, Myles. *The Cycles of the Kings*. Oxford University Press, 1946. Available online.

———. *Early Irish Literature*. University of Chicago Press, 1948.

Dillon, Myles, with Nora Chadwick. *Celtic Realms*. London, 1967.

Diringer, David. *The Alphabet: A Key to the History of Mankind*. Philosophical Library, 1948.

———. *The Alphabet*. 2 vols. Funk & Wagnalls, 1968.

———. *Writing*. Praeger, 1967.

Doblhofer, Ernest. *Voices in Stone*. Viking, 1961.

Ellis, Peter Berresford. *Dictionary of Celtic Mythology*. Oxford, 1992.

———. *The Druids*. Wm. B. Eerdmans Publishing, 1994.

———. *A Dictionary of Irish Mythology*. Oxford, 1987.

Farmer, David Hugh. *Oxford Dictionary of Saints*. Oxford University Press, 1992.

Fisher, Adrian. *The Labyrinth*. Crown, 1990.

Fremantle, Francesca, and Chogyam Trungpa, trans. *The Tibetan Book of the Dead*. Shambhala, 1987.

Gadon, Elinor. *The Once & Future Goddess*. Harper Collins, 1989.

Gaster, Theodor. *Festivals of the Jewish Year*. Quill, 1978.

Getty, Alice. *Gods of Northern Buddhism*. 1914. Dover, 1988.

Gikatilla, Rabbi Joseph. *Gates of Light*. Circa thirteenth century. Trans. Avi Weinstein. Harper Collins, 1994.

Gimbutas, Marija. *Civilization of the Goddess.* Harper Collins, 1991.

——. *The Goddesses & Gods of Old Europe.* University of California, 1982.

——. *Language of the Goddess.* Harper & Row, 1989.

Golowin, Sergius. *World of the Tarot.* Weiser, 1988.

Goodrich, Anne. *Peking Temple of the Eastern Peak.* Monumenta Serica, 1964.

Gordon, Cyrus. *Ancient Near East.* Norton, 1965.

Grahn, Judy. *Another Mother Tongue.* Beacon Press, 1984.

Graves, Robert. *Greek Myths.* Vol. 2. Pelican, 1982.

——. *The White Goddess.* Farrar, Straus & Giroux, 1966.

Green, Miranda. *Symbol & Image in Celtic Religious Art.* Routledge, 1992.

Gregory, Lady. *Gods and Fighting Men.* 1902. Macmillan, 1976.

Grimal, Pierre. *The Concise Dictionary of Classical Mythology.* Basil Blackwell, 1990.

Gundarrson, Kveldulf. *Teutonic Religion.* Llewellyn, 1993.

Hadamitzky, W., and Mark Spahn. *Kanji & Kana.* Tuttle, 1994.

Hallam, Elizabeth. *Saints.* Simon & Schuster, 1994.

Harris, Tod. "The Word Made Flesh," *Parabola* 20, no. 3 (August 1995): 20.

Harrison, Jane. *Prolegomena to the Study of Greek Religion.* 1908. Princeton, 1991.

Hawkins, Gerald. *Mindsteps to the Cosmos.* Harper Collins, 1983.

——. *Stonehenge Decoded.* Doubleday, 1965.

Healey, John F. *The Early Alphabet.* University of California Press, 1990.

Henshall, Kenneth. *Guide to Remembering Japanese Characters.* Tuttle, 1993.

The Herder Dictionary of Symbols. Chiron Publications, 1986.

Herodotus. *History of Herodotus.* Trans. George Rawlinson, 1928. Tudor, 1947. Available online.

Hollander, Lee, trans. *Old Norse Poems.* University of Columbia Press, 1936.

——. *The Poetic Edda.* University of Texas Press, 1962.

Holst, Sanford. *Phoenician Secrets.* Santorini, 2011.

Hoppin, James. *Old England.* Houghton Mifflin, 1867.

Hull, Eleanor. *Poem-book of the Gael.* Chatto & Windus, 1913.

Hyde, Walter Woodburn. *Ancient Greek Mariners.* Oxford, 1947.

I-Ming, Liu. *Awakening to the Tao.* Trans. Thomas Cleary. Shambhala, 1998.

Imperial Record Department [of Great Britain]. *An Alphabetical List of the Feasts and Holidays of the Hindus and Muhammadan.* Superintendent Government Printing, India, 1914.

Ions, Veronica. *Egyptian Mythology.* Newnes Books (1965), 1983.

Jackson, Kenneth. *A Celtic Miscellany*. Routledge & Kegan Paul, 1967.

———. *Studies in Early Celtic Nature Poetry*. Cambridge, 1935.

Jacobsen, Thorkild. *Treasures of Darkness*. Yale, 1976.

Jacq, Christian. *Fascinating Hieroglyphs*. Sterling, 1998.

Jaschke, H. A. *Tibetan English Dictionary*. 1881. Motilal Banarsidass, 1980.

Jean, Georges. *Writing: The Story of Alphabets and Scripts*. Abrams, 1992.

Jensen, Hans. *Sign, Symbol & Script*. Putnam, 1969.

Johnson, Buffie. *Lady of the Beasts*. Harper, 1988.

Jones, Alison. *Larousse Dictionary of World Folklore*. Larousse, 1996.

Joyce, P. W. *A Social History of Ancient Ireland*. 2 vols. London, 1903.

Kalweit, Holger. *Shamans, Healers, and Medicine Men*. 1987. Shambhala, 1992.

Kaplan, Aryeh, trans. *The Bahir*. 1176. Weiser, 1990.

———. *Sefir Yetzirah*. Weiser, 1997.

Kelly, Edward. *The Theatre of Terrestrial Astronomy*. 1676. Alchemical Publishing, 1988.

Khanna, Madhu. *Yantra*. Thames & Hudson, 1994.

King, R. J., et al. "Differential Y-chromosome Anatolian Influences on the Greek and Cretan Neolithic." *Annals of Human Genetics* 72, no. 2 (February 5, 2008): 205–214.

Krupp, E. C. *Beyond the Blue Horizon*. Harper, 1991.

Lamy, Lucie. *Egyptian Mysteries*. Crossroad, 1981.

Lao-tzu. *Tao Te Ching*. Trans. Sam Hamill. Shambhala, 2005.

Lao-tzu. *Tao Te Ching*. Trans. D. C. Lau. Penguin, 1963.

———. *Tao Te Ching*. Trans. John Wu. 1961. Barnes & Noble, 1997.

Ledbetter, C. W. *Freemasonry and Its Ancient Mystic Rites*. 1926. Quest, 1986. Available online.

Legge, James. *I-Ching*. 1882. Bantam Books, 1969. Available online.

———. *Li Chi: Book of Rites*. Part 1. New York University, 1967.

Leland, C. G. *Gypsy Sorcery and Fortune Telling*. 1889. Anthony Naylor, 1993.

Lemoine, Jacques. *Yao Ceremonial Paintings*. White Lotus, 1982.

Levi, Eliphas. *La Clef des Grands Mysteres*. Trans. A. E. Waite. 1896. Weiser, 1992.

Lissner, Ivar. *Man, God, and Magic*. Putnam, 1961.

Logan, James. *The Scottish Gael: or, Celtic Manners as Preserved among the Highlanders*. Harford (1831), 1846. Full text available online.

Lorenz, Megaera. "The Significance of the Folded Cloth in Egyptian Funerary Iconography." (March 7, 2020). Abstract of lecture given at the Oriental Institute of the University of Chicago.

Lurker, Manfred. *The Gods and Symbols of Ancient Egypt.* Thames & Hudson, 1984.

Mackey, Albert G. *Encyclopaedia of Freemasonry and Its Kindred Sciences,* rev. ed., vol. 1. Masonic History Company, 1913.

Magnus, Albertus. *Book of Minerals.* Circa 1300. Trans. D. Wyckoff. Clarendon, 1967.

Manjo, Guido. *The Healing Hand.* Harvard, 1975.

Matthews, John. *A Celtic Reader.* Aquarian, 1992.

———. *Hallowquest.* London, 1990.

Matthews, John, and Bob Stewart. *Legendary Britain.* London, 1993.

McKenna, Terence. *Food of the Gods.* Bantam, 1993.

Melaart, James. *Catal Huyuk.* McGraw Hill, 1967.

Miller, Crichton E. M. "Celtic Cross Ancient Science." *Heretic Magazine* (2016). Available on Academia website.

Moore, Patrick. *Stargazing.* Barrons, 1985.

Motoyama, Hiroshi. *Theories of the Chakras.* Quest, 1981.

Murphy, Gerard. *Early Irish Lyrics.* 1956. Oxford, 1960.

Napier, A. David. *Masks, Transformation, and Paradox.* University of California, 1986.

Naveh, Joseph. *Early History of the Alphabet.* Magnes Press, 1987.

———. *Origins of the Alphabets.* Cassell & Co., 1975. (Also published by Jerusalem Publishing Palphot distribution.)

Neugebauer, Otto. *Exact Sciences in Antiquity.* 1952. 2nd. ed. Dover, 1969.

Neumann, Erich. *The Great Mother.* 1955. Bollingen Press, 1991.

Ni, Hua-Ching. *The Book of Changes.* Seven Star, 1983.

Nichols, Sallie. *Jung & Tarot.* Weiser, 1980.

Northall, G. F. *English Folk Rhymes.* London, 1892. Full text available online.

Novello, Adriano. *The Armenians.* Rizzoli, 1986.

O'Curry, Eugene. *Manners and Customs of the Ancient Irish,* vol. 2. Williams and Norgate, 1873. Available on Google Books.

Opie, Iona and Peter. *Lore and Language of Schoolchildren.* Oxford, 1959.

Oxford Universal Dictionary. (1933), 1955.

Page, R. I. *An Introduction to English Runes.* Boydell Press, (1973), 1999.

Palsson, Hermann, and Paul Edwards, trans. *Egil's Saga.* Penguin, 1988.

Pennick, Nigel. *Secret Games of the Gods.* Weiser, 1989.

Plato. *Plato in Twelve Volumes,* vol. 9. Trans. W. R. M. Lamb. Harvard University Press and William Heinemann Ltd., 1925.

Poe, Richard. *Black Spark, White Fire: Did African Explorers Civilize Ancient Europe?* Prima Publishing, 1997.

Pollack, Rachel. *Seventy-Eight Degrees of Wisdom.* Aquarian, 1983.

Poole, A. L. *From Domesday Book to Magna Carta.* Clarendon Press, 1951.

Potter, Samuel. *Compendia of Materia Medica.* 1913. Blakiston's, 1917.

Pritchard, James, ed. *Ancient Near East.* Princeton, 1958.

Rätsch, Christian. *The Encyclopedia of Psychoactive Plants.* Park Street Press, 2005.

Reader's Digest. *Magic and Medicine of Plants.* 1986.

Rees, Alwyn, and Brinley Rees. *Celtic Heritage.* Thames & Hudson, 1991.

Rhie, Marylin, and Robert Thurman. *Wisdom and Compassion: The Sacred Art of Tibet.* Abrams, 1991.

Rohde, Eleanour Sinclair. *The Old English Herballs.* 1922. Dover, 1989.

Rolle, Renate. *World of the Scythians.* Trans. F. G. Walls. University of California Press, 1989.

Rose, Carol. *Spirits, Fairies, Leprechauns, and Goblins: An Encyclopedia.* W. W. Norton & Company, 1996.

Rutherford, Ward. *Celtic Lore.* Aquarian, 1993.

———. *Celtic Mythology.* 1987. Sterling, 1990.

Sanders, Seth. *The Invention of Hebrew.* University of Illinois Press, 2009.

Schimmel, Annemarie. *Mystery of Numbers.* Oxford, 1993.

Scholem, Gershom. *On the Kabbalah and Its Symbolism.* 1960. Schocken, 1996.

———. *Origins of the Kabbalah.* Trans. Allan Arkush. Princeton, 1990.

Schwartz, Howard. *Tree of Souls.* Oxford, 2004.

Shaw, Miranda. *Passionate Enlightenment.* Princeton University Press, 1995.

Skelton, Robin, and Margaret Blackwood. *Earth, Air, Fire, Water.* Arkana, 1990.

Spalinger, Anthony. "Epagomenal Days in Ancient Egypt." *Journal of Near Eastern Studies* 54, January 1995.

Stone, Adam. "Nanna/Suen/Sin (god)." *Ancient Mesopotamian Gods and Goddesses.* Oracc and the UK Higher Education Academy, 2016. Accessed on the Open Richly Annotated Cuneiform Corpus website of the University of Pennsylvania Museum of Archaeology and Anthropology.

Strassfeld, Michael. *The Jewish Holidays.* Harper Row, 1985.

Sturluson, Snorri. *Heimskringla: Saga of the Norse Kings.* Trans. Samuel Laing. Dutton, 1961.

———. *The Poetic Edda.* Trans. Carolyne Larrington. Oxford U. Press (1996), 2014.

———. *The Elder or Poetic Edda, Commonly Known as Sæmund's Edda: The*

Mythological—Poems. Trans. and ed. Olive Bray. Viking Club, 1908. Also available online.

———. *The Elder Edda: A Selection.* Taylor, Paul B., and W. H. Auden, trans. Vintage Books, 1970.

———. *Edda.* Trans. Anthony Faulkes. Everyman (1987), 1995.

———. *Prose Edda.* Trans. Jean Young. University of California Press, 1954.

Swadesh, Morris. *Origin and Diversification of Language.* Aldine, 1971.

Swiggers, Pierre. "The Iberian Scripts." In *The World's Writing Systems,* eds. Peter T. Daniels & William Bright. Oxford, 1996.

Thomson, George. *Studies in Ancient Greek Society.* Citadel, 1965.

Thorsson, Edred. *Runelore.* Weiser, 1988.

Titchenell, Elsa-Brita. *Masks of Odin.* Theosophical Press, 1985. Available online.

Tolstoy, Nikolai. *The Quest for Merlin.* Little Brown, 1985.

The Torah, A Women's Commentary. Edited by Tamara Eskenazi and Rabbi Andrea L. Weiss. URI Press, 2008.

Ulufudu. *Zulu Bone Oracle.* Berkeley, 1989.

Vigfusson, Gudbrand, and F. York Powell. *Corpus Poeticum Boreale.* 2 vols. Clarendon, 1883. Available online through Internet Archive.

Walker, Barbara. *Secrets of the Tarot.* Harper Row, 1984.

———. *The Woman's Dictionary of Symbols and Sacred Objects.* Harper Row, 1988.

Walters, Derek. *The Alternative I Ching.* Aquarian Press, 1987.

———. *Chinese Geomancy.* Element Books, 1989.

———. *Chinese Mythology.* Aquarian Press, 1992.

West, John Anthony. *Serpent in the Sky.* Quest, 1993.

Wethered, H. N. *The Mind of the Ancient World: A Consideration of Pliny's Natural World.* Longmans, Green and Co., 1937.

White, David Gordon. *Tantra in Practice.* Princeton Press, 2000.

White, Lynn. *Medieval Technology.* Oxford, 1962.

White, T. H., trans. *Book of Beasts: Being a Translation from a Latin Bestiary of the Twelfth Century.* Putnam, 1954.

Whitlock, Herbert P., and Martin L. Ehrmann. *Story of Jade.* 1949. Sheridan, 1965.

Wilson, Ian. *Before the Flood.* St. Martins, 2002.

Wolkstein, Diane, and Samuel Noah Kramer. *Inanna: Queen of Heaven and Earth.* Harper & Row, 1983.

Wong, Eva, trans. *Cultivating the Stillness.* Circa 200–589 CE. Shambhala, 1992.

Woolf, Jo. "Tree Folklore: Birch, the Lady of the Wood." Folklore Thursday website (April 14, 2016).

Index